THE WORLD OF OBSESSIVE-COMPULSIVE DISORDER

The World of Obsessive-Compulsive Disorder

The Experiences of Living with OCD

Dana Fennell

NEW YORK UNIVERSITY PRESS

New York

NEW YORK UNIVERSITY PRESS
New York
www.nyupress.org

References to Internet websites (URLs) were accurate at the time of writing. Neither the author nor New York University Press is responsible for URLs that may have expired or changed since the manuscript was prepared.

Library of Congress Cataloging-in-Publication Data
Names: Fennell, Dana, author.
Title: The world of obsessive-compulsive disorder : the experiences of living with OCD / Dana Fennell.
Description: New York : New York University Press, [2022] | Includes bibliographical references and index.
Identifiers: LCCN 2021013306 | ISBN 9781479881406 (hardback) | ISBN 9781479872343 (paperback) | ISBN 9781479820320 (ebook) | ISBN 9781479869909 (ebook other)
Subjects: LCSH : Obsessive-compulsive disorder.
Classification: LCC RC533 .F46 2022 | DDC 616.85/227—dc23
LC record available at https://lccn.loc.gov/2021013306

New York University Press books are printed on acid-free paper, and their binding materials are chosen for strength and durability. We strive to use environmentally responsible suppliers and materials to the greatest extent possible in publishing our books.

Manufactured in the United States of America

10 9 8 7 6 5 4 3 2 1

Also available as an ebook

To all those who have helped me find my way, especially my mom.

CONTENTS

Introduction

More Than a Neat Freak

> I check things a lot, think I've hit people when driving, seen bodies in bushes, have contamination fears. . . . My OCD is mostly focused on preventing any harm coming to other people.
> —Miles

Aged thirty-nine and living in the United Kingdom when we chatted, Miles recounted how obsessive-compulsive disorder (OCD) manifested in his life. He might be driving and worry that there was a body on the side of the road. "Common sense tells you it was a carrier bag. But OCD says it's a person, and that if I don't go back that person will die. And it will have been my fault," he told me. Miles and others with this type of OCD can get caught up in a cycle of checking to make sure they did not hurt someone, without evidence something bad occurred.

Miles came to believe OCD entered his life in his teen years. He felt that he had a good childhood, and when he first experienced aspects of OCD, he did not know what was going on: "I thought maybe everyone thought/acted like I did but that people just didn't talk about it. I also thought that maybe I was being punished by God." Years later, in his midtwenties, he read the book *The Boy Who Couldn't Stop Washing* and came to perceive himself as having the disorder. "Once I had a label for it, I felt better," he said. "It meant I could read/talk about it."

Miles was diagnosed with OCD and depression. He took medication, avoided certain situations, and prayed for the strength to deal with his OCD. His symptoms came in peaks and troughs. He described episodes of being entangled with the OCD: "It causes great anxiety and has a physical effect—I get hot, sweat, and I think my pulse must race. It's very tiring and you want to get away from it in your head but can't." He referred to it as something outside of him, "like it was in a box next to me and would come out at times, beat me up and then get back in the box. Or like a gray cloud that follows me around and sometimes rains on me and sometimes doesn't."

Miles viewed himself as exhibiting "odd" behavior and having troubling thoughts, explaining that OCD "affects your self-esteem and makes me feel less of a man." He avoided careers that might interest him such as working as a paramedic. Miles's fear of harming or offending others manifested in worries that he had written obscenities on company materials. He left one job because he kept worrying about this and checking to make sure he had not committed such an act. He tried and was often successful in covering up or hiding his OCD from others, but it impacted his life in profound ways. If people noticed him engaged in OCD-related behaviors, he believed that they tended to think of him as meticulous in his work. They were not able to see into his inner world. As a result of having OCD, he felt motivated to help others. He told me, "I want to help others and feel that I can put my OCD experiences to good use. I'd like to work in this area if possible."

Miles felt that many people either did not know about OCD or had a misperception of the disorder, which made it hard for them to understand. Before letting me interview him, he ensured that his answers would be kept confidential. He believed some of what he said could sound "bad" to others who do not know about the disorder. "I don't mind talking about it but worry about the judgment that is made on you when you have a 'mental' condition.'" However, he did have supportive people in his life. At the time we communicated, Miles had a girlfriend who told me, "I am keen to help him overcome his anxieties." She explained that she accepted "it is part of what makes him who he is. I don't even begin to understand where the impulses come from, but accept that if he needs to look in that ditch for an abandoned baby, that's what we will do." Miles exclaimed, "The irony is that my girlfriend sometimes asks if something I've done is because of my OCD and it isn't!"

Miles represents the way obsessive-compulsive disorder takes a myriad of forms that go well beyond the stereotypes of quirky neat freaks who want to eradicate an extra dust bunny, tackle germs, and appreciate an organized home. Obsessive-compulsive disorder and associated terms and phrases are referenced more publicly today than in the past, and as I wrote this book I became attuned to these mentions. On television, in books, on social media, and in casual conversations, people say they are "so OCD" or have OCD for liking things organized a particular way.[1] Memes exist on the internet consisting of pictures with something out of order or asymmetrical, with accompanying words joking that such details must arouse people's OCD. As I was writing this, I found a phone app described as a fun OCD game in which the player is presented with ice cream cones in multiple flavors and must sort them so that scoops of the same flavor are nestled adjacent to each other. In online stores, I encountered an "obsessive compulsive action figure" with marketing material that read, "Have You Washed Your Hands? But Have You Done It 20 Times Today? Yes? Then You're Weird."

Obsessive-compulsive disorder appears to be almost commonplace these days, even serving as a source of humor. Memes, products, and commentary about OCD along these lines can frustrate those with the disorder when these cultural products emphasize that the public does not understand the disorder and seems to minimize and ridicule it. This is a kind of trivialization, the process by which a condition is made to "appear less complex, less severe, and deserving of mockery."[2] The Mighty, an online community focused on empowering people with health issues and disabilities, therefore felt the need to put together a list of some "OCD-approved" memes to make those with OCD "laugh" and feel "understood."[3]

In actuality, OCD can take a host of forms, and the impacts on a person's life are wide-ranging. Having OCD means that a person experiences obsessions and/or compulsions.[4] These affect the person's functioning and/or cause them distress. A person with obsessions experiences various thoughts, images, or urges that at some point in time they deem "intrusive and unwanted,"[5] and which in many cases foster anxiety. This includes people who are concerned about blaspheming against God, worried that they might hurt their children, preoccupied with thoughts about contamination, troubled that they might not love their partner, upset by feelings that something just is not right, and more. The disorder can play on people's worst fears. Fred Penzel, an OCD therapist, wrote, "Sufferers tend to mistakenly believe that the obsessive thoughts are their own real thoughts, and therefore must be important and paid attention to, rather than actually being irrelevant

and the product of bad brain chemistry."[6] The OCD therapist and researcher Leslie J. Shapiro explained further:

> OCD seems to turn what the sufferer finds most objectionable into obses-
> sions, then vilifies the sufferer for having them. . . . People who have OCD
> are naturally people of good conscience. . . . Because the disorder leads
> them to doubt their "goodness," they perform rituals to compensate for
> any "badness" and to prove that their obsessions are not intended. You
> can see that having compassion (and self-compassion if you are a suf-
> ferer) for people who have OCD . . . is the most appropriate and humane
> response.[7]

As Shapiro indicated, in concert with obsessions or without, a person
with OCD may engage in certain ritual-like physical actions or mental
acts, which are called compulsions.[8] Compulsions go beyond washing
one's hands, checking the stove, or avoiding cracks in the sidewalk. They
may be performed in an attempt to relieve the obsessions or anxiety or
to prevent a negative situation. Inside that person avoiding the cracks
in the sidewalk may be a feeling that doing this will prevent harm from
befalling a loved one. Or, someone may feel an irrational urge to avoid
certain numbers even at the cost of getting calculations wrong at work.
The compulsions do not really make logical sense or are excessive.
(Although OCD involves thoughts, urges, images, and so on, for brevity
I will often use thoughts/behaviors as shorthand to refer to this more
encompassing list.)

People with OCD sometimes seem to have a better quality of life than
people with some other major mental disorders, but research has revealed that their quality of life, especially in terms of social functioning, can be the same or worse compared with those with panic disorder
and schizophrenia; in some studies, OCD has been associated with increased risk of suicide.[9] These results are shaped by the insight people
with OCD have, and how they may compare themselves against others
without mental illnesses. According to research on quality of life: "Patients with OCD in contrast to patients with schizophrenia have insight
into their behavior and are aware of the senselessness of their behaviors
leading to severe impairment of their psychological well-being."[10] OCD
can reduce psychological well-being, inhibit functioning at work and

in leisure activities, and negatively impact social relationships. Those experiencing obsessions and/or compulsions below the threshold to be diagnosed with OCD can face some negative health outcomes as well.

For many years, Miles did not perceive himself as having OCD; even when he did, he tried to cover up some aspects of it when interacting with others, fearful of how they might respond. As you walk down a street in any part of the world, you may be passing people who have OCD but not realize it. You may have friends or coworkers such as Miles and not be cognizant of their mental struggles. Research on OCD has increased, and we now recognize the disorder as affecting greater numbers of people than was thought decades ago.[11] Millions of people, likely at least one in fifty in the United States, will face this disorder at some point in their lifetime (lifetime prevalence rates varying across the world between .07 percent and 4.6 percent).[12]

Medical doctors, psychologists, and psychiatrists have been working on how to understand and treat the disorder, yet in the meantime, people must live with their OCD. Hence, I was drawn into studying it. OCD is treatable but lacks a surefire cure. I have long been interested in health, especially people's practices that can be referred to as complementary and/or alternative (CAM) to Western medicine. I took a job at a local health food store in South Beach, Florida, while working my way through college. My experiences there ordering organic foods and talking to people about their supplement usage inspired studies I carried out in graduate school. I interviewed farmers about their choices on whether to farm organically or using genetically engineered crops. In other studies, I examined how people conceptualized their health practices, especially complementary and alternative ones, and whether certain groups like people of a particular age or health status were more likely to use supplements such as vitamins and herbs. Next, I crafted a schedule of questions asking people with OCD about their lives and how they treated their OCD, anticipating that I might elicit tales of unique uses of complementary and alternative strategies and coping mechanisms. I got so much more. Without much prompting on my part, people opened up to me. People with OCD shared their hopes, fears, and intimate aspects of their lives, sometimes things they had not even told their doctor or therapist. I learned about their techniques for managing the disorder and how they hid it from others. I learned about what they wanted from doctors and therapists. Moved by their experiences, I broadened my research on OCD. I asked more questions and talked to more people. A few of them have stayed in touch with me over the course of years.

This book is based on the stories of more than fifty people who had, or thought they once had, OCD. It is designed to provide a full-spectrum picture of the "career" of having OCD. By that I mean the paths of those with OCD: from the beginning before they perceived themselves as having the disorder and when the phrase "obsessive-compulsive disorder" may have held little meaning for them, to their learning to live with OCD—and all the twists and turns in between.

Background

It might seem odd for a sociologist to study something that appears at first glance to be the purview of medicine, psychology, or psychiatry. However, sociology is at heart the study of people, and issues of health and illness are central to the human experience. People make sense of themselves as healthy versus sick, and they give meaning to their experiences as they interact with others in society. People's interactions with others vary during times of wellness versus illness; people who are sick may be unable to work, may enter into new and different relationships with healthcare professionals, may encounter stigma, and more. We can see commonalities in the experiences of those with a particular health concern. As the sociologists Joseph W. Schneider and Peter Conrad explained, *disease* has to do with physiology, but *illness* is "social."[13]

Sociologists and social psychologists have long studied issues of health and illness.[14] In recent decades, sociologists have pushed for further understanding of the entire illness experience. Having a health problem does not end when one leaves the doctor's office. Valuable books have been written, for example, on living with AIDS, Alzheimer's, epilepsy, fibromyalgia, and depression. These are studies of people's lived experiences and the meaning they give to such.[15]

When we provide people the opportunity to speak to us in their own words, the depth and complexity of the topic grow. In the space of our silence we make room for someone to tell us their truth, to tell us something that may not be easy to hear, and which we may never have thought was significant. The sociologist Arthur Frank wrote a beautiful book that recognized how stories of illness link us together in a shared experience. Frank wrote, "Sooner or later, everyone is a wounded story-teller. In postmodern times that identity is our promise and responsibility."[16] I like to imagine his words mean that at some point in time, we all encounter something that profoundly affects our lives and wounds us, such as illness. When we attempt to give voice to what is happening, to put language to the body, we create a story of who we are.[17] When we tell our story to others, we gain recognition and ideally empathy. As Frank pointed out, "Because stories can heal, the wounded healer and wounded storyteller are not separate, but are different aspects of the same figure."[18]

Further, people telling their own stories of illness or sociologists recording such narratives provides a more comprehensive picture of health and illness. Doctors in the past talked intimately with people (including about their lifestyle and morals) in order to treat them.[19] When we arrive at the doctor's office now, healthcare professionals have a range of tactics to diagnose our problems that do not necessitate talking to us about our lives but focus more on having a conversation with our bones, blood, and genes. According to Frank, "Folk now go to paid professionals who reinterpret their pains as symptoms, using a specialized language that is unfamiliar and overwhelming. . . . The chart becomes the official story of the illness."[20] But this is not the complete story. Frank contended that we have moved past the period in which patients had to passively surrender themselves completely to professionals and into a period in which "ill people recognize that more is involved in their experiences than the medical story can tell."[21]

Obsessive-compulsive disorder has been relatively neglected. Self-help books on OCD exist. Studies on how to diagnose and treat the disorder have been conducted, and more recently autobiographies have been written by those with OCD about their personal experiences. However, little research has systematically looked for patterns in the lived experiences of those with OCD from a social perspective. My goal in writing this book is to do just that. It is particularly important because many people with OCD hide their obsessions and compulsions and fear stigma; it seems only a minority may have received treatment in some contexts, and even those who seek help do not always receive adequate treatment.[22] I believe the lives of people with OCD have lessons for us all, including insight into the times in which we live.

Opening the Door to Understanding OCD

In order to break down stereotypes of OCD, I sought to interview as diverse a group of people as possible. I initially recruited people from a multitude of online groups, asking them to answer a list of questions over email and keep a journal of their daily experiences with OCD for two weeks if they had time; after that, I could follow up with a real-time conversation. Soon I realized that potential participants had obsessions and rituals that made particular forms of interaction difficult, or they feared stigma and were wary of certain forms of contact. Ultimately, I communicated with people through various mediums. I spoke to the majority of people face-to-face or over the phone.[23] I communicated with others via email or online chat or exchanged letters in the mail.[24] There was no support group for OCD in the city where I lived, so I attended five meetings for a group in another city (which met one or two times a month) when I traveled out of town periodically, listening to what people said and interviewing eight members.

I collected detailed information from 55 participants, as well as additional data from informal conversations with people who said they had OCD (e.g., people who did not complete the study). The core group of 55 people were located primarily in the United States (43 persons) and the United Kingdom (10 persons), with one person each from India and Canada (although included within my informal conversations were persons from Asia and Latin America). I spoke to 23 men and 32 women. Their ages varied widely at the time of our initial interview: 18 were between 18 and 30 years old; 26 were between 31 and 50 years old; and 11 were 51 or older.[25] They were married, divorced, single, and cohabitating. It was a relatively educated group, with many in college or having completed some years of college, but the yearly individual income was wide-ranging, from $0 to more than $250,000 (from being on governmental assistance for OCD to multiple people earning more than $100,000). The group was largely made up of people who identified their race/ethnicity as White/Caucasian,[26] although I spoke informally to people of other races and ethnicities. Those who were employed held various types of jobs, from government positions with the military and the Department of Homeland Security in the United States to some in the healthcare field. While the majority were diagnosed by healthcare professionals, I did include people who were not (although some were being treated by a professional). These included a few people who expressed uncertainty about whether they had OCD, such as a couple of people who hoarded.[27] I was eager to speak to them because I wanted to understand how they came to perceive themselves as having the disorder and why they did or did not utilize traditional avenues of support. Much research emphasizes conventional treatment, and historically, studies of mental illness have commonly involved people who were hospitalized; we do not know as much about non-help-seeking and other paths. When I introduce someone in the book, I specify if they have been diagnosed with OCD by a professional. A number were diagnosed as children, but I interviewed one man who was diagnosed in his retirement years in his seventies. The rest of the interviewees were diagnosed at various stages of life.

Anxiety disorders are among the most prevalent mental disorders, and OCD was previously classified in the *Diagnostic and Statistical Manual of Mental Disorders (DSM-IV-TR)* as a type of anxiety disorder.[28] The *Diagnostic and Statistical Manual of Mental Disorders (DSM)* is arguably the reigning way of classifying mental disorders. Some people refer to it colloquially as the psychiatric "bible."[29] Historically, it has fostered consensus among professionals regarding how to conceptualize particular mental disorders, and it has helped give legitimacy to psychiatry as a branch of medicine.[30] Professionals in the field of mental health questioned whether OCD-related disorders should form their own category,[31] and so in the most recent version of the *DSM* (the *DSM-5*, published in 2013) they do. Obsessive-compulsive disorder, hoarding, and other related disorders are categorized under the heading of "obsessive-compulsive and related disorders" rather than anxiety disorders.[32] Many people I interviewed were diagnosed before changes were made to the *DSM* and the conceptualization of OCD, so a handful of interviewees who were diagnosed with OCD in the past might today be reclassified by a healthcare professional as having an obsessive-compulsive and related disorder such as one involving body-focused repetitive behavior. Previously, hoarding was not directly listed in the *DSM* (although it was sometimes considered an OCD symptom by professionals),[33] but now "hoarding disorder" is outlined under the heading of "obsessive-compulsive and related disorders." This explains how the interviewees who hoarded thought they had or might have OCD.

In general, comorbidity (occurrence of OCD and another disorder) can be high.[34] Of those individuals I communicated with who had been diagnosed, more than 75 percent were diagnosed with depression or some other disorder (including attention-deficit/hyperactivity disorder [ADHD]) in addition to OCD. (Some of these diagnoses of other disorders could be misdiagnoses of OCD).[35] When I introduce someone, I indicate whether they were diagnosed with other mental disorders.

I complemented the interview data with a few other sources. I interviewed eight family members of those with the disorder. Six of these individuals were family members of someone with OCD whom I interviewed; the seventh was a mother whose daughter (with OCD) was unavailable to interview; the eighth had a young child with OCD. Although some of the people I interviewed with OCD worked in the mental healthcare field, I also interviewed three therapists about their experiences treating the disorder. Along with them, I interviewed the developer of an app for OCD that connects people to help for the disorder and also conversed with the administrator of an online group for OCD. When I was writing about the importance of information and social networks for people with OCD, I collected and analyzed 150 posts on an online forum for people with the disorder. In order to consider public perceptions of OCD, I conducted a web search for the phrase "so OCD" and analyzed the content of the first fifty hits. To assess public perceptions of OCD, I surveyed more than five hundred undergraduate students.

As the sociologist David A. Karp indicated when writing about depression, as did the sociologist Peter Conrad when lecturing on medicalization, a social scientist can focus on how categories such as "OCD" are created and used by those in society.[36] I recognize the power of society in labeling and shaping people's experiences, from broken bones to mental disorders, but I also know the torment people with OCD can feel and do not consider the disorder a figment of people's (or the healthcare profession's) imaginations. My goal is to explicate how obsessive-compulsive disorder becomes a meaningful explanation and category in people's lives, including if and how that label means different things to different people. I take what social scientists call a symbolic inter-actionist perspective in the book overall. A dog may represent danger to one person, while serving as a symbol of humanity's best friend to another. Things have no single meaning in and of themselves.[37] In in-teraction with others, people give meaning to everything from objects to experiences. Over time, society has come to observe and recognize things called "obsessions" and "compulsions," although not always in the same way. I am interested in how people with OCD respond to current medical/psychological/psychiatric conceptions of the disorder, and the meanings they give to OCD beyond this, as "OCD" shapes their work and family lives. I care about how OCD affects their sense of self. People construct a sense of who they are as they tell narratives about them-selves,[38] as they did in their interviews with me. There may be many people who experience what a psychologist would label "obsessions" and "compulsions," but for whom the label "OCD" has no meaning, and who never question whether they have a problem or disorder. However, these are not the people with whom I interacted, and so such issues are largely outside the scope of this book.[39]

My experiences studying OCD have been different from those I had when researching other topics over the years. I have spent time with Buddhists, Quakers, pole dancers, and circus performers, often partici-pating in activities with them. However, much of OCD takes place in the mind. Even those aspects that do not, such as compulsions, left me wondering how people felt as they performed them and how they in-terpreted what was occurring. In a sense, I asked people to open up their minds to me. They did so because they wanted the world to better understand and accept them. One of the goals of this book is to let them speak and give other people a chance to hear them at length in their own words. It will also help those with OCD who told me they yearned to hear more about the experiences of others who are similar to them. I as-signed everyone an alias, allowing their stories to be connected through-out the chapters. Although this book is not just for people with OCD and their loved ones, my sincere hope is that the book will help them see that they are not alone.

Career

Hearing the life stories of people with OCD, I noticed a career-like quality to what they were saying, as if coming to see oneself as having OCD is a process consisting of stages that people cycle through (sometimes repeatedly). These stages are coming to see oneself as having a problem, defining the problem as OCD, seeking help, and learning to live with the disorder. There can be a chronicity to having OCD. Some people I interviewed felt they had conquered their obsessions and compulsions. However, even when people's OCD was in remission, sometimes they remained vigilant, waiting and watching in case it returned, or else monitored their children's behavior for signs of obsessions and/or compulsions.

It might seem unconventional to call having an "illness" a career. However, for decades sociologists have fruitfully used the idea of a "career" as a means to understand people's experiences and their transitions into, within, and out of various roles and activities.[40] Just as people move through stages and transitions in their work lives, they similarly do so when they get sick and seek treatment. Consider how becoming a lawyer or a medical doctor involves an occupational path; achieving this position requires particular training and credentials, as well as moving through transitional positions such as internships. Beyond conventional careers, researchers have studied the trajectories associated with various roles and have revealed patterns in other activities, including becoming a marijuana user or gym-goer. The career framework is a nuanced way of understanding the stages people go through, and how people's understanding of themselves (and others' treatment of them) changes over time. Sometimes models emphasize people's paths as patients. Because not everyone with a mental disorder seeks help, and their paths are not purely linear, I map commonalities in the experiences of those with OCD while paying critical attention to the complexity of people's individual lives. For instance, some people whose thoughts and rituals were diverse went through particular stages again depending on the form their OCD took. There was no one final end point everyone shared, and some individuals stopped at a particular stage or skipped a stage.[41]

This career framework has been especially useful in understanding the experiences of those with illnesses. In his book on depression, Karp theorized that those with depression go through various stages, which involve moving from experiencing "inchoate feelings" without labeling them depression, to perceiving that "something is really wrong with me," to a "crisis stage that thrusts them into a world of therapeutic experts," and finally to "coming to grips with an illness identity."[42] Furthermore, Karp explained how career stages often involve a change in how one perceives the self: "Much of the depression career is caught up in assessing self, redefining self, reinterpreting past selves, and attempting to construct a future self that will 'work' better."[43] When I read Karp's book, it changed how I perceived depression as it helped me put myself into the shoes of the people he interviewed. It made me more empathetic when interacting with students and friends who have depression. My hope is to provide a similar book, but one about OCD.

The career model lets us see how the OCD experience evolves. I have designed the bulk of this book to take the reader through each of the different stages named earlier. For instance, we do not know much about what having obsessions and compulsions means to people with OCD, including how they came to perceive their entanglement with these intrusive thoughts as problematic and constituting a disorder. I spoke to a therapist in Malaysia who told me:

> I have encountered a lot of individuals in the traditional Asian role of a housewife that appear to have suffered from OCD for decades (excessive cleaning for hours to the point where their hands bleed, etc.), but their symptoms went unnoticed (or are even praised) because culturally, it's considered part of their duties, even though they caused them a lot of physical and emotional distress.

We perceive OCD as a more widespread mental health issue today than in the past because it has become medicalized and psychologized, in other words, conceptualized as a diagnosable mental disorder that can be treated by psychiatrists and psychologists. Many authors highlight how processes such as medicalization shape people's perception of themselves as sick with a potentially stigmatizing condition, when before they may not have even believed they had such a problem.[44] In the face of the power of the medical establishment, "patients" can appear passive, docilely listening to their doctors and therapists as they are depersonalized by technological diagnostic probing and testing.[45] However, we are also living in a period that has pushed us to manage risk and take individual responsibility for our health. Commentators from a variety of disciplines have argued that many patients are now more active, veritable "co-creators" of their health. In the case of OCD, medicalization and psychologization were valuable processes for many interviewees and ones that they promoted themselves. Many of the people I interviewed (as well as those I observed in online groups) actively diagnosed themselves, eagerly sought professional information, and/or reiterated the value of current therapies for the disorder among themselves. They did this in the face of a healthcare profession that itself sometimes lacks knowledge of and misdiagnoses OCD.[46] They were regularly active consumers, including advocating for more shared relationships with healthcare professionals. (Terminology surrounding the "doctor-patient" relationship is controversial, and there does not appear to be a substitute term that all interested parties agree on, such as "service user" or "consumer." As a result, I will use different terminology throughout, selecting the term that best fits the literature or context to which I am referring.)

Trivialization and Stigma

A theme throughout the book, and one that cuts across the various stages of the OCD career, is the difficult position people with OCD and their allies are in, navigating a tangled web of trivialization and potential stigma. Janet was a woman in her forties living in the United Kingdom whose therapist told her that she probably had OCD; thus, Janet perceived herself as having been diagnosed. (Her therapist said there might also be "elements of depression," and in the past a psychiatrist had told Janet that she had a minor mood disorder. She further described herself as having anxiety-related and somatoform disorders.) She revealed to me just how complex social interaction can be for people who feel they experience obsessions and/or compulsions:

> I am on a journey that I never asked to take, and without the appropriate equipment, desperately trying to do my best. . . . Society does not view people with OCD in the true sense because it is so carefully hidden.

When they are forced to look at it, there can be a range of reactions including distaste, fascination, pity or even amusement at its peculiar
nature. . . . In, out, in, out—does the world want to see it or not? Pull it
out for the medics to see if they can sort it, now put it back in so it doesn't
affect your productivity, let's have it out again so I can indulge my curios-
ity and horror, now back in because you are reminding me how vulnerable we all are. . . . There is still fear and misunderstanding about [mental
illness]. . . . The mentally ill make us all reflect about what is normal and
about our own mental fragility. Perhaps that is their ultimate crime. . . .
Make your mind up, world. I am not a side show.[47]

Mental disorders are not one-size-fits-all. The public stereotypes
disorders differently from each other, considering some as less serious
and less stigmatizing than others. In this way, society has constructed a
social acceptance hierarchy—or, considered from the other side of the
equation, a stigma hierarchy. This is an underused concept by scholars,
but people with OCD show how there are unique aspects to living with
a particular disorder.[48]

The obsessions and compulsions people with OCD have are at once
potentially subject to minimization and positive stereotypes, as well as
negative exaggerations and judgments. Even the types of obsessions and
compulsions that people have are viewed differently by the public, as
some generate more misunderstanding and fear on the part of the public than others. For instance, consider how the public might respond
to someone who has a fear of germs and illness versus a fear that they
might be a pedophile (even though this type of OCD is not actually associated with pedophilia or pedophile interests).[49] People with OCD are
caught between a rock and a hard place. They are caught between fears
that people will stigmatize them in the traditional sense by seeing them
as weird, crazy, abnormal, and dangerous—and frustration when people
minimize and belittle having obsessions and compulsions or otherwise
trivialize the disorder.

Trivialization and stigma at first glance appear to be different, perhaps even opposites; one interviewee referred to trivialization as "reverse
stigma." Stigma involves a difference that is viewed negatively by society, linked to negative stereotypes, social distance, and discrimination.[50]
Self-stigma happens when people apply those negative stereotypes to

themselves, resulting in negative outcomes.[51] A past commentary in the *American Journal of Public Health* began with the statement, "Individuals with mental illness experience disparities in health care, education, and employment outcomes, and the stigma associated with mental illness is a central contributing factor to these disparities."[52] Trivialization, meanwhile, is associated with minimization of the disorder. Relatively little research has examined the trivialization of mental disorders by the public and its effects, but doing so is critical. Many people with OCD and their allies are frustrated by trivialization. They believe that it misrepresents the disorder, is demeaning, and makes it hard for people with the disorder to receive the professional help they need (much less gain understanding from the general public, friends, and family). One person I interviewed with OCD who works in the healthcare field felt that even professionals make fun of those with OCD and do not treat the disorder as seriously as they should. I argue that trivialization can lead to microaggressions and potentially even stigma, for instance, if people with OCD are belittled as being too sensitive and exaggerating their problems unnecessarily.

At the same time, trivialization intriguingly also appears to grant people with OCD certain privileges. Misunderstanding of the disorder may keep those with OCD from facing some of the negative stereotypes and stigma people with other disorders face.[53] In other words, if OCD is constructed as a quirky personality trait, it hardly leads people to run for the hills screaming in fear and discriminating against those with the disorder.

The tricky part, then, is determining how best to help those with OCD. Emphasizing the seriousness of the disorder may reduce trivialization and alter people's sense of the disorder as quirky and not a big deal. On the flip side, I recognize that it may trigger some people's fears and potentially foster an increase in negative stereotyping and the stigma that arises from such. In writing this book, I have had to consider that increasing public knowledge of OCD may further stigmatize those I want to help. I credit Mick, who has had OCD since age five and has become a sounding board for my working ideas on OCD, for encouraging me to take notice of this issue. Mick first wrote me in 2003, when he was almost forty. After I did research on representations of OCD in the media, he contemplated my report. When he contacted me to discuss my findings, Mick brought up how some people I interviewed were frustrated that the media did not represent the full spectrum of OCD and wanted to see more representations of the diverse forms that it can take. Mick said that he too would like to see the various fears and worries people experience within media portrayals, but he wondered about misunderstandings that might result if such were to be shown to the public:[54]

> But (1) how, oh how, do you represent something like that? Something so internal? So perceptual? And (2) how do you do it without your audience getting the wrong idea, wondering whether the show is going to end with harm to "his neighbor's little boy" or the bus driver being hailed with a racial epithet? Because, of course, there is no molestation and there is no insult; it is the unrealistic fear of these happening and the fear of losing control that one means to portray. Yes, perhaps I'd sooner leave the issue alone.

Instead of seeing people's worries for what they are, Mick was concerned that viewers might mistakenly view people with OCD as harmful to society.

My hope is that by showing what OCD is like for people with the disorder, this book will illuminate the problems of trivialization while providing enough information to promote empathy and understanding. More specifically, I illustrate how it behooves us to see people's experiences of obsessions and compulsions on a continuum and not incomprehensible and wholly alien from the experiences of those without the disorder. This is important because even you may have experienced unwanted intrusive thoughts or urges, as it appears the majority of people experience them to some degree.[55]

I am not denying the serious struggles unique to those with OCD, nor evidence of neurobiological foundations of the disorder, but I am pointing out that the fears of those with OCD, just like everyone else's, can reflect the problems of our society. Contemporary society has been characterized as one of risk, and potentially one of anxiety or increasing psychological distress.[56] The thoughts and rituals of people with OCD, therefore, do not appear so radically different from everyone else's. This is especially evident considering the international COVID-19 pandemic. Mick, whose OCD included fears about being contaminated and causing contamination, told me that people have been making jesting remarks to him given that now the world must take precautions to prevent the spread of COVID-19. His mother, with whom Mick lives, said something akin to "Now we're all like you!" Interestingly, Mick's anxiety has not been extraordinary during the pandemic. He noted, "It is easy for me to eschew touching my face, to remember to wash whatever hand touched public surfaces, to avoid people on the street. Indeed, it's quite natural." According to Nathaniel Van Kirk, the coordinator of clinical assessment at the McLean Institute for treating and researching OCD, because people with OCD are used to feeling fear and uncertainty, they may be more prepared for the pandemic.[57] Another interviewee said that since the onset of the pandemic he actually feels safer, as more people are taking precautions. However, there is evidence that people with OCD have experienced a worsening of symptoms as a result of COVID-19, and not just those related to contamination, potentially due to stress resulting from the pandemic.[58] Further, the pandemic may increase the general public's understanding of OCD, as more people are having to manage this kind of risk and uncertainty.[59] "Everyone is getting a sense of what it's like to live with obsessions and anxiety every day," said Van Kirk.

Recent research on stigma suggests that perceiving mental illness on a continuum (i.e., that there is a continuum between everyday distress that the general population experiences, and having a mental illness) may help take the bite out of stigma by increasing empathy and social acceptance. Some workplaces train employers to view mental health along a continuum to better target help for their workers.[60] As some people I interviewed explained, we all have our problems.

The Book's Organization

The book is organized into two parts. Part I provides background information on obsessive-compulsive disorder. In chapter 1, I begin by briefly reviewing how "obsessions" and "compulsions" have been viewed historically. In contrast, within chapter 2 we start to perceive the world through the eyes of those with obsessions and compulsions. This chapter relies heavily on extended quotes to bring people's thoughts and feelings to life.[61] In the process, we hopefully can break down stereotypes and public misperceptions of OCD. Chapter 3 reviews the available treatments for the disorder.

In part II, I move to depicting the "career" of having OCD, and the rest of the book is organized by each successive stage. Chapter 4 begins with what life was like before those I interviewed realized they had OCD. We have to consider people within social contexts, for instance, examining the behavior of those around them to evaluate themselves, at times hiding what they were experiencing, and using their existing knowledge to give meaning to their thoughts/behaviors. This encompassed various explanations, from believing it was just them (an aspect of their personality or self and thereby with no solution), to supernatural causes such as Vodou (the religion).

In chapter 5, I examine the shift that occurs when people go from perceiving themselves as having a personality issue, spiritual problem, or other type of difficulty to believing they have OCD, a mental disorder. Unlike situations in which an "illness career" begins when a healthcare professional labels a person with an illness or disorder, some interviewees took on this role themselves. However, sometimes years passed between interviewees deciding they had a "problem" and coming to this label, in part because of stereotypes and lack of information about the disorder. It is within this chapter that I depict how diagnosis can be a double-edged sword, giving people with OCD an explanation for their self-perceived problematic thoughts and behaviors, but also labeling them with a stigmatizing condition. The shift in identity that comes with being labeled is not entirely unique to OCD. However, I argue that aspects of this process are distinctive for each disorder, bringing into play the concept of a stigma hierarchy. In this chapter I develop how people with OCD navigate a complicated context involving both trivialization and stigma.

Chapters 6 and 7 are about help-seeking. These chapters explore what people do after they see themselves as having OCD. Karp argued that when people with depression begin taking medication, it is akin to forming a relationship. Building on his idea, I argue that people have metaphorically formed a marriage with their OCD. For example, they have been using compulsions and other coping tactics—everything from avoiding things related to their thoughts to exercising—to manage their thoughts. I refer to this as the "daily grind." Professional treatment commonly involves attempting to give up aspects of this relationship to form a new one with medication or taking their thoughts and behaviors to therapy, hoping to revamp the relationship. I explore how difficult this can be, especially when people confront their fears in therapy and recognize how certain coping behaviors can reinforce the OCD. As part of this, I delve into how family and other people close to those with OCD have also formed a relationship with the OCD, such as when people with OCD ask those around them to clean the house in particular ways or engage in other rituals with them or for them. Treatment is a social process.

In chapter 7, I discuss how resources, specifically social and cultural resources or capital, help people with OCD build connections with others, follow evidence-based techniques for coping and treating their OCD, and maneuver within the healthcare system. For instance, some of the biggest roadblocks to treatment include lack of access to knowledgeable and affordable treatment for those with OCD. While there was not always much people could do to address the cost of help, I show how interviewees used information and experience to advocate for what they wanted out of the treatment experience and in their relationships with healthcare professionals. Recently, research has been examining the potentials of self-guided treatment protocols and technology-based applications. Despite benefits, there can be downsides in the search for information and social support for those with the disorder, such as when searching for information becomes an obsession unto itself.

Chapter 8 describes the last stage in the OCD "career," which involves learning to live with OCD. I discuss how people's sense of themselves in relation to the OCD evolved over time and study their interactions with others more closely. This includes considering the long-term impacts of OCD, such as how parents sometimes monitored their children for traces of the disorder. Importantly, interviewees did experience stigma but not as much as they feared and anticipated, although this is partly because they engaged in multiple strategies of subterfuge and obfuscation within social interactions. They commonly sought understanding and, all told, received quite a bit of warmth and support from others. The people with whom I spoke often saw OCD in a relatively individual light, as a medical or psychological problem they needed to manage.

As a sociologist, I questioned to what degree they perceived OCD as a larger social issue. Their answers were complex. They appreciated and utilized their connections to others with the disorder and wanted to increase the public's knowledge of the disorder. Yet they expressed some hesitation at identifying too closely with the label, much less advocating for the rights of OCD people as a group.

I conclude the book by considering the implications of the forgoing chapters. How do we improve the lives of those with obsessive-compulsive disorder and others who have been diagnosed with mental disorders? Certainly, to understand OCD, we have to see people with the disorder as more than individuals with defective brains or quirky people who like to clean. In the conclusion I tie together ideas on trivialization and stigmatization, continuum models, and living in our contemporary risk society. I concur with interviewees who hoped for and envisioned institutions that take into account the needs of everyone along the mental health continuum. Improving the lives of those with OCD and other health concerns involves more than getting them better medications and therapy, or their perceiving it as a personal trouble. I believe we would benefit from more flexible institutions that meet the needs of diverse populations whose members may not want to disclose that they have been diagnosed with a mental illness or who experience problems at a subthreshold level, enabling them to be happy and productive.

One goal of this book is to represent the experience of OCD from the perspective of those with the disorder. To this end, quotes and excerpts from persons are abundant.[62] One example is the following passage from Kelcie, who lived in the United States and was diagnosed with OCD and an eating disorder:

> [If I could speak to the world, I would] want people to know that OCD is more than just washing hands a million times and keeping every[thing] neat and orderly. As I keep moving forward, I need to remember all that I have gone through. . . . I believe that all of this will make me a stronger person. It will make me appreciate life so much more. Life is challenging, but at the same time it is so beautiful and wonderful. All I can say to life is bring it on. I will not be defeated by OCD.

PART I

The Misunderstood

1

What Is OCD?

Most of the public . . . they don't see OCD. . . . The [film about Howard
Hughes] *The Aviator* . . . does display some of the worst symptoms and
possibilities of OCD. . . . That's something you don't see in many depictions like *Monk* the [TV] series or [the film] *As Good as It Gets* where he's
just basically walking over sidewalk cracks and it's kind of comedic. . . .
[I watch] all those shows and I have to laugh even though I can relate
to some of those symptoms. . . . If you can't laugh about some of the
most terrific things and some of the most difficult things in life, then
you're going to be a very dreary [person]. . . . [But] they don't show the
life-shattering consequences of it. And, it trivializes OCD in the public
mind. . . . That can be a problem because that's how . . . people are exposed to the idea of OCD. . . . [There are also times where media represent OCD as very deviant and] they speak about it like it is some kind
of contagious disease. . . . [I saw one Dr. Phil show where an audience
member looked at the person with OCD] like she was an animal, like she
was just from another planet.
—Destin

Destin points to how obsessions and compulsions have a variety of
public faces in contemporary society. Destin was diagnosed with OCD
and ADHD, and thought he might have been told by professionals that
he had depression or bipolar disorder. At the time we spoke, he was in
his twenties and in graduate school. Destin had a unique approach in
communicating with me. I would send him questions by email, and he
would send me audio recordings and emails of his musings on the topics
I raised. He told me about how he experienced a variety of obsessions
and compulsions, referring to his symptoms as free-floating in that they
could latch on to what he saw others do. At one point he avoided media
representing OCD in order to impede this process.

When he did engage with this type of media, he noticed how humorous fictional characters traipsed across the big and small screen, capturing the attention of viewers, for example, Monk in a show by the same name. Other people I spoke to mentioned how the homes of hoarders have been treated as spectacle and opened up for viewing in the American reality TV show *Hoarders*. I have seen movie trailers about obsessed characters, with their attachments to former lovers, sex, and more. Do these representations reflect how healthcare professionals perceive obsessions, compulsions, and what people with OCD experience?

Destin indicated they do so only partially, leaving a public that he felt did not truly understand OCD. Destin told me, "Thank you for attempting to give voice to those with OCD." He believed it would be hard for people without the disorder to make sense of it. "If I didn't have it, I kind of feel like it would be hard for me to believe that others are being truthful about their experiences. . . . How can they relate to somebody who has numbers and ideas and thoughts of wickedness or whatever, flying through their heads twenty-four hours a day?"

Therefore, this chapter provides an overview of how OCD has been defined and represented in society. People who see themselves as having OCD are impacted by what official experts such as psychiatrists and psychologists say, what the media represent, and other understandings of OCD in a particular culture. The thoughts and behaviors that today define a person as having obsessive-compulsive disorder have a varied history. We have not always understood it in the same way, and we will likely come to understand it in different ways in the future.

Public Perceptions

I recently saw an image on the internet. Within it, objects in a store were neatly organized, accompanied by the message "OCD is pleased." When I went online later to try to find the picture for a closer look, I encountered a different "ecard" that depicted a woman cleaning, accompanied by the words, "Some people call it OCD. I call it 'not being a fucking slob.'" OCD is discussed more publicly today than in the past.[1] For example, media attention to the disorder appears to be increasing, so much so that you have probably seen casual references to OCD being made outside of medical contexts, as I did in the media. You may have encountered online memes joking about obsessions/ compulsions, such as having a fondness for organizing things. You may have heard people, even celebrities, say they are "so OCD" when sometimes they just mean that they are a little excessive in their organizing or their concerns about cleanliness. Two researchers of communication, Rachelle L. Pavelko and Jessica Gall Myrick, wrote about how people on social media refer to themselves as having OCD when they engage in everyday nonclinical organizing-type behaviors.[2] There was even a makeup company called Obsessive Compulsive Cosmetics, for which "obsessively craft[ing]" makeup for those who compulsively buy such cosmetics was stated as a positive purpose.

Such ways of representing and talking about OCD suggest the disorder is commonplace in society and can imply that it is akin to a personality trait. OCD ends up appearing potentially positive and humorous and not particularly serious. This stands in contrast to the stigmatizing ways mental disorders are often represented in the media.[3] People in society do not always have direct experience with a mental disorder or know of someone with a mental disorder. The media can serve as a primary source of information about mental disorders, shaping people's views and behaviors. Although more complex representations of mental disorders do exist in the media, many studies indicate that the media misrepresent people with mental disorders by stereotyping them as dangerous and violent. A study of US television images revealed how the rate of characters with mental disorders committing violent crimes was nine times higher on the television programs compared with actual crime rates.[4] Other negative representations have portrayed people with mental disorders as unpredictable, unkempt, not trustworthy, self-involved, childlike, and unproductive social failures who are unable to hold down jobs and have difficulty interacting socially.[5] Tweets on social media have even been analyzed by researchers, revealing that mental health conditions were stigmatized more than physical ones.[6]

Media representations of mental illness as well as healthcare professionals influence public perceptions of mental illness, help-seeking, and stigma.[7] For this reason, I argue that it is important to pay attention to how *particular* disorders and symptoms are represented. Although the public and the media can treat obsessions and/or compulsions as quirky and humorous, media representations of obsessed stalkers do exist, suggesting that people with obsessions can be dangerous.[8] A popular understanding of the term "obsession" is the hungering for something desirable, as in obsessive love. For healthcare professionals, this construction of obsessions is inaccurate as obsessions are unwanted and commonly distressing.[9] In a similar way, compulsions in popular culture are sometimes understood to involve people being unable to stop doing something pleasurable, such as gambling. Meanwhile, healthcare professionals argue that people with OCD do not find performing compulsions pleasurable. However, a search on the Internet Movie Database easily yields examples of these popular constructions of obsessions and compulsions, and other instances exist in magazines.

While media representations of OCD appear to have increased over time,[10] and use of the term "OCD" seems to have entered our everyday conversations, people cannot necessarily identify someone with the disorder. In one study of American adults, only a third of respondents recognized a vignette as depicting OCD.[11] The vignette portrayed a person with worries about bad things happening such as a stove catching on fire, so the person engaged in checking behaviors. The character in the vignette was also afraid of germs and washed his hands. In a different study, a small sample of students in a high school in Spain were shown a vignette about a person with order-related OCD as well as an example of a person with obsessions related to self-harm. The vast majority labeled the first vignette as OCD, while less than a quarter identified the second example as OCD.[12] This research suggests that while the public may not necessarily recognize obsessions/compulsions, which are more commonly represented in the media, they have more knowledge of those. A few years ago, My colleague Michael Boyd and I studied portrayals of OCD in fictional films.[13] I conducted this research in part to see what types of obsessions and compulsions are shown in films. Around the same time, a researcher in the field of psychology examined representations of OCD in films for their dissertation.[14] The most common compulsions represented in the films, according to these studies, were ordering, washing/cleaning, and checking, and the most common obsessions were contamination and ordering obsessions. Therefore, the diversity of forms that obsessions and compulsions can take do not appear to be commonly recognized by the public or represented in film.

However, people with OCD and their allies, including healthcare professionals, are using online resources and social media to represent OCD and break public stereotypes. I observed creative online videos during the COVID-19 pandemic that discussed mental health and encapsulated how OCD impacts people. This included video creators verbalizing the thoughts in their heads as they physically went about their days, singing about symptoms the public may not associate with OCD, showing their rituals, talking about how OCD is not a joke, and generating satire that juxtaposes what the public thinks versus what people actually experience.

Professional Conceptualizations

People have all types of thoughts that zip in and out of their minds. These include bizarre thoughts and impulses that interrupt the stream of our thoughts, which we shrug off. A psychologist gave the example of someone jogging across a bridge and feeling an urge to jump off.[15] Further, many of us have our auspicious rabbits' feet, lucky shirts, various "quirks," or superstitions, which are sometimes centered in the myths of our culture. These thoughts/behaviors are generally not considered abnormal by society, so what makes OCD any different?

Following diagnostic criteria, OCD is considered to be something more than this. According to the *Diagnostic and Statistical Manual of Mental Disorders* and the World Health Organization's International Statistical Classification of Diseases and Related Health Problems, having OCD means a person experiences obsessions and/or compulsions.[16] The obsessions/compulsions take up a significant amount of time (more than one hour per day) or cause a person "clinically significant distress or impairment,"[17] as if those intrusive thoughts anyone might experience were ratcheted up to the nth degree. Obsessions include obsessional "ideas," "images," "convictions," "ruminations," "impulses," and "fears."[18] A person with obsessions tries to forget about, suppress, or neutralize them. Compulsions refer to "purposeful, meaningful, and deliberate behaviour that the person feels driven to carry out repeatedly, and is usually performed according to certain rules or in a stereotyped fashion."[19] However, these acts do not make rational sense (i.e., they are not related to what they are designed to relieve) or are overmuch, and a person with OCD does not find engaging in them enjoyable; this makes OCD different from activities that give people pleasure and are associated with some other mental disorders.[20]

People with OCD are not simply quirky (although people I interviewed sometimes saw themselves as such); the disorder can be quite serious and have real impacts on a person's daily functioning. The psychiatrist Peter D. Kramer referred to OCD as "among the most terrible of psychiatric disturbances" and "distinctive and relentless."[21] It can be frustrating for people with OCD and their therapists to hear someone say they are a "little bit OCD." However, there is increasing evidence that people can experience thoughts/behaviors that do not meet the diagnostic criteria for OCD (for instance, having intrusive thoughts/rituals that take up less than one hour per day or lead to moderate distress or impairment), but which still cause difficulties for them in their lives (so perhaps being a "little bit OCD" is possible).[22] The impacts of the obsessions and compulsions on the wider society, therefore, may be larger than current estimates of the prevalence of OCD suggest, and it is useful to perceive the level of people's obsessions and compulsions along a spectrum. The fact that researchers are studying obsessions and compulsions at the subthreshold level and considering early interventions for people experiencing these illustrates the increasing medicalization and psychologization of obsessions and compulsions through the extension of a more established diagnosis.[23] There also appears to be a group whom researchers have labeled "supernormals," people who experience a significant level of obsessive-compulsive symptoms but are not negatively impacted.[24]

When listening to interviewees or reading posts in online groups and forums, I noticed how people talked about particular types of obsessions and compulsions, such as checking compulsions or harm OCD. Researchers have similarly been trying to make sense of the heterogeneous disorder by categorizing obsessions and compulsions into subtypes or symptom dimensions, for example, contamination obsessions/cleaning rituals, religious obsessions (scrupulosity), and symmetry obsessions/ordering compulsions.[25] Presumably, these still share something that fundamentally makes them "OCD." However, intriguingly, some evidence intimates that symptom dimensions may vary in important ways, such as biological differences, variations in symptom onset, and variable treatment outcomes. In other words, certain forms of obsessions and compulsions may respond better to particular treatments, have different causes, and so on. People can and do have symptoms from more than one dimension.

When I started reading more closely about OCD a number of years ago, I found a variety of studies that suggested a neurobiological basis for OCD. Research on the topic has grown, and there are now neuroimaging studies that show potential differences in the size and functioning of different areas of the brain in people with OCD.[26] Twin studies have been conducted that indicate a potential genetic basis for OCD. According to one study, more than one hundred candidate genes have been linked to the disorder; however, "OCD polygenetic and multi-factorial typology makes hard to find single gene associations . . . [explaining] the difficulties of translating biological knowledge into preventive measures or clinical trials."[27] Although "structural and functional changes within the brain" have long been associated with OCD, we are not at a point where it is possible to diagnose OCD from a brain scan.[28]

Claims of links between mental disorders and biological processes in general have been on the rise in recent decades.[29] As one article phrased it, the "increasing biologisation of mental illness has shifted the psychiatric gaze towards the understanding of humans as neurological or neurochemical beings."[30] Yet, decades of research on psychiatric disorders directed toward hunting for their neurobiological foundations have seemingly not led to all the revolutionary findings psychiatry hoped for.[31] Despite the medications people take or therapeutic techniques they may try, improvements in outcomes may be due in significant part to other factors (such as the placebo effect).[32] Social and environmental factors influence treatments and their effectiveness.[33] One group of healthcare professionals and researchers wrote, "It is increasingly recognized that specific technical interventions, such as drugs, have a limited impact on the overall burden of serious mental illness."[34]

This is likely because so many factors are at play. If we look historically, the general link of mental illness to biology has existed in the past, with society seemingly alternating between thinking causes are biological versus attributing mental illness to some other cause.[35] More recently, various people from theorists to those in healthcare delivery have argued that we need new models for psychology and psychiatry.

We seem to be in the midst of a potential paradigm shift, perhaps toward a viewpoint that takes greater account of people within their larger environments.[36] Kamaldeep Bhui, editor of the *British Journal of Psychiatry*, spoke about the newer paradigm of "cultural neuroscience" that "asserts the co-evolution of genetic, biological, neural, social and cultural affordances, that improve the human capacity to communicate, cooperate, survive and adapt."[37] The sociologist Nikolas Rose wrote about the import of recognizing people within larger milieus, indicating that we need to turn away from the idea of disease classifications existing in and of themselves, outside of lived experience.[38]

Current theories consider that OCD may have a biological and genetic basis but that the environment can trigger OCD, for example, through the occurrence of stressful life events.[39] As it stands, it is likely that multiple factors affect OCD, including biological, psychological, environmental, cultural, and social ones.[40] Prevalence rates vary geographically, as we see more people with OCD at higher latitudes. Regrettably, research on social factors and their relationship to obsessions and compulsions is minimal. Research today outside of OCD is increasingly exploring the complex ways in which biology may relate to environment and culture; this includes epigenetics, which has shown how the environment can affect what a parent passes down to their children. Hopefully, we will soon know more about the complexity of OCD.

Despite the seeming clarity of professional conceptions regarding OCD at first glance, there are some ambiguities regarding what constitutes OCD, and where the line is between having OCD and not having OCD. First, are the thoughts of a person with OCD fundamentally different from those of a person without OCD? Researchers have confirmed that the majority of people experience intrusive thoughts.[41] As worded in a book on neuropsychology, "OCD symptoms are present to some degree in most people."[42] One hypothesis is that people with OCD are not unique in their experience of intrusive thoughts; what makes people with OCD different from others is how they respond to such thoughts, for instance, treating them as important. Researchers have explained this cognitive model as follows: "OCD and nonclinical individuals both experience similar intrusions. . . . People who appraise the occurrence and content of their cognitive intrusions as significant and meaningful on the basis of particular dysfunctional beliefs would develop OCD: the cognitive intrusions would escalate into obsessions. In contrast, nonclinical individuals would not consider the occurrence and content of cognitive intrusions to have a special significance, and therefore these cognitive intrusions would be easily dismissed."[43] Obsessions are more frequent, intense, upsetting, and apt to be tied to dysfunctional appraisals than are intrusions.[44] This theory is called the appraisal model. Another theory that has similarities to this focuses on metacognition and indicates, for instance, that the disorder is maintained by people's "metacognitive beliefs about the meaning and consequences of intrusive thoughts and feelings, and beliefs about the necessity of performing rituals and the negative consequences of failing to do so."[45] Metacognition itself "refers to knowledge of beliefs about thinking and strategies used to regulate and control thinking processes."[46]

A different theory also promoted by psychologists is the inference-based approach, which suggests that something more distinguishes "normal intrusions" from obsessions than is indicated within the appraisal model.[47] Intrusions and obsessions may differ by context, with obsessions being more likely to occur in situations without direct evidence to support them. In this view, people with OCD worry more about hypothetical possibilities than do those without the disorder. It is the difference between two people, both of whom are concerned their hands are dirty, but one watched someone cough, shook that person's hand, and then had this thought (intrusion based on direct evidence); the other heard a news report on the radio about germs that day, began to think about times they had caught a cold from others, and then worried about their hands being dirty (obsession based on an internal monologue beyond what is currently accessible to the senses using past experiences and abstract facts). The person with OCD gets caught up in their imagination, rather than what is actually present, and there is a distrust of the senses; they can "experience physiological reactions, feelings of anxiety, and compulsions that are concordant with the imagined scenario."[48] The result is to "confuse a possibility with reality and to act as if this possibility were true."[49] According to this theory, obsessional doubt is the crux of the problem, and researchers are also exploring how people with OCD can become hypervigilant as a result of fears about their "selves" (who they might be or could become).[50] Note that "it has been shown that eliciting such 'what could happen' scenarios in non-clinical participants induces OCD-like cognitions."[51]

A second ambiguity regarding OCD is that there is a social element built into its definition. According to the *DSM*, to be diagnosed with OCD, an individual must be distressed or have thoughts/behaviors that affect functioning.[52] This means OCD is not simply the equivalent of particular thoughts or actions but is affected by what is considered functionally "normal" in a particular culture, and what constitutes distress to a particular person. For instance, Judith L. Rapoport, a psychiatrist who has treated and studied OCD, recounted an example of a woman who spent hours a day washing walls in her residence, but did not label her as sick.[53] Rapoport explained that this woman was able to maintain close social relationships, do well in school, participate in extra activities, and hold a part-time job. Rapoport confessed later in her book, "The more I learn about OCD, the less sure I am about where true disorder ends and the spectrum of 'compulsive' styles, habits, and predilections begin."[54] Making a related point, Lennard J. Davis, who wrote a book focused on obsession, argued: "If your behavior, say the meticulous lining up of objects, is seen as an oddity, you will be distressed that you do it. If it is seen as the useful quality of a master bricklayer then you will not be distressed."[55]

Such makes one wonder if the types of thoughts and behaviors people with OCD experience can be exacerbated by social conditions or are more likely to occur (or be perceived as problematic) in certain societies or time periods. Currently the evidence demonstrates that OCD is not exclusive to one nation, although the terminology used to describe the disorder and people's knowledge of it can vary by context.[56] One licensed mental health counselor with whom I spoke referred to OCD as a "multicultural phenomenon." However, he maintained that symptom type and content are affected by one's stage of life. For instance, a mother might have thoughts or compulsions related to her child, such as fears of the child becoming contaminated. The prevalence or content seemingly varies by culture or group. In a handbook on OCD, researchers wrote that "cultural variations in adult OCD do exist and should be considered in the conceptualization and treatment of OCD."[57] There is already quite a bit of evidence that "obsessional content stems from that which is culturally relevant to the sufferer."[58] For example, researchers are looking into whether cultural attitudes toward sex and conflict may affect the rates or content of obsessions and compulsions.[59] A group's religious beliefs may affect religious thoughts/behaviors, socioeconomic factors facing a particular group may affect hoarding, and so on.[60] Cultural factors can even affect the ways in which people try to control their thoughts.[61] Further research is needed to better explore these possibilities, including the experiences of different ethnoracial groups such as African Americans.[62]

OCD in Historical Context

Until recently, professionals say, not much was known about the disorder.[63] Are the obsessions and compulsions of today a new manifestation? The answer is complex. Labels and diagnoses are names that account for some phenomenon that is noticed and of interest to society. In a book on this topic, the clinician and sociologist Annmarie Goldstein Jutel wrote, "Diagnosis provides a cultural expression of what a given society is prepared to accept as normal and what it feels should be treated. We might chuckle to think that witchcraft . . . and the tendency of slaves to run away (drapetomania) . . . were once seen as diseases. . . . [But] the knowing chuckle is misplaced. . . . Might there be similar contemporary examples that will look as droll and as value laden to those who will read our books and diagnostic manuals one hundred years hence?"[64] Jutel pointed to the way in which diagnoses are not just plain for all to see but are to some degree affected by societal understandings of what is important and normal versus deviant. This applies whether we are talking about something physical or psychological. That is not to say that society makes up problems out of thin air. Instead, it shows that what is noticed, how it is conceptualized, and whether it is considered a problem can shift and change.

Put into perspective, this means that what might today be labeled OCD was perhaps not always recognized or considered a problem, much less a medical one.[65] However, according to Davis, this has not stopped some writers today from creating a history for the disorder, citing ancient peoples with the disorder and purporting OCD has been around since "time immemorial" with limited evidence.[66] It is hard to assess the history of OCD because one must decide whether to trace the history of the label or the history of the thoughts/behaviors. The latter is tricky. How do you assess the thoughts/behaviors you are reading about before labels such as "obsession" and "compulsion" existed? For example, are the same thoughts/behaviors those that would later come to be classified under such labels?

In the case of OCD, scholars have found that people described what appear to be obsession-like and compulsion-like examples prior to the 1800s.[67] In his book, Davis maintained that in the third and fourth centuries such thoughts/behaviors were linked to being attacked by supernatural forces. An interesting example from Saint John Climacus in the sixth century describing blasphemous thoughts reads: "This atrocious foe has the habit of appearing during the holy services. . . . these unspeakable, unacceptable, and unthinkable words are not ours but rather those of the God-hating demon who fled from heaven. . . . This deceiver, this destroyer of souls, has often caused men to go mad. . . . If you have blasphemous thoughts, do not think that you are to blame. God knows what is in our hearts. . . . Those unclean and unspeakable thoughts come at us when we are praying, but, if we continue to pray to the end, they will retreat."[68]

German E. Berrios, a professor of psychiatry, commented that "medieval terms such as *obsessio, compulsio,* and *impulsio* seem to have referred to behaviours redolent of obsessions; and so have vernacular words such as *scruple* . . . which since the 1500s (if not earlier) named repetitive thoughts of a religious nature."[69] Considering the Renaissance, Ian Osborn, a psychiatrist who studied Christianity, argued that obsession- and compulsion-like thoughts/behaviors became an "epidemic"[70] as a result of increased personal responsibility in salvation, growth in confession and how it was conducted, and the belief that thoughts can be sins.

Professor of linguistics Patricia Friedrich claimed that throughout history "obsessions" appear to have existed, but the concerns that shaped those obsessions "cannot be separated from the general issues and fears of that era. As a consequence, in more god-centered times a clear tendency existed for religious obsessions not only to be more present, but also to be more discussed and addressed. In turn, times of economic uncertainty or health crises tend to bring about greater preoccupations in those realms."[71] Indeed, in the past people had obsessional fears about diseases of their time such as the plague.[72] Fears about viruses developed at the end of the 1800s as belief in germ theory grew.[73]

In the 1800s obsession-like behavior was medicalized. According to Berrios, "The *medical* concepts built into this diagnosis were tooled in Europe during the second half of the nineteenth century."[74] More specifically, Davis wrote that "one begins to see obsessional behavior as a cultural problematic that starts with modernity. This isn't to say that such behavior did not exist before, but it was not seen as problematic before except in the major area of religion."[75] There was a period in which such behavior was viewed as an aspect of melancholia.[76] Sigmund Freud played an important role in the history of OCD, although his understanding and treatment of the disorder have since been critiqued, with psychoanalytic treatments often rejected as ineffective for use in treating the disorder.[77]

Note that after being perceived as an "illness" in a medical framework, obsession-like behavior came to be viewed through a psychological lens, where "for the first time a nonpathological, nonreligious view of obsessions and compulsions was offered."[78] For this reason, researchers Stanley Rachman and Ray J. Hodgson stated, "The concept of obsessions has survived three historical stages—religious, medical, and psychological."[79] The conceptualization of OCD has continued to go through changes, up until the present day, where to some degree it is being viewed again from a more medical perspective (here I am thinking of biological psychiatry and the popularity of medications to treat mental disorders).

These changes in the conceptualization of OCD, from being viewed as a supernatural manifestation to a medical concern, align with larger shifts in society. The historian Roy Porter argued that madness may be as "old as mankind,"[80] and cited early examples of "madness understood as divine or demonic possession."[81] Over time, religious understanding of "madness" shifted to become a "matter of psychopathology,"[82] (a shift from "sin" to "sickness," as sociologists Patricia A. Adler and Peter Adler referred to it).[83] We witnessed medicalization, but "although the mad were institutionalized, certified by physicians, and more and more were considered to be sick, there is little evidence that anything resembling *medical* treatment was carried out."[84] Therapies utilized by physicians in the 1700s were not the most forward-thinking and included bloodletting and starvation. Nonetheless, "by the late 18th century the concept of mental illness was becoming the dominant definition of madness."[85] More recently, we can speak of a dominant medical or neuroscientific framework, although there are also theories that consider social and psychological factors and origins.[86] (Note that the "madness" has not always been judged negatively; there have, for instance, been depictions of it as creative and prophetic.)[87]

Yet, even into the 1970s and 1980s, little was known about OCD, which was perceived as affecting few people.[88] More recent studies indicate the disorder is much more common than previously realized, to the point that in 1989 Michael A. Jenike, a researcher and the founder of the OCD Institute at McLean Hospital, referred to it as a "hidden epidemic" and asked, "How can so prevalent a disease remain largely hidden from physicians?"[89]

2

But What Is It Really Like?

> How do you describe something that's very subjective? . . . The only thing
> these people see [if anything] is the outward manifestations of the be-
> havior, of the obsessions and compulsions. . . . I could go into a biologi-
> cal explanation, physiological explanation, but, what exactly good would
> that do? I want people to understand when I explain to them just how I
> feel. . . . That's important to me, because if they can understand that, then
> I think they can empathize more and be more understanding.
> —Destin

The psychologist Jonathan Grayson wrote in a self-help book for individuals with OCD, "One of the greatest problems for those of you who
suffer from this disorder is the disparity between your inner world and
the outside. For all of us, the person we show the world is not exactly
who we are. . . . But, for you, the gulf is greater."[1] This gulf provides one
explanation for how OCD remains hidden at times from the public and
even from healthcare professionals. To overcome this gap, descriptions
of the inner worlds of people with OCD such as Destin can help and are
the focus of this chapter.

As I sat down to talk to people with OCD, often I did not notice
anything out of the ordinary. Our conversations were not interrupted
by people reorganizing the room. I did not find people so caught up
in their thoughts that they were unable to express themselves. In general, their words were thoughtful, and they were able to recount their
experiences, often quite eloquently. I follow people with OCD on social
media. Their posts are similar to those of my other friends. They post
pictures of their families, their pets, and their travels.

Much of "OCD" takes place in the mind and is hidden from view,
which likely helps breed stereotypes regarding what constitutes the disorder. Because OCD is not worn on the skin, the people I interviewed

experienced a relatively hidden otherness. People with OCD can have obsessions as well as mental rituals or compulsions, such as reviewing an event over and over in their mind (or even repeatedly praying). These may or may not become apparent to others.

I remember talking to Monty over the phone. He lived in the United States and at that point was happily married and had a child. He had been diagnosed with OCD, attention deficit disorder (ADD), and anxiety. He had held jobs that were dangerous, such as being a firefighter. He told me, "I've run into burning buildings. I carried a firearm. None of it bothered me, but if I'm sitting by myself I can scare myself to death." He described getting caught up in fears, such as those of being sick. People found out about these if he decided to share them, such as when he brought them up to his parents when he was a child. However, he had a hard time explaining what was in his head, and he assumed his parents chalked it up to childhood fears.

More obvious are the compulsions or rituals that people with OCD physically enact. Clara, who had been diagnosed with OCD and was eighteen when we corresponded, told me that when she was a child in India she tried to force her parents to engage in her compulsions. This included not going to certain places or using certain objects. When we spoke, Jeff was in his thirties, lived in the United States, had a PhD, and was diagnosed with OCD. (He also wondered if he might have ADD or ADHD.) When Jeff was in grade school, his teachers noticed some of his behaviors. For example, he did a "class project about dinosaurs and while I was talking, the teacher told me that I didn't have to keep interrupting my presentation by mentioning that scientists were not absolutely sure about all the details [as his symptoms at that point involved concerns about deceiving people]. At one point, I didn't even want to use the phrase 'he or she' in my talk because it seemed incomplete, in case there were any other genders I hadn't heard of yet."

Those with whom I spoke regularly looked at themselves through the lens of what they perceived as the larger society that does not have OCD. They employed a variety of tactics to hide or cover up their OCD for fear of how people would perceive them (I discuss these tactics in more depth in chapter 8). For instance, at times they engaged in compulsions when others were not around. Sometimes people with OCD have the ability to hold off rituals until a later time, and thoughts do not have to be said aloud. However, even when people could hide their specific thoughts and rituals, the impacts could be felt—although an outside observer might not attribute such to OCD. For example, consider that people with OCD may avoid situations that relate to their fears or may lose hours of their day to obsessions and compulsions. Friends might notice the loss of time or lack of engagement in particular activities.

Therefore, the outer worlds of people with OCD *can* but do not necessarily reflect their inner turmoil. Interviewees moved through society, at once part of the flow, for their obsessions and compulsions did not overtake and seep into all of their thoughts/behaviors, but at the same time also standing apart. They saw themselves through their own eyes as well as through the lens of the larger society (imagining how others might perceive them), experiencing a type of double perspective on the world.[2] This was compounded by the way in which OCD can manifest as thoughts and urges that exist but feel somehow wrong to those with the disorder, and which do not reflect how they truly feel.

Heterogeneity and Control

Before I started talking to people with OCD, I knew obsessions and compulsions could take a few forms. Somewhere in the course of growing up, I learned that people with the disorder might be worried about germs and contamination, or that something bad will happen. As a result, they might wash their hands excessively or engage in rituals to stop harm from befalling others, such as checking the stove to make sure it is turned off or repeating a phrase in their mind over and over. I did not realize, however, that people with OCD can face obsessions about whether they are gay, have images of themselves hurting others pop into their minds, experience seemingly unrelenting questions about whether they love their spouses, feel urges to rearrange objects, have songs repeat in their minds, get caught up in questioning the nature of their existence, suffer extreme guilt, confront fears about the "self," and so much more. I certainly did not realize the host of compulsions in which people with OCD might engage. The same person might even have a variety of obsessions and compulsions. Some of the obsessions and compulsions described herein may seem foreign, but others may feel familiar. The disorder can involve fears related to topics of central concern in contemporary society such as health and contamination, sexuality, and aggression. As one group of researchers phrased it, "The more inconsistent the contents of an intrusive thought are with someone's core beliefs and values, the more likely it is that this intrusive thought will become an obsession."[3] In one interviewee's words, "It takes the fun out of God, food, and sex."

As I listened to people with OCD, I began to see that despite the difference in content of their thoughts and behaviors, control and agency was a repeated theme.[4] I am referring to the feeling of an ability to enact our will on ourselves and our surroundings. Agency has to do with "the sense that I am the one who is causing or generating an action or a certain thought in my stream of consciousness" and includes one's "sense of control."[5] People with OCD seem to want to make the world more understandable, controllable, and safer for themselves and others, and many social theorists have questioned if our self feels less anchored in today's global and technological postmodern society.[6] Of course, control is an important issue with regard to any illness. We try to control risk factors for particular health problems, although we sometimes face medical problems over which we have little control. We struggle to maintain our dignity and ability to carry out everyday functions as we present ourselves to others in social interaction.[7] However, I suggest the issue of control is more central to OCD.[8]

People with OCD implicated control in a variety of ways. They depicted their OCD arising as a result of feeling a lack of control, their OCD making them feel a lack of control, their OCD being their attempt at gaining control, and having to give up control in order to get better. For instance, one woman who lost a number of family members in the space of a few months when she was young said: "My OCD went off the charts because it's when I felt no control over my life around me. And in some sort of small way this [the OCD] was my mind's way of saying, you know, you can make order out of this world, you can control things." The theme of control I heard from people with OCD has gained recognition in psychology. As one example, research has suggested that concerns over losing control may lead people to perform checking behaviors.[9]

The people I communicated with commonly described efforts to take seemingly excessive control of themselves and their circumstances, including to control their thoughts, to control everyday life events, and to attempt to control a number of aspects of their lives that other people likely do not worry about or that are largely outside of control. I am not saying that people with OCD are a danger to society. For example, those with harm thoughts, such as described later in this chapter, are no more likely to behave in a harmful manner than those without OCD and without these thoughts.[10] Instead, Grayson explained that people can move through life feeling a sense of certainty about things, for example, that someone they talked to ten minutes earlier is alive or that the sun will rise.[11] This is a bit of an illusion because it is not 100 percent certain, but people treat it as truth and act based on that until they receive information otherwise. With OCD, the reverse can occur; instead of waiting, people with OCD may try to seek out certainty. This is complicated by how people with OCD take notice of things in the world in finer detail.[12] Treating the disorder can involve getting people to accept uncertainty.

Argh! Those Troubling Thoughts, Images, and Urges

Jesse, who has had OCD since he was a child, described what obsessions felt like in his head:

> I can't just stop the thoughts. I hate them and don't want to think about them, but the harder I try not to think them, the more I think them. By the time I get home from work I'm a mess, mentally drained, nerves shot, depressed, and just emotionally tired. Sometimes the images come with questions and doubts. . . . [I sometimes think] these kinds of thoughts represent some of my deeper fears, which makes me feel anxious. I seek reassurance and ask questions with the hope that I can perhaps hear something that will change the scenarios in my head to something easier to live with. But it never works and usually just gets me more stirred up.

Jesse indicated that he had thoughts that he disliked, and which he perceived as invading his mind in a way he could not control. The problem, then, for Jesse involved the quality or type of thoughts he had, how often they recurred, and his inability to stop them from coming. Jesse was almost fifty, lived in the United States, was married, and had a graduate degree. He had been diagnosed with OCD, ADHD, and depression. His prepubescent OCD symptoms were related to symmetry. He also described tic-like behaviors like squinting and a repetitive pattern of nose rubbing. His obsessions after puberty were focused on his romantic relationships, thoughts about the past sex lives of the people with whom he was romantically involved.

Other interviewees described obsessing about incestuous thoughts, sexually molesting children, being gay or lesbian, philosophical issues such as whether humans have free will, wondering whether or not they had done something to offend God, and more. The contents of their thoughts/urges/images were different than Jesse's, but there were similarities in how they conceptualized what was happening, their response, and the issues concerning control.

Percy experienced thoughts about being gay. He lived in London, was in his twenties, and had not been formally diagnosed with OCD. However, he believed that he had OCD (as well as felt he might experience depression and was a mild sufferer of body dysmorphic disorder [BDD]).

> Out of nowhere popped the thought, "Am I gay?" Although quiet at first, it became more of a nuisance as the week progressed, forcing me to find solitude and think about it. . . . By the end of the week I was attempting to find logic in the situation. . . . [I] question[ed] whether I had issues with my sexuality. . . . To fight the thought, I would look at attractive woman in the office and check that I still found them a turn-on. . . . It rattled my brain night after night. Unable to change my thought pattern, I started to feel out of control. . . . I still can't stop the endless visualizations of checking to see whether I want sex with men. . . . At the time [all this started], I was twenty-three years old and had enjoyed a purely heterosexual lifestyle with the normal coming-of-age thoughts about sex and sexuality as I was growing up. . . . [Since then] I have not been myself. Unable to escape the thoughts streaming through my brain, I felt like my life was being taken from me into a world of insanity, where my ideals and beliefs no longer existed.

Sean was also in his twenties and was living in Scotland. He had been diagnosed with OCD and depression, and told me that his OCD had come in three main forms. At various points throughout his life, he would constantly monitor his breathing, "to make sure that I was doing it properly. This could sometimes last for up to three months without stopping." Later he developed fears about being gay. "Sometimes I would visualize these acts in my head between five hundred and a thousand times a day. . . . I knew that it wasn't true; however, I couldn't stop it." Then he experienced relationship fears. "I thought, 'Well, if I'm gay, why have I been in a relationship with a female for four years?' This sent my thought processes into overdrive. I couldn't get the words 'it's over' out of my head. Again, there was absolutely no control. It was horrible looking at the person you love with your mind telling you that you didn't and that your relationship with her was over."

Despite differences in content, all three of these interviewees described having thoughts/urges/images they did not desire. For instance, unable to dismiss or control their thoughts, Percy and Sean questioned if they might really be gay, yet, they felt they were not truly gay.

Chris's experience held similarities to theirs, even though the contents of his thoughts/urges/images were of harm. Chris had been diagnosed with OCD, was in his twenties, and lived in the United Kingdom when we first chatted online. He told me that he chose to speak to me because he was "fit for bursting." He not only had hidden his thoughts, urges, and behaviors from most people but also had hidden himself away physically, reducing social contact.[13] In Chris's words:

It's difficult to get out of the house even to go to work. I can't keep on meeting people in case I do something to them. . . . I'm scared of harming people. It occupies my mind all day. . . . I don't want to hurt people. . . . I would have thoughts of raping [my girlfriend] and I would be anxious all the time. Deep down I know I would never do such a thing but the thoughts are always there. . . . For the most part I prayed. I kept it all to myself. . . . [Sometimes I feel I have an urge] to run people over, so I drive as far from the pavement as possible. . . . Although I resist these urges, they are there and worry me. So that's why I am always checking the rearview mirror to see if the pedestrian is still there. . . . [The checking] causes anxious symptoms such as heart racing, sweating, lack of concentration and shakes. . . . I can see there is no dent or dead body . . . [but] my mind imagines there is, and the thoughts become very real.

I asked Chris about treatment, and he mentioned the one thing that helped him was realizing that everyone can have bizarre thoughts and urges. "He [my psychologist] showed me that all people get 'bad' thoughts and urges. He said that people without OCD are able to dismiss these thoughts as nonsense and carry on with their lives—whereas people with OCD feel ashamed of having that thought in the first place and can't get rid of it. Knowing that everybody gets 'bad' thoughts was quite comforting." For Chris, treatment involved "analyzing how stupid my thoughts and urges were and understanding that no one with OCD carries out the awful things that their mind is urging them to do." Years later, when we chatted again, Chris depicted himself as living a "productive life" and no longer needing the medication or visits to a therapist; he had the OCD under control.

People such as Chris can have unwanted thoughts that they find repugnant and which feel at odds with their sense of self. In other cases, such as Jesse's, people have thoughts that in isolation are not at odds with a thought they might expect to have. For instance, they want to protect the people close to them, or make sure that their hands are clean, but their thoughts and/or behaviors are excessive and irrational. Although this did not happen to Chris, people with OCD can also face obsessions about self-harm and suicide. These "involve repetitive, unwanted thoughts of suicide that cause severe distress . . . that do not reflect a 'true' intention to kill or harm oneself but rather reflect a repetitive thought loop that gets stuck."[14] (However, a word of caution: in some studies OCD is associated with a higher risk of attempting or dying by suicide, which is different than what I am describing here.)

No Longer Taking the Mind and Body for Granted

Clearly, OCD can impact one's sense of self. An association between the illness experience and how one sees the self is not unique to OCD.[15] Two sociologists explained, "The body, which in many social situations is a taken for granted aspect of the person, ceases to be taken for granted once it malfunctions and becomes more prominent in the consciousness of self and others."[16] People with self-described obsessions sometimes indicated how their mental processes came to the foreground and could no longer be taken for granted. People with OCD probed their thoughts, examining which ones they felt appeared "normal" versus those that did not. They questioned why they would have thoughts that felt alien, what other people would think, and more. They were using their minds to analyze their minds and feelings and were unable to think and live their lives in a usual manner. Their engagement in compulsions made them question their behaviors as well. Sociologists have begun considering how parents may have minds that are full of to-do lists and schedules— that is, "contaminated time"—reducing their ability to enjoy the present.[17] People with OCD face another type of mental contamination.

But What to Do? The Experience of Compulsions

Obsessions are different from compulsions. For instance, one woman I interviewed said that when she was young, she would line up her plastic horses and other items symmetrically on a shelf. In the vast majority of cases, compulsions are done in response to obsessions.[18] As an example, if your obsessions have to do with contamination, you may engage in cleaning compulsions.

The people I interviewed engaged in a host of tactics to deal with their thoughts. The mental checking of some of the men described earlier can be considered compulsions. At one point Jeff became preoccupied with whether ghosts and devils were inside himself or surrounding objects. When he had a bad thought, sometimes he would walk backward to correct it. One man told me that when he was younger and masturbated, he would have thoughts about getting AIDS and would "have to say various compulsive phrases in my head, or picture my blood as immune to the disease to fend off the scare." People described many types of compulsive and neutralizing behaviors; here, I am only able to scratch the surface, but at least you can see what it feels like for people.

Kirstyn, who was fifty-three when she talked to me, had been diagnosed with depression and post-traumatic stress disorder (PTSD). At age forty she had major depression, and her OCD got out of control to the point that she quit her job and spent time in bed. She recalled memories of OCD from as far back as age four. She said obsessions are like an "itch" that you scratch with a compulsion. "You have the thought. It causes discomfort . . . so you do the ritual to make it stop." She said that having OCD is like having two minds. You have your "normal mind," but the OCD mind keeps giving you the feeling of *what if.* "The best way I can describe it is have you ever gone out, and . . . you can't remember if you locked the door . . . and it's bothering you. . . . [OCD is like] that nagging feeling that 'I got to go back and check.'" She said you can do the ritual even if you know it seems illogical. At the age of seven, her ritual was to touch doorknobs and light switches a particular way and count in her head. "If you were to come and ask me 'Do you really think you can prevent your father from dying by touching that light switch five times?' Of course I would say no. . . . But when you have OCD it's like this other voice is in your head telling you 'well if you do this thing then it won't happen.' . . . You just have to do it anyway."

Therefore, compulsions can be tied to things people feel strongly about or fear, such as preventing harm to others, and things about which they want to feel certain. Chris's compulsions were motivated by a desire to protect people and make sure he had not already harmed them and would not endanger them in the future. Chris sometimes got caught up in a cycle of checking in which he sought certainty but ended up feeling uncertain.

> [Sometimes] although I have looked at the bonnet [hood] and seen that there was nothing there, I would feel the need to get out and feel the bonnet for a dead body. . . . I would have to examine the bonnet in great detail. . . . My mind would start obsessing about "Have they gone over/ under the car"? . . . I couldn't trust my own thoughts, sight, and hearing. . . . I stopped riding it [motorbike] because I was convinced that there was someone hanging off the back, although there was no passenger reflection in passing shop windows, no performance degradation due to extra weight. . . . [I] would stop, get off and look at the pillion seat for hours, looking to see if anyone was there, even putting my hand on the seat to prove that there was no one there. This of course was not enough proof. . . . Looking back, it was irrational and stupid. I knew it at the time, too, but I couldn't stop looking . . . because of "What if?" "What if there was someone there?"

People colloquially refer to the type of OCD in which you believe you have potentially hit someone in the road (without evidence this occurred) as "hit-and-run OCD."

The approach Chris described taking in response to his thoughts is not unfamiliar. If you were worried you hit something with your car, you might look in your mirror to check. Compulsions seem like they will reduce anxiety or make a person feel better, and sometimes they provide a bit of relief.[19] However, researchers have argued that in the long run compulsive behaviors like checking may only make things worse (for people with or without OCD). For example, you might believe that checking something will make you feel more confident in your knowledge of the situation, yet research has shown that compulsive checking may encourage distrust in memory. Instead of feeling more certain, your confidence in your memory can dwindle, and maybe your accuracy, potentially fueling more checking, especially when those with OCD feel a sense of personal responsibility.

Avoidance was another common strategy interviewees described using to cope with their thoughts, and involved avoiding things that they felt could trigger their anxiety or OCD; avoidance could function as a compulsion.[20] For instance, someone who is afraid of hurting a loved one with a sharp object might avoid these objects. Phineas got to the point that he was avoiding so much that he felt as if his sense of self was altered. He was in his early thirties when we first started communicating, lived in the United States, and had been diagnosed with OCD and depression. With a life he described as 24/7 nonstop obsessing about a variety of topics, he avoided many things, including close relationships. He told me, "No one has any clue how much torture is inside my head. They think they all know me, what I like and dislike, but they don't." People saw him through the lens of what he avoided. However, that is "the Phineas that OCD has made. They have no clue who the real Phineas is, and neither do I."

Compulsions can be a part of people's lives for years. Laveda lived in the United States, was thirty-eight and married, and worked part-time in a professional job when we first spoke. She was diagnosed with OCD. When she was a child, she began to feel that a classmate was contaminated. Laveda maneuvered her body at school in such a way to prevent him from bumping into her, but she still felt contaminated and would shower after returning home. She had rituals to stay clean at home, so much so that she was afraid to spend time with her family because she might get recontaminated. She said, "The worst thing I did to not get

contaminated was urinate in my bed so I wouldn't have to get recontaminated stepping on the floor." A few years later, Laveda's fears about
contamination transferred from the classmate to a friend. She was afraid
that if she was contaminated by this friend, she might turn into a lesbian.
Laveda began to completely avoid this person, even skipping class, and
of course lost them as a friend. At the time of our interview, Laveda had
grown up and had children of her own, yet she still feared becoming
contaminated and regularly walked up to people and asked if they were
this former friend.

Rodney provided another example of how OCD impacts those
around people who have the disorder. Rodney was from the United
States and in his fifties; he was diagnosed with OCD, depression, and
obsessive-compulsive personality disorder (OCPD), although he disagreed with the latter. Among other thoughts/behaviors, he spoke to me
about being afraid of getting sick, especially with cancer. He even described being afraid of salmonella "because that would mimic something
that I could mistake for stomach cancer." At restaurants he would go back
into kitchens and question the employees, "You sure you couldn't have
touched the chicken after you touched my food, after you were touching
raw chicken? You sure? Maybe you wiped your hands on your apron, but
germs could be on your apron." He told me that he turned this scrutiniz-
ing of restaurants' food practices into a routine: "If I got chicken that I
thought was [problematic] I called the health department and tried to
describe the chicken. Sometimes if it was a restaurant I didn't know, I'd
call later on and ask the manager [questions]." He also encouraged other
people to read things more than once. Because he read things multiple
times, he felt that by doing this other people were "sharing in my compulsion," and he did not have to "feel quite as ashamed."

Kirstyn, Chris, Laveda, and Rodney all described different compulsions. However, each shared a feeling of needing to perform acts that
they (at least as adults) recognized as not making sense, and/or as varying from cultural standards or what was typical for them. Rodney told
me that he "always knew there was something wrong, something that set
me apart from the rest of the world." These people depicted OCD as taking away some of their agency. At the same time, their actions embod-
ied attempts to exert control over themselves and/or their environment.
People with OCD can have feelings of imperfection, that something is

"not just right" or incomplete, driving them to engage in compulsions until the situation feels more right to them.[21]

Also note that researchers have recently been considering whether there is a subtype of OCD that includes a tic disorder, characterized by early onset and other elements.[22] One of the family members I interviewed, Clyde, lived in the United States and realized his eleven-year-old son had an unexpected problem that he could not identify when his son started having what appeared to be full-body seizure-like tics. His son was eventually diagnosed with anxiety and OCD, and Clyde was told the tics were associated with the OCD. Clyde's son grew out of the tics after puberty.

Additionally, someone once contacted me asking if I knew of anyone with symptoms involving the cutting of hair. At that point, I had not, but later I interviewed Karla, who was in the United States and had been diagnosed with OCD; she also thought she had BDD and had become agoraphobic. She told me that in the past, out of nowhere, she found herself stuck in the bathroom cutting her hair, one strand at a time, trying to make it even, sometimes for days. She was hospitalized various times, where she was diagnosed with different disorders. I came to learn that trichotemnomania involves the obsessive-compulsive practice of cutting or shaving of hair.

Heterogeneity

OCD is heterogeneous not just in content but also in symptom severity and course of symptoms. I talked to people like Kirstyn who could not remember a point in their lives without OCD. Other people's compulsions started when they were older, such as one man who began experiencing symptoms when he was seventy-four years old. Researchers have found that the age of onset of OCD for most people tends to be before age twenty-five.[23] Onset in childhood is quite common, with pediatric OCD "one of the most ubiquitous childhood psychiatric illnesses," while onset in one's later years (age fifty-five and older) is relatively rare.[24] According to one article, "Although OCD in women typically begins in their early 20s, for males, onset commonly occurs in middle adolescence, and can have profound developmental effects that disrupt education, socialization, sexual experience, and employment."[25]

One question I asked people was how many hours a day they spent on obsessions and/or compulsions. Although the *DSM* specifies that for thoughts/images/urges/behaviors to count as OCD, a person has to be distressed or spend more than an hour a day on them, this question stumped some people. They did not always see the OCD in these terms. It was possible for interviewees to feel that OCD operated 24/7, constantly in the background. Others talked about the OCD as being more episodic. They experienced periods where they fought their OCD until it was beaten back, or where it seemed to naturally give them a reprieve—at least until the next episode, "wave," "attack," or "frenzy," as they called it.

Martin explained the despair that came as the next wave of OCD arrived: "The little ones I could always deflect. . . . Once a 'big one' got me . . . you know what you're in for. . . . It's the most awful feeling in the world. . . . You don't know how long it's going to stay. It might stay a day. It might stay a year. It might stay ten years. You don't know. All you know is you're fucked, bad. And that is possibly the most disheartening aspect of OCD." Martin lived in the United States, was in his fifties, and diagnosed with OCD, depression, panic disorder (and other disorders he felt were misdiagnoses).

People I interviewed sometimes became focused on their thoughts and rituals to the point they ignored everyday commitments in their lives. Others were able to manage family and work roles, although these could be hampered by their OCD. Aiten, a man in his thirties living in the United Kingdom and diagnosed with OCD, planned his whole day around using the bathroom. He told me:

> I can use the public loos to urinate because I stand up and don't need to touch anything. To do the other, I can't do it. . . . [To manage this] I won't eat a great deal until later in the day. . . . If I am going to be out all day then I take some antidiarrhea tablets. . . . If I am caught short when out and need to use a loo, I feel contaminated [the] rest of the day and I often throw all my cloths away when I get home. . . . If I know someone else has been to a loo I avoid them too. . . . On a good day I might be able to touch a door handle. On a bad day I can't. . . . This is the strange part. I can't put my finger on what I fear if I don't, other than I will feel uncomfortable.

As Chance (who lived in the United States) and I talked in person, his attention was not fully on me, although if he had not told me, I would not have been aware of what was occurring. He explained, "It [OCD] causes a hesitation in my speech when I'm talking, almost like a stutter because I count the syllables of the words that I use. Sometimes I'm even known to flex my joint with each syllable. And if it's bad enough, or the day is awkward enough, I'll actually count the letters of each word and I can't stop doing it. . . . You and I are having a conversation right now. I'm thinking about my speech." Chance was in his forties, was married, and identified himself as American Indian; he had been diagnosed with OCD and bipolar disorder.

Life in Metaphor

Another way to convey the inner worlds of people with OCD is through metaphor, as it reveals important ways in which people conceptualized the disorder and their relationship to it.[26] Looking at the metaphors people use when they speak can tell us a lot about how they view a topic.[27] Imagine two people talking about marriage. One refers to marriage as akin to an old tree, something that grows strong under the nourishment of respect and love. The other person sees marriage like a war, with two parties trying to win over the other. Each of these people is viewing the same institution but through a different lens, likely shaping their interactions.

One common way in which people with OCD metaphorically conceived of their OCD was to "other" it in some way, to distance it from their sense of self. Some therapists have suggested that people give their OCD a name as part of treatment. John March, a professor of psychiatry and a researcher, with writer and editor Christine M. Benton, instructed families with children who have OCD in doing so, writing, "It's Germy, Mr. Stupid, Dodohead—or just an illness with its own name, OCD. The thoughts, urges, images—whatever pops up when OCD hiccups—have no real meaning . . . that you can learn to ignore safely."[28] The idea here appears to be using the power of a label to distinguish OCD from people's sense of identity and remove some of the disorder's influence.

Figure 2.1. *Self-Portrait* by Hannah Hillam

For people with OCD, the disorder grew arms, legs, and teeth. It cajoled, attacked, beat, and battled them. They referred to OCD as a nemesis, bully, goliath, and plague. One man perceived OCD as a gremlin soaked in water after midnight that attacked him. One woman described it as an evil twin, and yet another interviewee referred to it as a sadistic monster. Multiple people described OCD as devilish, and as making life hell or nightmarish. Justine, who was in the United States and was self-diagnosed with OCD and traces of social anxiety disorder, said, "OCD to me is a nightmare" that takes over your mind "and you become a victim, weak minded and afraid." In these ways, people with OCD conceptualized the disorder as something other, something outside of themselves and negative.

Justine's words echoed what a number of those I interviewed described metaphorically feeling, that of being dominated, stunted, or paralyzed. One man compared having OCD to feeling like an "insecure, scared adolescent." Two interviewees compared it to the feelings people must have after being sexually abused. One woman said it was as if someone took over her body, and then later she had to go clean up this person's messes. Another interviewee referred to herself as like a dog on a short leash, and others spoke about feeling tortured or imprisoned. People with OCD used quite a bit of battle imagery. When asked what OCD meant to her, Nancy, who lived in the United Kingdom, was diagnosed with long-term stress, and had diagnosed herself with OCD, said, "It means the biggest struggle in my life. . . . It's something I had to fight almost every waking minute for such a long time—something I am still fighting today."[29] These metaphors show how people with OCD were attempting to construct or demarcate a true self as something other than the OCD.

However, OCD is particularly difficult for people to deal with, as what they are fighting is not really outside of themselves even though they may metaphorically envisage it as such. They know OCD is not really out there like an object controlling them. They acknowledged this within some of their metaphors, as well as when considering the limits of metaphors. Kelcie told me, "I guess on some level I was trying to separate myself from the OCD by imagining that my OCD was some evil monster. . . . That did not really work because I have trouble sometimes distinguishing what's OCD and what is me." I show later in the book how some people came to perceive the OCD more as part of themselves over time.

In this way, people with OCD struggled with both othering and identifying with the OCD,[30] a recurring theme in the book. This makes sense because people's "awareness" of their OCD was not uniform. Some people told me they were able to clearly and swiftly identify and distinguish their OCD symptoms from what they saw as their true thoughts/behaviors, while others were not able to draw this distinction. Ego-dystonicity is often a hallmark of OCD, where people reflect and perceive what they are experiencing as outside their sense of self. For instance, an ego-dystonic thought would be perceived "as occurring outside the context of one's morals, attitudes, beliefs, preferences, past behavior and/or one's expectations about the kinds of thoughts one would or should experience. The thought gives rise to considerable emotional distress and is resisted."[31] This stands in contrast to disorders in which people view their thoughts/behaviors as desirable or reflecting their values, as well as a long history of considering it impossible for people who were "mad" to be cognizant of their "madness."[32] Insight has to do with how accurately people with OCD perceive the beliefs that underpin their thoughts/behaviors.[33] For example, a person who believes that they really can prevent someone from dying by flipping a light switch three times would not be characterized as having good insight. The most recent edition of the *DSM* indicated that many people have "good" or "fair" degrees of insight, although some people may have poor insight (and a few exhibit "absent" insight), and that degree of insight can change over the course of the disorder.[34]

It is interesting to note that if everyone I interviewed could wave a magic wand and rid themselves of their OCD, not everyone would. Therefore, we cannot become too complacent in assigning certain thoughts/behaviors as universally problematic.

3

Treatments, Old and New

> We all exist in a perpetual state of fear because we can't control any-
> thing. . . . It's scary. Who is to say a religious whack won't board this train
> fitted with explosives chanting, "God is great." Who is to say the jungles
> won't cough up a deadly malady worse than AIDS or Ebola, one our bi-
> ologists won't understand. . . . I want to experience life. I need to stop
> asking questions. . . . Living involves submitting oneself to uncertainty.
> —Patrick

Patrick lived in the United States, was in his twenties, and had been
diagnosed with OCD and depression. His words are those of someone
who has been to therapy. Working to accept uncertainty and to avoid
compulsions and reassurance are common refrains in contemporary
methods for treating OCD.[1] Patrick experienced a few types of OCD
symptoms, including philosophical and religious obsessions. According to Penzel, "Existential OCD involves intrusive, repetitive thinking
about questions which cannot possibly be answered, and which may be
philosophical or frightening in nature, or both. The questions usually
revolve around the meaning, purpose, or reality of life, or the existence
of the universe or even one's own existence."[2] Patrick's handwritten journal contained musings on elements that make up the body, free will, and
God's existence. He described trying to curtail his researching of these
topics, which exacerbated the problem, and instead accept uncertainty.

Remember that for interviewees the disorder was linked in complicated ways to losing as well as maintaining control. People with OCD
are sometimes attempting to control things that are not easily controlled
or not commonly thought of as within people's control. For instance,
how much control does anyone have over their thoughts? As some people with OCD explained, if you were told not to think about something,
how easy would it be for you?

This conundrum is not new. The novelist Fyodor Dostoyevsky raised the issue, and in the 1980s the psychologist Daniel M. Wegner and colleagues ran an experiment in which they tested what happens when people try to suppress their thoughts. People were unable to completely suppress the thought, and paradoxically these attempts could potentially produce an obsession.[3]

According to therapists, while the thoughts/feelings/urges people have are not necessarily controllable, people can gain control over their OCD. Doing this involves learning how to respond to thoughts/feelings/urges, not engaging in compulsions, avoidance, or reassurance, for example.[4]

However, OCD was not always perceived and treated in this manner. This chapter reviews current and past treatments for OCD and provides context for later chapters' accounts of people's help-seeking experiences.

Older Approaches

Prior to the 1970s and 1980s, OCD was often viewed through the lens of psychoanalysis and unconscious motivations.[5] In an article for the International OCD Foundation, a group of psychologists warned readers about the dangers of potentially harmful treatments for OCD. They included psychodynamic/psychoanalytic approaches in this list, where they said that "clients are left to speculate about possible connections between their symptoms and some other prior events or personal history."[6] Rapoport has written that it "remains one of the great ironies in psychiatry that obsessive-compulsive disorder, the illness most cited to illustrate the fundamental principles of psychoanalysis, should be the disorder that benefits the least from this treatment."[7]

When I interviewed him, Rodney beseeched me to consider the potential negative impacts of telling someone with OCD that their thoughts/behaviors are repressed desires. His parents first sent him to a psychiatrist in the late 1960s, who he felt subscribed to Freudian theories. As Rodney recalled:

> [My dad] sent me to a psychiatrist when I was around thirteen or fourteen, [but I was not diagnosed until later]. . . . Every conversation I'd have [with him] he kind of picked up on the fact that I didn't have any relations with women. . . . And he would always kind of steer me into this type of

direction where he would be telling me in somewhat crude, somewhat not like a professional, but more like a peer would in school . . . to go and just take a girl out . . . like buying her a Coke, reaching under the table and feeling her up and getting her hot and bothered. . . . Can you imagine if I would have . . . told him that I had a fear that I was going to be homosexual? They'd all be telling me I need to come out of the closet and go down to some gay bar and act out. . . . Freud was like the worst thing that ever happened to OCD. . . . I was so embittered by this experience that I revolted at even the thought of ever wanting to see a shrink as long as I lived. . . . [OCD then] was not known to be caused by a biological malfunction as it is today. . . . You would not dare tell a therapist your sexual intrusive thoughts since . . . you would be told your intrusive thoughts were "latent" desires. . . . Those horrendous intrusive OCD thoughts are magnified and given more credibility in your mind.

Rodney was so "embittered" that he "revolted" at the idea of seeing a "shrink" again, and he later tried church-oriented counseling in order to avoid questions about sex.

As Rodney indicated, researchers have turned away from the theory that obsessions are repressed desires. Researchers Jedidiah Siev, Jonathan D. Huppert, and Shelby E. Zuckerman wrote, "The obsessions specifically target things most disturbing or concerning [to the person], not most secretly desired. . . . OCD can be described as a bully, who says things just to be provocative."[8] Further, approaches that encourage doubt can be harmful to people with OCD.[9]

Psychoanalytic approaches are still utilized at times. For instance, Professors Gail Steketee and Teresa Pigott, with practitioner Todd Schemmel, wrote that psychoanalytic approaches "may help some patients work out early traumatic experiences that may be troubling to them in other spheres."[10] Authors looking at the experiences of young people with OCD have questioned whether traumatic experiences may be important in the development of the disorder.[11]

Medications

Things have changed, notably the growth of biomedical explanations for mental disorders. We have seen the proliferation of medications, professionals prescribing them, and people taking them. Americans consume so many medications that the anthropologist Joseph Dumit proclaimed, "Americans are on drugs."[12] Kramer wrote that we have seen a broadening of what constitutes the boundaries of OCD to encompass people who would not previously have been considered to have a problem.[13] According to Kramer, "Once reserved for the most obviously ill patients, 'obsessional' and its contrasting counterpart, 'hysterical,' came as the period of psychoanalytic dominance progressed to be applied to people's social styles. The advent of biological psychiatry . . . with the discovery of new biological treatments, the operational definition of OCD is expanding once again, in part because what responds like OCD comes to be called OCD. 'Obsessionality' and 'compulsiveness' are now used by those who treat illness with medication to encompass what in earlier days would have seemed mere personal idiosyncrasy."[14] As a psychiatrist, he documented how much of an impact medications like Prozac could have on people, including on their personalities.

One of the commonly utilized treatments for OCD today is medication. The group of drugs called selective serotonin reuptake inhibitors (SSRIs) are regularly prescribed for OCD; fluvoxamine (Luvox) proved efficacious for OCD in 1989.[15] Before 1960, monoamine oxidase inhibitors (MAOIs) were reported as beneficial for OCD.[16] Clomipramine (Anafranil) was the first medication approved by the Food and Drug Administration (FDA) for OCD in the United States.[17] It is a tricyclic antidepressant and is sometimes referred to as a serotonin reuptake inhibitor (SRI). Later, the FDA approved SSRIs for OCD, and these drugs gained popularity. These include fluoxetine (Prozac), which was first available and used for depression in the United States in the late 1980s but was approved for OCD in 1994.[18] Other SSRIs are sertraline (Zoloft) and paroxetine (Paxil).

Many people (in some studies more than 70 percent of participants) receive some benefit from taking medication. However, it is possible that only 10 to 40 percent achieve remission through taking medication, and benefits do not necessarily last in the long term.[19] SSRIs are even prescribed to children and adolescents, yet an analysis of multiple studies involving people under the age of eighteen found their overall effectiveness to be small.[20]

Despite the growth in numbers of people taking medications for all types of health concerns, the solid knowledge we expected from investment in neurobiological research has not been as epic as hoped, and some companies are de-investing in the development of psychiatric drugs.[21] Researchers have raised questions about their safety and effectiveness,[22] and the mechanisms by which medications work are not perfectly clear.[23] Experts tout how more effective treatments have been developed for OCD over time. They may not have improved remission rates for the disorder as much as we like to imagine, though.[24]

CBT and CAM

The other main type of treatment recommended for OCD today is cognitive behavior therapy (CBT). Research suggests cognitive therapies and/or behavior therapies are equal to or more effective than available medications,[25] but of course they can be used in combination: "The combination of cognitive and behavioral interventions has become the treatment of choice for OCD according to international guidelines."[26] Some treatments labeled as CBT can be unhelpful for OCD, and some professionals warn that therapists should be trained in therapies specific for OCD or else such may contribute to obsessive-compulsive symptoms.[27] (For instance, the method of thought-stopping is not very effective for OCD and can potentially make symptoms worse. According to this method, a mild stimulus such as a snap of a rubber band on the wrist is made every time the concerning thought arises, and eventually the client moves to saying "stop" to themselves without the rubber band.)

One of the first books I read about OCD, *Brain Lock*, by psychiatrist and researcher Jeffrey Schwartz with Beverly Beyette, was described as useful by some interviewees. These authors argued that people with OCD can change their brain chemistry and taught readers how to become their own cognitive behavioral therapists.[28] On the back cover of the book are images of before and after PET scans of the brain, visually demonstrating to the reader the changes that apparently take place as a result of this method. Such is one version of CBT.

Behavior therapy (BT) arose in the period between 1950 and 1970, in parallel developments by researchers in the United Kingdom and the

United States.[29] Early theories recognized the importance of the environment and learning in the development of mental disorders. Behavioral treatment for OCD is "based on the hypothesis that obsessional thoughts have become associated, through conditioning, with anxiety which has subsequently failed to extinguish. Sufferers have developed escape and avoidance behaviors (such as obsessional checking and washing) which have the effect of preventing extinction of the anxiety."[30] The BT of exposure and response prevention (ERP), sometimes called exposure and ritual prevention, involves exposing the person to the thoughts and so forth but without letting them engage in the rituals, avoidance, and so on.[31] Some therapists pair this with relaxation techniques, but there are questions over whether this inhibits the treatment's effectiveness.[32] Cognitive therapies (CTs), on the other hand, highlight belief systems, such as people's maladaptive thoughts and cognitive distortions, which CT works to modify.[33] This includes beliefs about the power to change things or inflated responsibility, overvaluation of controlling thoughts, overestimation of a threat/undesirable outcome, and thought-action fusion, which includes the belief that thinking of something makes it more likely to happen. In the journal *Cognitive Behaviour Therapy*, researchers explained, "Although there are several cognitive models, most are similar in their formulations. . . . Contemporary OCD models propose that obsessions arise when these intrusive thoughts are misinterpreted as having serious implications, for which the person having the thoughts would be personally responsible. Compulsions are conceptualized as instrumental behaviors for averting or undoing harm, or for reducing one's perceived responsibility for aversive outcomes."[34]

Cognitive and behavioral approaches are commonly combined. CBT combines CT with some type of behavior therapy like ERP. ERP can involve interventions "regarded as cognitive . . . [such as] therapist-patient discussion about dysfunctional beliefs."[35]

Researchers are still studying the causes and maintenance of OCD, which will likely lead to changes in how the disorder is treated.[36] One treatment that is distinguished from exposure and other commonly used forms of CBT is inference-based therapy (IBT). I explained in chapter 1 about the inference-based approach (IBA). Following this theory, treatment focuses on "teaching people with OCD to identify the reasoning errors that lead to obsessions" and "how to trust reality in OCD trigger-ing situations, not by repeated exposure to feared objects to habituate to it."[37] For example, imagine a person sought help for fears that they would put their garbage in the recycling bin, or for fears that they were homosexual. ERP might involve purposefully having the person place garbage with the recycling (which could go against their values as well as violate the law in some countries), or having the client watch hours of pornography. Instead, IBT stresses that "the OCD doubt is pathologi-cal not normal doubt and is created subjectively not based in reality."[38] Therapy involves figuring out what is supporting and feeding the doubt. Cognitive approaches or this type of treatment may be helpful to people who are reluctant to try ERP or who drop out of treatment; there are therapists who are hesitant about using ERP as well.[39] ERP is often said to be associated with a high dropout rate, but the rate may not actually be higher than that for other forms of treatment.

Expanding clients' options, third-wave CBT has arisen, which can be combined with ERP and other forms of CBT.[40] According to an article on these approaches, "Third-wave therapies largely include concepts such as mindfulness, emotions, acceptance, relationships, values, goals, and metacognition. Here, the focus is on modifying the relationship one has with one's inner experiences (thoughts and emotions) and not the content of that experience."[41] Acceptance and commitment therapy (ACT) is one such approach.[42] ACT turns away from focusing on tra-ditional psychiatric diagnostic categories and proposes that everyday psychological processes and symbolic communication are the source of humanity's achievements as well as its problems. ACT helps people not get caught up in attempts to avoid and control distressing mental con-tent (much of which cannot be regulated anyway) and to focus more on the present.

One reason I find cognitive behavior therapies interesting is because some of them incorporate complementary approaches to medicine. Complementary and alternative therapies encompass a diverse array of theories and treatments, including herbs, acupuncture, and prayer. We have seen growing interest on the part of governments and research-ers to evaluate these therapies' safety and effectiveness. For instance, in the United States, the National Center for Complementary and Alterna-tive Medicine (NCCAM) was established in 1998 to study the safety and effectiveness of CAM; it has now been renamed the National Center for Complementary and Integrative Health (NCCIH).

The most obvious incorporation of complementary approaches in treating OCD appears to be how some CBT therapies draw from Buddhist concepts.[43] Buddhist techniques for training the mind have been extracted for use outside of religious contexts, for instance, to help people with depression or to help soldiers deal with the stresses of battle. In the case of OCD, Schwartz and Beyette's approach involves "mindful awareness."[44] Mindfulness in Buddhism can be extraordinarily complex. We might say it means keeping something in mind (personal communication with Buddhist nun).[45] According to the Majjhima Nikāya, there are four foundations to mindfulness, which involve contemplating the "body as a body," the "mind as mind," "feelings as feelings," and "mind-objects as mind-objects, ardent, fully aware, and mindful, having put away covetousness and grief for the world."[46] Schwartz and Beyette's instructions ask people to distinguish their OCD thoughts/behaviors, labeling them "obsessions" and "compulsions" and distinguishing such from their "true self."[47] They tell readers that the statement "It's not me—it's OCD" effectively becomes a weapon.[48] Overall, the process involves employing reflexivity to gain control.[49] More recently, OCD specialists Jon Hershfield and Tom Corboy published a workbook specifically on mindfulness for OCD.[50]

More research is needed on other potential alternative and complementary therapies for OCD. At this point, there is some evidence that nutrients like N-acetylcysteine, and plant-based supplements including valerian root and milk thistle, can be helpful for OCD.[51] Initial studies suggest that mind and body practices such as meditation, acupuncture, and kundalini yoga might be helpful for OCD. However, it does not look like St. John's wort, eicosapentaenoic acid (EPA), or meridian tapping is effective.

Additional Treatments

Other methods sometimes used in the past to treat OCD were electroshock therapy or neurosurgical procedures.[52] These techniques have changed/advanced over the years, and people who do not see improvement with other treatments may turn to non-invasive brain stimulation or contemporary neurosurgical options such as neuroablation and deep brain stimulation (DBS). DBS is a procedure that is somewhat reversible and usually involves implanting electrodes to stimulate the brain connected by wires that run under the skin to a pulse generator. Studies indicate that this treatment can be effective in reducing OCD symptoms, although complications and side effects are relatively common. Research is evolving as researchers work out the best stimulation sites and the mechanisms for how DBS works. DBS can be used in conjunction with ERP to improve effectiveness.

I only interviewed one person who had tried DBS. They were surprised and a bit offended when a healthcare professional first suggested neurosurgical options for treating their OCD. However, they had tried other treatments and eventually turned to DBS, candidly describing the day of surgery as follows:

> I felt like a VIP the moment I got into the surgery prep area. There were so many doctors who were going to help out and a bunch of students watching. . . . They had to screw this huge metal frame around my head. That activity was what hurt the most that day. . . . Since there are no pain receptors in the brain I was not knocked out. Also, I needed to be awake just in case they touched something that they were not supposed to and I was left unable to talk or something like that. I was given some minor pain meds but nothing major.

The interviewee had a penchant for taking note of the quirks of everyday life such as when they noted, "I really did not know when they started cutting into my brain because I was concentrating on the fact that I had to go to the bathroom." Later they described the everyday impacts of this treatment, such as charging the pacemaker: "Basically I have this recharger that is a charger, long cord, and then circle thingy. The circle thingy goes on my chest right where the pacemaker is." This interviewee faced some unexpected battery malfunctions in which the system turned off. Without realizing what had happened, they noticed the difference in their mental state, demonstrating the impact of this treatment. They told me that when the system was not on or did not operate, the world seemed to grow darker and they felt depression creeping in; once the system was functioning, things immediately seemed brighter.

Less invasive ways of stimulating the brain exist and have been approved by the FDA. These include transcranial magnetic stimulation and transcranial direct current stimulation, which do not require an incision.[53]

Options

Clearly, research on how to treat OCD has been growing. A variety of treatments are available now that were not available a couple decades ago, and some people experience remission of symptoms to levels where they would no longer be diagnosed with the disorder. However, there is not a magic pill that works for all people who have OCD.

Family and others who are close to people with OCD may become involved in compulsions and coping and can play an important role in treatment. A therapist I spoke to emphasized that treatment is a family affair: "Whenever you treat somebody with OCD, you have to work with the family. There are no ifs, ands, or buts about that." Some treatments such as CBT can require significant investment on the part of those with OCD and those around them, as we will see in later chapters.

PART II

Living with OCD

4

Is It Me or Is There a Problem?

> I think my first memories [of OCD] were like third grade. And then it kind of got progressively worse and worse and worse as I got older. I didn't know that it was OCD at all. . . . It's such a horrible thing when you're young. I just felt like a bit of a freak, like an underachiever because every time I would read a book, every time I'd get to a hyphen in a page—and you can imagine how many hyphens are in a page. . . . I would have to count a certain pattern in my head. I mean I'd get through half a page and be literally exhausted because the patterns wouldn't just stop with one pattern. . . . [So I would] just fall asleep with the book open. My parents thought I was lazy or shouldn't read in bed. . . . [People said I wasn't] studying hard enough. . . . I thought they were right! Because I hadn't read the chapter.
> —Zelda

There are certain patterns in Zelda's life that I saw repeated in the accounts of other people with OCD. I label these stages of the OCD "career": *coming to see oneself as having a problem, defining it as OCD, seeking help,* and *learning to live with OCD.* People with OCD do not experience their troubling thoughts and rituals and necessarily jump to the conclusion they have OCD. Zelda, like a number of other people I interviewed, spent much of her life *not* thinking that she had OCD. I discussed what OCD felt like for interviewees, but theirs were the words of people who had already come to see themselves as having the disorder.

Prior to her diagnosis, at times Zelda felt some of her thoughts/behaviors made her life difficult and were not what she referred to as "normal," so she tried to hide them. She described doing "avant-garde" rituals, where she would go to a corner of a room and put her hands in a particular position and look a certain way. As she did this, she thought to herself, "Why can't I stop?" and "This is crazy. I mean, why am I doing this?" She did not want people to see her and so she would tell herself to do the rituals later when everyone in the house was asleep. She told me that the smaller rituals did not really make her feel "freakish," but with respect to bigger rituals, she could not ignore how "this was something different." She did not really frame it as a problem that could be treated, though.

Zelda recalled a time when her OCD skyrocketed. Her stepbrother died on his motorcycle; prior to this she had a thought about him dying. She said, "I wasn't so out of it that I thought I was personally responsible. But somehow I felt like there was a connection."

The more she engaged in rituals, the more trouble she had functioning in school, and the more she questioned whether others had these same thoughts. When she was in college, she did not have to hide what she was doing from others.

> I was able to really ritualize to my heart's content. . . . So I would just get stuck. . . . Everything had a ritual. . . . I had this threshold in my apartment and for some reason it just always gave me a lot of trouble, so I would be late going to school. I would just have to go over it and over it and over it. And that's really when I started thinking this is just problematic. My hands were getting chafed from washing so much. I was exhausted from even washing my face. . . . So it became this jail cell for me.

Zelda happened to have a conversation with her brother who was studying psychology, which proved pivotal. She asked if he ever made promises to God so that some future negative event would not occur. He picked up on the OCD and gave her a book to read titled *The Boy Who Couldn't Stop Washing*. At that point Zelda began to move from the first stage of the OCD trajectory, where she had come to see herself as having a problem, to the next stage of labeling it OCD. Zelda told me that she went on to read the book and began crying. Her tears were partially the result of relief because she had judged herself negatively for years. She had perceived her thoughts/behaviors as a personal flaw. She explained:

> It was very emotional just to realize this was an issue. This was something. This wasn't, you know, who I am. It was a very very very sad but happy moment as well. . . . The OCD limited me on so many levels and

I always felt like such a misfit in some ways, an underachiever. . . . I was always kind of suicidal when I was a kid. . . . It was just nice to know that this is actually a problem that could be fixed, or at least to have a name. So it wasn't my whole, my identity. It was something that was a part of me, but I wasn't just this lazy person and I wasn't just this freak.

She sought professional help in the form of an OCD specialist, where she continued her emotional journey of reflecting on her childhood experiences and recasting them in a new light that involved less self-blame. She began to replace ideas that she was unintelligent and a bad student with recognition that the OCD inhibited her. She sought to get ahold of her thoughts and behaviors, to see what life might be without them. This is the third stage of the OCD "career," help-seeking. When Zelda and I spoke on the phone, she was thirty-three years old and had been diagnosed with OCD, body dysmorphic disorder, depression, and an eating disorder.[1]

Although we can call this a history or narrative of her life with OCD, it is only in retrospect that Zelda can tell this story. She went from perceiving her thoughts and behaviors as part of who she was, to distinguishing some as obsessions and compulsions, akin to a separate entity. She and those around her reinterpreted her past in light of this information, a "retrospective" interpretation or labeling.[2] "I guess everyone just thought I was very superstitious and a little eccentric. And turns out my maternal and paternal grandfathers had OCD and everybody looking back on it was like, 'Ooohhh, ah, I guess that's what it was.'" Not everyone immediately does something with this information. Zelda did by seeking specialized professional help.

Over time, she went through further changes, the stage of learning to live with OCD. For Zelda, this stage of the OCD trajectory included her coming to see herself as having a chronic disorder called OCD shared by others, and her being more open about her OCD when interacting with other people. At the time of the interview, her experience had come full circle. Bearing in mind a potential genetic link to OCD, she was no longer just watching her own thoughts and behaviors but also observing her child, trying to distinguish expected behaviors for a kid from any potential ritualistic OCD behavior—as children commonly engage in rituals and grow out of them.[3]

Illness Careers

Why should we look at illness in the form of a career? We know that illness often disrupts people's lives.[4] In the most basic sense, we can imagine a period before the illness insinuates itself into our existence, a treatment phase in which we attempt to bend it to our will, followed by time after treatment. This can be termed a career because it has different stages. It is true that compared with the past, many people are experiencing chronic health problems rather than a temporary sick role. People's bodies and mental states may never go back to some pre-illness way of being, leading to uncertainty and unique questions about how to perceive their self and engage with others.

I utilize the idea of a career to show how having an illness does not have a singular turning point. In the case of OCD, different stages were linked to shifts in information and alterations in how people perceived themselves, interpreted their thoughts and behaviors, sought help, and reacted to potential stigma. Stages did not form a generically linear process with professional treatment and/or remission at the end. Instead, some people never went through all the stages, such as those who never sought professional help. Others went through one or more of these stages at once.

Further, we cannot assume "symptoms" are the only driving force of illness trajectories. Sociologists studying illness have exposed some bitter truths. They have found that what leads someone to become a patient, be labeled as ill and/or hospitalized, and fall under the gaze and care of a medical professional is not always due to the person's "symptoms." Previously, I assumed that people who end up involuntarily committed to psychiatric hospitals engage in significantly different activities from those who are not hospitalized. However, within sociologist Erving Goffman's classic study of people involuntary hospitalized in "mental institutions," published in the late 1950s, he wrote that for every behavior that resulted in hospitalization, many cases existed where similar behaviors did not lead to hospitalization.[5] He wrote about how people went through a series of definable stages he called a career, but discovered how "career contingencies" existed outside of symptoms.[6] Factors such as people's socioeconomic status and available resources affected what happened to them. More recently, in a study of Alzheimer's disease, the sociologist Renée Beard illustrated how there are social consequences to being diagnosed regardless of "symptoms."[7]

Therefore, I discuss how people's lives and sense of self changed at the different stages of the OCD career, rather than just focusing on symptoms. Interviewees are mothers, fathers, husbands, wives, friends, colleagues, business partners, and more. The sociologist Talcott Parsons explained long ago how being labeled as sick affects these identities and how the people surrounding us interact with us.[8] Looking at illness as a career can help us take into account how the social is intertwined with the biological and psychological.

Importantly, the symptoms of OCD are diverse, so it is possible to go through stages again for each form of OCD. For example, a person may perceive their thoughts of harm immediately as problematic, but not define other thoughts/behaviors in this way. I witnessed this process when in the course of an interview a person would contemplate whether a certain thought or behavior of theirs was obsessive and/or compulsive. I recall sitting with Chance when he mentioned discovering information on complementary treatments for health problems. He had begun the interview by telling me about how his OCD manifested. Later in the interview he described himself as a "compulsive reader." "I read everything. I can't walk past something and not read it. I have to know what everything says," he told me. He reflected on what he had just said, questioning if his reading was a symptom of OCD. Chance's next words were "I guess that's another OCD I didn't even realize."

As a multifaceted disorder that is stereotyped and trivialized in the media, OCD provides a valuable case for looking more closely at how people define a health problem in their lives and the factors that affect professional help-seeking. In a study of patients with OCD at two outpatient clinics in Spain, 46 percent of participants did not believe they had a problem soon after "symptoms" began.[9] The first stage of the illness career may be an important piece of the puzzle regarding why many people with diagnosable mental disorders, especially OCD, are not receiving the most effective treatments currently available for disorders.[10] It is a period to which researchers do not always direct much attention, instead focusing on the turning point of diagnosis.

We do know from surveys and interviews that people's recognition of themselves as having a problem and/or help-seeking for OCD appear linked to factors such as age of onset, race/ethnicity, number of symptoms, type of symptoms, perceived ability to handle or control symptoms, impact of symptoms on their lives, how people and those around them interpret their thoughts/behaviors, comorbid diagnoses, fear of stigma, misdiagnoses, and lack of information about OCD.[11]

This chapter takes us beyond the numbers and into people's lives to contemplate why factors such as these matter. The rest of this book is designed to examine each of the stages of the OCD "career" in turn. We travel the twists and turns of people's paths before and after diagnosis, tracing the trajectory of OCD. In this chapter I focus on the first stage in order to look at the diversity of ways people made sense of their "obsessions" and "compulsions" before they saw them as "symptoms" of a disorder, essentially the pre-OCD experience. By starting at the beginning, we can look at if/how/when people start to see themselves as different from others, or as troubled in some way and having a problem. I define "problem" here as a gap between the person you are and the person you want to (or feel you should) be, in other words, a gap between the real and virtual self.[12] These gaps can be neutral or positive (such as when a person believes their OCD makes them excel at their job), but only become a problem when there is a negative gap, something that a person believes needs fixing.

Every person I interviewed, except one, eventually came to the conclusion that some of their thoughts/behaviors constituted a problem. Yet, they did not immediately deem it a psychological or psychiatric one. As Martin said, "Oh, I definitely knew there was something weird going on. But I didn't know what it was. In fact, it was my deepest darkest secret."

Is This "Normal"?

The central question for people at this first stage was "Am I experiencing sensations, thoughts, urges, behaviors, and so forth that are 'normal' or not?" That aided them in assessing if such was a problem. It was a question that people tended to cycle back over. One day at a support group for people with OCD, Riley, an enigmatic man and regular attendee, posed an issue that cut to the heart of how hard it can be to define a strict line between "normal" and "OCD." We later conversed about the topic through mailed letters. Riley felt mosquitoes hunted him because they preferred the taste of his blood more than the blood of others. He engaged in rituals to deny them the ability to feast on his flesh. Were those rituals an expected response to mosquitoes finding him particularly suitable prey? Riley appeared middle-aged and had been diagnosed with OCD and considered himself to have a complex set of problems and disorders (potentially ADD). Although diagnosed with OCD, he still went through this stage of questioning whether something he was doing was emblematic of OCD and a "problem" or not. He once wrote me to say:

> My reaction to mosquitoes, which includes "whopping" around with large plastic bags before entering the house from the outside, and spending 15 minutes before bed each night to stand outside my bedroom to try to draw biting bugs out of the room, then "whopping in" with a couple towels, and rapidly closing the bedroom door and sealing it with the towels underneath the door, may be considered an "OCD" thing, itself. But as you know, some people actually ARE more attacked by mosquitoes and other biting bugs than average. Which brings me to my "continuum theory": there is a continuum between a "normal" level of precautions on one end of the spectrum and an OCD level, on the other end. It is not a clear diving line.

His words provide food for thought. When people face sensations, thoughts, and behaviors that seem atypical for them or for a particular social context, they work to give such meaning. The diverse nature of obsessions and compulsions, especially the way they can insinuate themselves into people's minds and seem so real, while at times remaining sneakily hidden from others, complicates this process.

There was no one event, thought, behavior, emotion, or urge that everyone with OCD pointed to as signifying that they had a "problem." Many of us probably subscribe to the idea that we know "normal" when we see it. Yet, defining this and distinguishing it from what is outside social norms can be difficult, especially when considering mental concerns versus, say, the more obvious broken bone. Much sociological research indicates that there may be no single act, thought, or feeling that identifies a mental disorder as such. Instead, people without a diagnosable disorder can experience anxiety and depressive symptoms under certain conditions. Professionals admit that "in the absence of clear biological markers or clinically useful measurements of severity for many mental disorders, it has not been possible to completely separate normal and pathological symptom expressions contained in diagnostic criteria."[13] Hence, they turn to the idea that a diagnosable disorder leads a person to feel distress or to have issues in functioning.

In general, sociologists have pointed out how society and culture shape people's perceptions of wellness as well as illness. People's sense of who they are and what they are experiencing is inextricably connected to the larger society in which they live. Our hopes and dreams, our sense of who we are, what is right and wrong, normal versus deviant—they are not decided in a vacuum but are built brick by brick as we interact in society. Defining "normal" versus "deviant" is a mercurial target that can vary by context and change over time. A bottle of alcohol can be discussed as a temptation at a meeting of alcoholics, a means of demonstrating skill to a group of brewmasters, an illegal activity to police cracking down on underage drinking, or a fun night out to a group of pub crawlers. Meaning is not given in the bottle itself.[14] Even the franchisers of McDonald's came face to face with this when they expanded to other countries.[15] Lining up in a queue, knowing how to eat a hamburger, associating a smile with friendly customer service are not universal social norms—so McDonald's educated consumers. In Moscow, employees at the start-up of a McDonald's reportedly stood outside with bullhorns announcing that employees would be smiling to indicate their willingness to help rather than because they were laughing at customers.[16] In today's society, what counts as "normal" has become even more varied.[17] We face the "'uncertainties' of contemporary life and living."[18]

Establishing a Baseline

The knowledge that we have of the world provides us with ways to understand and talk about ourselves.[19] To establish a baseline for judging their thoughts/behavior, people with OCD looked at the world around them and drew on their knowledge of social norms.[20] They compared their thoughts/behaviors to those of others, critically appraised others' responses to their thoughts/behaviors, and directly asked others for feedback on thoughts/behaviors. This makes sense in light of how, decades ago, the sociologist George Herbert Mead revealed how the self develops in interaction with others.[21] Explicating Mead's ideas, sociologists James A. Holstein and Jaber F. Gubrium wrote, "Experience provides the means and meanings through which one becomes conscious of what one is."[22]

Without evidence to the contrary, some people I spoke to assumed what they were thinking and doing was typical. Delia and I chatted at a mental health center, and she told me that her mom raised her "to be a clean person." She was married with children, lived in the United States, and was diagnosed with OCD and bipolar disorder. Earlier in her life, she assumed that her cleaning and organizing around the house (which also involved counting) were the same as what everyone else was doing. She admitted that when she went into people's homes, "I just thought well maybe they just aren't finished for the day. Surely they don't . . . keep their house this way." It was Delia's daughters who came to her when she was in her twenties and told her that she was "an obsessive-compulsive person." That began Delia's path toward seeing things differently. Looking back, she felt she got OCD from her parents, who engaged in some of the same behaviors.

Meghan's baseline was her work and family. Meghan lived in the United States, was married, and had been diagnosed with OCD, depression, and an eating disorder. When Meghan worked as a nurse, her coworkers praised her. She explained to me, "In my field . . . checking and double-checking and triple-checking is a good thing in nursing. And I've actually kind of made a good reputation for myself for being anal and being a nitpicker." She was in her thirties at the time we chatted. Diagnosed the previous year, she had come to feel she had had OCD for as long as she could remember. She recalled counting, ordering, and performing other compulsions when she was younger. However, she said her family "was kind of like that," so she did not perceive the behavior as out of the ordinary. She imagined everyone else in her family could be diagnosed with OCD. Meghan continued, "It just seemed somewhat normal enough and we made jokes about it. My mom is a hoarder. We'd get on her [about it]. . . . But we just figured that was the way it was in everybody's family, I guess. I did. When I got older [we used the term] anal. Like my sister went through a very stressful time with her boyfriend. She would clean and wouldn't leave her house because she was cleaning all day every day. When she cleaned nobody could sit on any of the furniture. . . . But this whole time . . . her boyfriend lived with her. So he wasn't allowed to sit on anything in his own house, or she had to go back and clean it again."

Since these thoughts/behaviors were expected within her family, Meghan did not see herself as having a problem for quite a while. In this way, some people I interviewed experienced a potentially diagnosable level of symptoms but did not necessarily define what they were experiencing as a concern. Later things got worse for Meghan, to the point that she kept checking her husband and dogs to see if they were breathing, and checking the locks on the door. This checking was taking up her whole night, and she would worry all day. At that point she decided that she had a problem but could not yet put a name to it.

There are some similarities here with the career of other mental disorders. Feeling as if something is off but being unable to decipher such can be part of having depression. Karp found that people who were depressed went through an initial period of being scared and in discomfort without labeling it depression, what he called the stage of inchoate feelings.[23] In some cases this was because they did not have a "baseline of normalcy for comparison," for instance, a few interviewees who were raised in abusive families.[24] For people with OCD, one difficulty in establishing a sense of things is the way in which people do not walk around like cartoon characters with thought bubbles over their heads that reveal their innermost thoughts. Assessing what is a problem or not is therefore particularly hard when it involves thoughts or private rituals. This goes back to the gap between the inner and outer worlds of those with OCD.

As a result, the people I interviewed sometimes directly went to others to help solve this ambiguity. Monty was not shy, and he recounted being willing to talk to anyone who was willing to listen, including coworkers. He said if he and I were sitting on a bus and he felt like he did in the past, he probably would have asked me if I experienced thoughts about which he was curious. "Because I mean at that point in time, I wanted to find out what was causing it, and do other people have it, and why am I feeling this way." He continued, "I would literally talk to anybody that would listen."

Previous research has suggested that age at onset may be a relevant factor for OCD, with earlier age at onset of "symptoms" linked to delays in help-seeking. Age of onset may be linked to differences in people's perceptions of what they are doing as atypical and/or a mental health concern.[25] My research suggests that age matters because it affects the variety of meanings people can bring to bear on what they are experiencing.

The vast majority of people I interviewed were nineteen or younger when they first experienced what they now call obsessions and compulsions, although to be fair, some of them said this upon looking back on their lives and did not notice much at the time. Many of them were under age ten. As a result, they indicated that the resources from which they could draw to understand themselves were limited. Jeff and another person I interviewed explained how they could not consider themselves as having a psychological or mental problem when they were children because they had no knowledge of such. As we age, move in different social circles, take on various roles, and experience other cultures and ways of life, the resources we have to draw from can expand, with concomitant shifts in how we might act and perceive our thoughts/behaviors. One interviewee described how her sense of herself evolved: "I don't remember really having an idea of it as a kid. People would point out, 'Why are you doing this?' or 'What did you say?' but I would hear people say that to kids all the time. Kids do weird shit. I mean that's what kids do, so I guess I didn't really think anything about it. Why would I hide it? . . . Later on when people profusely were always like, 'Why are you still doing that?' . . . I did look around and say [to myself] 'OK, no one else is doing this but me.'"

People commonly turn to social networks for advice when they encounter concerns that are potentially symptoms of an illness.[26] Considering the tender age at which many people I interviewed said they first experienced symptoms, families obviously played a large role in helping to determine if a problem was occurring. Note that there is some evidence that children engage in somewhat different rituals than adults, and young children are also more likely to request family participation in some rituals.[27] OCD "in childhood is typically associated with significant functional impairment across multiple areas of a child's life. The time occupied by performing rituals often significantly interferes with a child's daily routine, which inadvertently also disrupts the entire family and family life."[28] Families can affect the course of the disorder, for example, with respect to whether they accommodate and participate in rituals.[29]

One controversial response on the part of families and social networks is what we can refer to as "finding the normal," or framing as a nonproblem.[30] These are times when people noticed thoughts/behaviors but decided to consider them as nothing out of the ordinary, neither a problem nor a boon, but simply within expectations for the context. For instance, Miles recalled having symptoms since age sixteen. He told me, "I did talk to my parents about it but they just said that they'd been like it. I don't think it was true but they were trying to make me feel better. . . . I thought maybe everyone thought like I did but that it just wasn't talked about. Maybe I hoped that everyone did!" This is not an unexpected response for within everyday, mundane interactions, people make assumptions; when situations are ambiguous, we try to make sense of them and "normalize" them to some degree.[31] In one study, families of youth at "high risk for psychosis" sometimes treated "atypical behavior" as evidence of the youth being teenagers or as manageable character traits.[32]

Researchers have disagreed over whether "finding the normal" is beneficial or problematic for those with potential mental health concerns. Some researchers are wary of labeling problems. Professor of psychiatry Allen Frances questioned what he perceived as overdiagnosis in contemporary society, saying, "In this brave new world of psychiatric overdiagnosis, will anyone get through life without a mental disorder?"[33] Other practitioners are eager to get people into what they perceive as helpful treatment sooner and would see this as an avoidable delay. Recently, researchers recommended that even people without symptoms, but who have a family history with OCD, engage in self-observation (or parental observation) and psychoeducation; for subthreshold symptoms they recommended workshops, meditation, and exercise.[34] Therapists are concerned that the duration of untreated OCD may be associated with worse treatment outcomes.[35]

Forcing people into treatment against their will can backfire, though. Sabina was forced to go to a healthcare professional by her school. She was in the United States and was twenty-one years old when we wrote to each other online, and she confessed how others labeled her as different and treated her negatively. She remembered that at around age seven or eight, she touched things repeatedly, hoarded little toys the teacher gave students, and engaged in checking behaviors. She labeled herself as weird but not necessarily as having a problem: "[Experiencing symptoms as early as age seven or eight,] I knew I wasn't normal . . . although I can't say I remember it as a problem exactly. . . . I didn't want to tell anyone. . . . I don't think my family really noticed anything. I really hid a lot of things. I didn't want people to think I was weird." She felt that other people, such as one of her classmates, noticed even though she was fairly successful at hiding. "Things got much worse when I was about twelve. It was very obvious [to family and people at school] that I had a problem, but no one would've guessed what. . . . Everyone [at school] thought I was weird. . . . It was fairly traumatic." She felt stigmatized and imagined they perceived her as "crazy." The school forced her to seek treatment. Sabina told me, "I didn't want to be someone who went to a therapist. That's why I wouldn't talk to her [and instead my mom talked to the therapist]. . . . Silly, but I was thirteen. . . . I wouldn't get out of the car at first." The therapist said she had anxiety and years later Sabina diagnosed herself with OCD. Sabina's comments illustrate how perceptive children can be in assessing and trying to manage what they perceive as behaviors outside of the social norm. Her story also demonstrates the power of stigma early in the illness career.

Interviewees who experienced obsessions and/or compulsions later in life, versus people who have never known themselves without obsessive thoughts and compulsive behaviors, described using their previous thoughts/behaviors as a baseline. As people age, they have not only learned more about the world but also learned about themselves. If you perceive yourself as straight and suddenly start having random thoughts in which you worry about being homosexual, it seems out of character. If you have never worried much about organization and germs, but increasingly find yourself cleaning and organizing, you might wonder what is going on. People have lived and gotten a chance to construct a sense of self without OCD and notice when they are thinking or acting outside of their own personal norms.

Sam was seventy-four years old when his obsessions and compulsions turned him into someone that he, as well as his wife, did not recognize.

He wrote me that prior to this he may have always had tendencies. An important factor that led Sam and his wife to conclude that he had a problem was that they knew what he was like in the previous sixty-plus years. His wife narrated to me over the phone:

> We were traveling and he was driving and . . . all of a sudden, he says, "I think I hit that bumper back [there at the restaurant.]" . . . I said, "No, you didn't. I was in the car with you. You didn't." [He said,] "No, no I have to go back and check. I have to go back and check." Then all of a sudden it came to me: all of a sudden he's doing this repetitive kind of behavior. Then we went out to a dinner with some of his relatives and [he got upset at someone who said they were copying a video for a friend.] . . . He was going to call the police on them that night. And I go, "Wait a minute, wait, where are you coming from? You're never like this, you know." He said, "I think something's wrong with me. I think something's wrong in my head because I just have all these compulsions I feel I have to do."

For Sam and his wife, OCD was a life-changing biographical and familial disruption, making it more obviously a problem. He lived in the United States and was diagnosed with OCD and depression.

Note that while assessing their thoughts/behaviors as outside of social norms was often linked to interviewees perceiving these as a problem, this did not occur in all cases. For instance, keeping things clean was in some ways a positive aspect of having OCD for Delia. Her house was certainly cleaner than her sister's or brother's house, she proclaimed. Cleaning served as a form of therapy for her, even though it caused some strife in her family.

Symptoms

Although what people perceive as a "symptom" is somewhat mutable, research has acknowledged type of "symptoms" and "symptom severity" as factors that may influence problem recognition, especially the degree to which they inhibit people's ability to function.[36] I found that the way in which people's thoughts/behaviors waxed and waned shaped their perception of the "problem."

Interviewees were sometimes able to ignore or tolerate a variety of thoughts and behaviors, whether or not they perceived them as "normal." Sabina thought she was acting oddly but did not make the mental leap to thinking she had a problem until it worsened. People could refer to points in time when they understood their thoughts/behaviors to be less of a "problem" and instead more "annoying," "irritating," or "no big deal." Instead of labeling themselves or their thoughts/behaviors in a serious and negative manner, some chose more lighthearted titles such as "sillinesses," "habits," and "quirks," especially before diagnosis. However, thoughts and behaviors that became more severe or impaired daily functioning acted as pushes, nudging people to notice them and look for answers and possible solutions. Although certain thoughts/ urges sometimes disappeared for periods of time and ritualizing became less severe, the reverse could happen. Or, compared with the severity of other things the person was experiencing, including other disorders, the OCD did not seem like as much of a problem.

Concealing behaviors was driven by "symptoms" as well as social concerns like stigma. Rapoport theorized that "secrecy is part of the disorder."[37] What struck me in my interviews was how some people, at a very young age, began to hide their self-perceived "abnormal" thoughts and behaviors. However, as Monty showed us, before he realized what he was doing might potentially be perceived as outside social norms, there was no pressing need to go out of his way to hide it. Having decided they were thinking outside the cultural box or engaging in deviant behaviors, the people I interviewed commonly developed techniques for hiding their thoughts/behaviors from at least some others.[38] Interviewees referred to themselves as manipulators and performers, although with varying levels of skill in masking their odd thoughts/behaviors. Ashamed, confused, and fearful of stigma, they found ways to disguise their abnormal thoughts/behaviors and avoid the public's gaze. Mick explained how hiding does not just mean avoiding public disapproval or stigma. "[I learned] over the years how to appear more 'normal' than my OCD is, and now do so without conscious thought. . . . My main motives, however, were (1) to avoid causing my family distress (and myself guilt over their distress), and perhaps even more urgently (2) so that I could actually do the compulsions with a minimum of interference/ distraction."

Assigning Meaning to the Problem

Once people felt they had a "problem," what did they perceive as the cause? They drew from the resources and knowledge available to them. They blamed everything from God to themselves. Their perceptions of the problem were shaped in part by whether they believed in their thoughts and behaviors, and the degree to which they perceived their thoughts/behaviors as an intruder or alien to their sense of self, rather than as part of who they were. OCD has historically been associated with ego-dystonicity and having insight, although not all people with OCD have insight.[39] Children, especially, may be prone to less insight or not finding the OCD as senseless.

Some interviewees declared OCD, especially at this stage in their OCD career, could seem relatively believable or made them question themselves. For instance, Adrian, a man from the United States in his thirties who had not been diagnosed (but thought he might have had OCD or at least at one point was developing it), told me that when he was a child he believed he really was controlling and preventing people from coming to harm by engaging in certain ritualistic behaviors. He thought he was doing something beneficial. Certainly, some interviewees recognized the irrational nature of their thinking. However, people's perceptions of their thoughts/behaviors could fluctuate and be uncertain. Although all of us can have bizarre thoughts, people with OCD can misinterpret unwanted intrusive thoughts as revealing something about their "self."[40] They sometimes view these as revealing a hidden part of who they are, and they question their self-concept. For example, I talked to people with homosexual thoughts who questioned if they might be gay. Sean had these thoughts and at one point "firmly believed" that he was bisexual.

Monty, who had fears of contracting a disease, said, "Even though there was no practical reason how I could have had AIDS, I was convinced that I had AIDS and that I was going to give it to my girlfriend. And I remember when I came home, one of the first things I did is told my mom I wanted to be tested for AIDS. My mom was looking at me like 'What did you do?' And I'm like, 'Nothing.'"

People who had more insight might still fear not engaging in rituals. Kirstyn, who was not diagnosed with OCD until her thirties, believed her obsessions and compulsions started at age four. She said that before her diagnosis, she would have "never told anyone" because "I knew it's crazy. I mean it really is a crazy disorder. It makes no sense and I knew what I was doing was not [possible]; I couldn't make things happen or not happen." She said that she just had to do it anyway. At least some of rituals were designed to stave off negative events, so she told me she worried that if she told others about her thoughts/behaviors, those bad things would happen. The rituals wouldn't work. That motivated her to keep her thoughts/behaviors a secret.

Therefore, we can better understand how people sometimes attributed the cause of their problematic thoughts/behaviors to themselves. Rodney said, "Of course I could never explain to anyone what I was doing—at that time I did not know that there was a professional designation for what I had; I thought it was just me sui generis." Sometimes seeing what was happening to them as an expression of themselves made them perceive that something was wrong, but they did not perceive it as a type of problem they could change. In a sense, they were the "problem."[41]

One conclusion some interviewees drew was that their thoughts/behaviors were reflective of something about their personality, like a habit or trait. This helps explain why only 27 percent of the people I interviewed went to a professional for their obsessions and compulsions and were diagnosed there (although others said they were diagnosed when presenting themselves for related issues).

Janet and Jeff provided two other illustrations of this type of thinking. Janet told me, "I couldn't imagine that anyone else could have this problem. And as my parents reacted with bewildered annoyance, I became convinced that it was a personal weakness of mine, an inability to fully cope with things, a failure of character and will." Jeff said that around the fifth grade he "kept worrying that my bottom or my underwear weren't entirely clean. But at that time, I think I saw my tendency to obsessive thinking as more of a character or personality flaw, something that was wrong with my attitude but which I couldn't fix, than anything that you could go to the doctor for."

What other explanations did people turn to once they perceived they had a "problem"? Vodou, demons, an abusive home life, I'm crazy—I was not sure what explanation I would hear next. I realized the interviewees were just pulling from the resources they had at hand. Holstein and Gubrium argued this is how people make sense of things and build a coherent sense of self. Some people had religious knowledge, and instead of blaming themselves, they attributed their thoughts/behaviors to a spiritual cause. Monica (a woman in her thirties who lived in the United States, self-diagnosed with OCD and professionally diagnosed with depression) hypothesized that perhaps "somebody put Vodou on me or maybe somebody in my past . . . because [my family is] Haitian." As a child, Jeff questioned if he had been rejected by God. One day, he touched his parent's computer and the screen froze, "and I felt worried that this was a sign that there was so much evil or demons in me."

Finally, some people attributed their problems to medical ones, although the majority of people I interviewed did not. Missy was in her thirties, lived in the United States, was diagnosed with OCD, generalized anxiety disorder (GAD), and panic disorder, and said she had an eating disorder in the past. She initially considered physical explanations for her obsessions and compulsions because these were more familiar to her. She was young and her knowledge of mental disorders was limited. She told me, "Even fifteen years ago, people weren't talking about mental illness like they do now. So I knew something was wrong; I just didn't know what it was. That's why I kept going to usually those physical places. I have cancer. I have a heart attack. I'm dying."

Some people did turn to psychological causes, but not necessarily OCD. Most people I interviewed had limited knowledge of OCD at this point in their lives, and what they did know was often stereotypical and incomplete. Researchers have used the phrase "mental health literacy" to refer to people's recognition of contemporary medical/psychological perspectives on mental disorders.[42] This includes their ability to recognize "symptoms" and appropriate means of treatment. There is evidence that people's recognition of disorders is associated with seeking help from medical and psychiatric professionals.[43] Among those I interviewed, some were so young as to not even have a conception of what a psychological problem was.

Those who did suppose that they might have a medical or psychological problem sometimes were hazy on what specific disorder it might be. Quite a few people wondered if they were "crazy" or "nuts" or "insane." Sean told me, "I thought I was going mad." A woman from the United

States and diagnosed with OCD said that she "went really, really nuts. I mean I couldn't sleep." She said she could not stop thinking about the fears that she had. Another woman from the United States diagnosed with OCD and depression told me, "I frankly was really scared I was losing my mind. I was like, 'What is going on?'" These people did not seem to be using these negative words to mean they might have an actual diagnosable condition. Instead, it was as if they were trying to find some way to describe their fears about what was happening, or perhaps drawing from intensely negative media stereotypes. Sometimes they were indicating they felt they had a mental disorder, but one unique to themselves, something not shared by others.

For a number of the people I communicated with, at times they just could not make sense of their thoughts, feelings, urges, and behaviors. They struggled to find suitable resources to give meaning to their lives, to construct a sense of who they are, and to explain why they were acting in a particular way. It was as if meaning-making processes stalled, and their ability to build a consistent coherent narrative of their "self" was blocked. They were left with an ambiguous "something" they were experiencing. They engaged in behaviors they could not explain to themselves or others. They had thoughts that did not seem to make sense or be the kind of thoughts they expected to have. As a result, they said things to me such as the following:

All I knew was that it was stupid but I couldn't control it. . . . I had absolutely no idea what was wrong with me. (Sean)

So far as having a problem goes, there was no question of that. I thought I had a very serious problem that nobody could understand or explain. (Jeff)

I noticed it, yeah. I knew something was wrong, but I couldn't figure it out. And it's like all my life I've been hunting and hunting and searching and searching and searching . . . [for answers to] "Why do I feel like this?" (Merrill)

[When I was in school, students would see how I ate and ask me] "Why are you doing this?" . . . [I would say] "That's how I eat it. I don't know." And then it would be like an awkward, "Who knows?" (Mona)

They suffered, sometimes hiding their thoughts and behaviors, unable to make sense of what was happening to them. Sean and Jeff have been introduced previously. Merrill lived in the United States, was diagnosed with OCD and ADD, and at times believed that he had social anxiety disorder and depression. Mona lived in the United States and was diagnosed with OCD, ADHD, anxiety, and depression.

Mapping the Pre-OCD Stage

Social scientists Simonds and Elliott wrote, "One might conclude that people do not seek medical help for mental-health problems because they do not perceive them as medical problems."[44] The variety of explanations interviewees provided confirms this. The dynamics of this pre-OCD stage are presented in figure 4.1, which illustrates how interviewees were situated within larger social contexts that shaped how they perceived their thoughts and behaviors. Factors such as the type of thoughts/behaviors and their severity intersected with social factors to affect how people and their social networks noticed thoughts and behaviors and labeled them as a problem or not. These factors acted as pushes and pulls, in some cases pushing people and social networks away from noticing their thoughts/behaviors and other times directing them away.

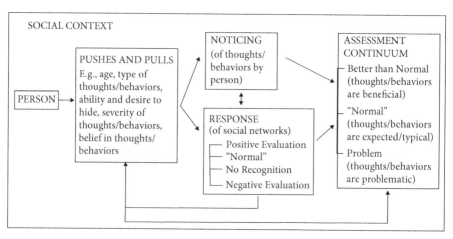

Figure 4.1. Dynamics of pre-OCD stage

Years went by before some people paid their thoughts and behaviors much mind. While in many cases interviewees came to label their own thoughts and behaviors as problems, at times they viewed these in a more neutral or positive manner. Furthermore, people could hold multiple perspectives at once, for example, recognizing some thoughts/behaviors as a problem and not others, or some thoughts/behaviors as beneficial in a particular situation but not others.

Once people noticed their thoughts/behaviors as troubling, they tried to give meaning to this "problem" and give meaning to their lives using various explanations. "Society's members . . . artfully put discourses to work to constitute their subjectivities," wrote the sociologists Holstein and Gubrium.[45] However, people expressed some uncertainty and confusion.

If they just had more information about OCD, some interviewees suggested, their OCD "career" might have been different and they would not have struggled so long for answers. Parents with OCD described hoping that if their children had the disorder, they could make things easier by taking advantage of their accumulated knowledge regarding the disorder. However, mental health literacy would not have changed everything completely. We can already see how people with OCD struggled with the question "Is what I am experiencing me, and is it 'normal'?" This is a recurring theme in the book. It did not necessarily disappear completely even after one had knowledge of OCD. Instead, the question could morph slightly to, "Is it me or my OCD?" Maeve, a woman from the United States and diagnosed with OCD and depression, said: "I never know what is 'normal.' . . . My number one struggle in life right now is to figure this out. It has become a new obsession of mine . . . trying to figure out if my thoughts are real or OCD."

5

Stigma and Trivialization

> One night I was watching the TV show *20/20*, and there was a segment on about people suffering with OCD. I started crying when I was watching it because I realized I had OCD. . . . [I want people to know] all the different possible issues that OCD can bring up in your life because I always just thought OCD was washing your hands.
> —Maeve

The moment of labeling/diagnosis is so pivotal that in recent decades sociologists have argued that we need to devote a special area of study to the sociology of diagnosis.[1] This chapter explores the dynamics of the second stage of the OCD "career," including how people came to perceive themselves as having OCD and the resulting implications for their lives. Like Maeve, many of the people I interviewed realized they had OCD after encountering information through sources such as the media. When Maeve saw that television show about OCD, she was in her early teens. The lack of public and sometimes professional understanding of the disorder, along with interviewees' fears of stigma, contributed to those I communicated with sometimes going years before labeling themselves with the disorder or getting diagnosed. After the show, Maeve's sense of her thoughts/behaviors was transformed. Maeve began separating her real "self" from the "OCD."

Maeve contacted me when she was in her midtwenties. She was in the United States and had recently earned a graduate degree and was working in the technology field. Over the years, she experienced a number of forms of OCD. Maeve's first symptoms involved fears of germs, and she described washing her hands practically nonstop. If she stepped into a restroom, she believed she was going to contract AIDS upon touching something. In her teens she went to a youth group. The minister or person in charge was "kind of fanatical and he told us this story about if we lied to our parents we were going to get possessed by demons." This led to obsessions that she might become possessed. Maeve told me that prior to watching the television show, "I had no idea why I was the way I was." After she saw the show, she did not have to fear that she was possessed by demons or had contracted AIDS; she instead chalked this up to OCD, a mental disorder with available psychological/psychiatric treatment.

Maeve told her mother right away that she had OCD upon viewing the television show. She talked to me about how she remembered begging her mom to take her to counseling because she felt severely depressed and was performing "constant OCD rituals." Her mom's response to this pronouncement was that Maeve did not have OCD. Maeve felt her mom acted angrily in response to her persistence about counseling and described her mom as "emotionally abusive."

At that age, Maeve could not pay for a therapist on her own and so she sought help from a guidance counselor at school and from other relatives, including one who worked in the healthcare field. They seemed to have no idea about what she was experiencing. It was years later, in college, that she was officially diagnosed. However, that diagnosis lacked impact, she said, because she had diagnosed herself years prior.

This process of naming one's thoughts/behaviors "OCD" is the next stage of living with the disorder. However, OCD is tricky. Throughout her life, Maeve experienced different obsessions and engaged in various compulsions/avoidance behaviors. She went through this second stage of the OCD career more than once, wondering if the new thoughts/behaviors reflected something about her or were the OCD. For instance, at one point she obsessed about being gay. She recalled:

I thought legitimately I was searching for whether I was gay or straight . . . when really it's just a symptom of OCD. . . . I kept almost trying to like prove it to myself that I wasn't. Like I'd start dating a guy just to be like, "Look I'm dating a guy. That means I'm not gay." . . . I did have a cousin who was married to a guy who also had OCD. . . . He was like, "Oh my gosh, that's a typical OCD obsession." . . . At first I didn't believe him. . . . When I started reading things about OCD, I saw that it was a common obsession that people have. Then it started to make me feel a lot better and then I didn't obsess about it as much anymore and then it eventually went away.

When Maeve and I were chatting over the phone, she confessed that she had been hiding a form of OCD she experienced from me. In the past she had experienced thoughts about molesting the children she babysat, and as a result she engaged in avoidance behaviors. She told me:

> I couldn't babysit them anymore because I was afraid just to be around them. . . . I kind of hid it from you because I was afraid I was going to molest those kids and that scared the hell out of me to say that to people because I was afraid people were going to think I was a child molester, and I could never say that to people. . . . At first I didn't know that it was OCD. . . . This is terrible, like there's something seriously wrong with me. . . . I thought I could actually do something to hurt somebody, and logically I know I wouldn't but I just kept thinking I would. . . . I couldn't see a psychiatrist for like a couple weeks because it took forever to get an appointment. . . . I thought if I went into the emergency room and got into a psych ward, I could talk to a psychiatrist right away and they could get me on medicine that actually works [but they didn't want to admit me or talked me out of being admitted. Eventually I saw a therapist and she said that] . . . what was happening to me was OCD. It wasn't based on anything real or my real true feelings. . . . [She told me,] "You're not going to hurt the kids."

Even after receiving a professional diagnosis, Maeve continued to have doubts about whether some of her thoughts/behaviors were OCD, reiterating why some people refer to OCD as the "doubting disease." In her words, "I just sometimes wonder, is this still OCD?"

Maeve demonstrated how words have power, even if they are not handed down formally from a professional to a patient in the form of a diagnosis. For some illnesses, the moment of formal diagnosis serves as the starting point of the illness career. The paths of the people I interviewed were sometimes a bit different. These individuals did not always wait for a professional but labeled themselves with OCD. Labeling/diagnosis is important but can be bittersweet. Labeling/diagnosis comes with benefits such as increased understanding of what one is going through, a sense of shared experience with others who have the same illness, and access to professional treatments. One downside is they have a confirmed health problem.

However, people labeled/diagnosed with OCD are in a peculiar position due to the disorder being both trivialized and potentially stigmatizing. After realizing she had OCD, Maeve was able to leverage the public's limited and stereotypical knowledge of the disorder in her favor to reduce stigma. She told some people that she had OCD, knowing that they probably did not *really* know what her life was like, and that they were likely relying on stereotypes of OCD as having to do with cleanliness and order.[2] She explained, "Certain friends I don't talk to about my OCD because I don't know if they'd understand. . . . Some of my friends think OCD is just checking to make sure you turned off the stove, or checking to make sure you unplugged an appliance. So those friends of mine always act like it's not a big deal. I just let them think that." At the same time, she desperately wanted the world to have a greater understanding of OCD, including all the ways OCD can manifest. That would presumably help people like her realize they have OCD faster and receive more knowledgeable help from professionals. The trouble is that improving the public's mental health literacy has a complicated effect. It could reduce delays in help-seeking and minimize people's trivialization of the disorder—but I will show how it may actually increase stigma.

Running into a Diagnosis

Maeve showed us how believing one has OCD requires knowledge of the disorder's existence and makeup, but the general public is not always familiar with OCD. Additionally, not all healthcare professionals are knowledgeable with respect to the disorder. This helps explain why only a little over a quarter of those I interviewed (27.3 percent) went to a healthcare professional for their thoughts/behaviors and were diagnosed there, while 40 percent began to consider they might have OCD after encountering information about OCD in the media or in a social context. (Another 16.4 percent saw a professional for something else or a related issue and were diagnosed.)[3]

Jeff posited how the problem with available information about OCD is that people find these sources only if they know to look for them. "I suppose that many of the worst-off people are getting no help at all because they don't know to ask. Therefore, it's really good when OCD is talked about on TV or other mass media." Jeff's analysis is telling. A number of the people I interviewed happened upon information in the media, which led them to believe they might have OCD. These media included nonfiction TV programs, a fictional TV show about hospital life, and books about OCD. I imagine that if I were to talk to a younger generation of people with OCD, online sources would have been more prominent.

In other cases, interviewees were active and on the hunt for information. Merrill fit this description. He was in his forties when we started talking. He told me that he looked for help in a variety of sources, including religious materials, philosophical treatises, and psychology books. He searched for nine to ten years and said it felt like he was searching his whole life (this is part of the reason there can be large gaps of time between when people feel they have a problem and when they seek professional help). Then, one day twenty years ago, Merrill happened upon a book about OCD called *The Boy Who Couldn't Stop Washing*, and things clicked (this is the same book that Zelda mentioned as being instrumental for her).

It is not that people with whom I communicated had never heard of OCD, although some had not. Their perceptions of the disorder were sometimes limited and steeped in stereotypical conceptions. If your best friend were to tell you that they had OCD, what would first come to your mind? Jesse told me that he was a psychology major in college. He had heard of OCD but was only aware of "classic symptoms" such as contamination fears. Therefore, he did not connect this to his own experiences. Maeve brought this issue to light at the start of the chapter, when she did not immediately recognize the different manifestations of OCD.

The ages of the people I interviewed were diverse, meaning some of them first encountered symptoms in the 1950s and 1960s. They suggested information was harder to come by in decades past. Confirming this, psychologist Otto F. Wahl, in his study of magazine articles representing obsessive-compulsive behavior over the period 1983–97, found no articles prior to 1987; he found more articles about other disorders, specifically, more than three times as many articles about depression.[4] Research about the nature and treatment of OCD picked up in the late 1980s and the 1990s.[5]

Even today, public and healthcare professionals' recognition of OCD can be limited.[6] I previously discussed public knowledge of OCD; for instance, in one study of American adults, a third of respondents recognized a vignette as depicting OCD, and that vignette depicted stereotypical forms of the disorder.[7] In a study of members of the American Psychological Association (APA), the overall rate at which respondents misidentified vignettes depicting OCD symptoms was 38.9 percent.[8] Professionals' ability to recognize OCD symptoms was particularly hampered for less-stereotypical forms of the disorder. The rate of incorrect responses was 15.8 percent for contamination obsessions; the rate of incorrect responses was the highest for obsessions about homosexuality, at 77 percent.

The impacts of what professionals know and think about OCD can be profound on people seeking diagnosis and treatment. In 2004 Jenike wrote, "On average, people with OCD see three to four doctors and spend more than nine years seeking treatment before they receive a correct diagnosis. It takes an average of 17 years from the onset of OCD to obtain appropriate treatment."[9] Problems with diagnosis and treatment of OCD have continued. Professionals who lack knowledge of OCD may inadvertently traumatize and stigmatize people who have the disorder. This can occur if they misinterpret people's thoughts. Imagine that someone has obsessions involving fears of molesting children and seeks help; if they have OCD, they will likely be told by an OCD specialist to face their fears and continue to be around children.[10] Now imagine if they encounter a professional who misdiagnoses them with pedophilia. In the previously mentioned study of members of the APA, a vignette depicting someone with obsessions about homosexuality was mistakenly treated as depicting sexual identity confusion 65 percent of the time.[11] A vignette depicting sexual obsessions about children was misdiagnosed as pedophilia 37 percent of the time. The authors of the study wrote, "Individuals with OCD who have intrusive sexual thoughts about children experience significant distress from the thoughts; to have their worst fears of being a pedophile incorrectly confirmed by a mental health professional may induce greater impairment in functioning and depression. A further complication is that in some states clinicians are mandated to report individuals who they believe may harm an identifiable victim."[12] In another study, psychiatrists and psychiatry residents were asked to respond to a description of a person with aggressive obsessions about their child.[13] Many of the respondents recommended involuntary confinement and contacting child welfare authorities. The authors indicated this seems unjustified because OCD is not associated with a high risk of violence, but perhaps a lowered risk instead.

The studies just outlined surveyed people about hypothetical situations. However, one article I found documented two situations in which child protection proceedings were initiated and mothers' contact with their children minimized before someone realized that they had OCD.[14] Further, those I interviewed recounted meeting some healthcare professionals who had limited knowledge of OCD. For instance, Aiten, who had already diagnosed himself, faced a general practitioner in the United Kingdom who knew little of the disorder. After he told the general practitioner that he had OCD, the doctor's words were, "What is OCD?" Aiten was shocked. "I left feeling quite low, thinking I was still on my own." Kirstyn said that when she was in her midtwenties she told a doctor about her thoughts and rituals, and "he looked at me and scratched his head and walked out the door. He never said a word. That's the only time I mentioned it to anyone [in that period of time]. He was a psychiatrist, and so I thought ooookaaaay he doesn't even know. I'm not going to say it again. . . . [I] felt like a real idiot." A counselor told Percy that if he did not want to be gay, he did not have to be. Interactions like these with healthcare professionals can be shared over the internet, likely making others wary. Phineas described being upset by "stories I hear on the OCD board [online] about people who have doctors who either misdiagnose them or tell them that [they] might actually commit the horrible acts they are obsessing about." To be fair, people with OCD did not always give healthcare professionals full disclosure from which to make a diagnosis.

Double-Edged Sword of Diagnosis

Once interviewees perceived themselves as having OCD, things changed for them because their thoughts/behaviors were "medicalized," "psychiatrized," and "psychologized." By this I mean that OCD is considered a mental disorder treatable by healthcare professionals, the result of potentially biogenetic and/or psychosocial causes. Researchers have coined the term "medicalization" to refer to the process whereby something not perceived as a medical problem comes to be seen as such in society, including being depicted in medical terms or treated using medical knowledge.[15] Similarly, psychiatrization is the process whereby something not perceived as a psychiatric concern comes to be seen as such.[16] The medicalization of mental illness emphasizes the equivalency of mental illness to physical disease and has involved the search for their biogenetic underpinnings.[17] The psychologization of mental illness emphasizes psychosocial causes such as environmental stressors.

These "-izations" are societal patterns we have probably all felt or experienced in our personal lives. The birthing of babies has been medicalized, from use of genetic screenings while a woman is pregnant to the use of technology in the form of ultrasounds to capture an image of the baby in the womb. Issues we might have once viewed as more personal, such as heavy alcohol use or having many sexual partners, have been reformulated into addictions, with associated treatment facilities. It could be said that we have witnessed the "medicalization of life itself."[18]

Critiques of these processes abound in the media and exist in scholarly literature. For instance, you have likely encountered an article in the media about whether we should be dispensing prescribed pills to children to calm them down. It is not hard to find critics opining that children are naturally supposed to play and be inquisitive, even if this behavior does inconvenience their parents. They question whether we are turning expected behavior into a problem that needs to be labeled and altered through professional treatment. Effectively, what critiques like this tell us is that healthcare professions have had a lot of say over what we treat as typical and not worth noticing, versus what is deviant or unhealthy or dangerous—and scholars and journalists have been wary of this power.[19]

According to Dumit, "Analyzed as power conflicts, medicalization can be a coercive force turning people into patients in order to control and manage them. Alternately, medicalization can be a tactic by sufferers to become objects of attention and care through becoming patients."[20] When I reflected on how people with OCD came to perceive themselves as having this disorder, I realized that many of them took information from the healthcare professions and applied it to themselves. In contemporary society, we evaluate health through statistics and notions of risk and encourage people to monitor their health and health-related numbers such as their blood pressure readings. Websites hosted by treatment centers for OCD, as well as by organizations that offer resources for those with OCD, provide opportunities for people to test themselves for indications they might have OCD through filling out questionnaires about their thoughts/behaviors. Such self-labeling can fuel the medicalization/psychiatrization/psychologization of people's thoughts and behaviors.[21] Sociologist Kristin Barker stated that "we are increasingly active participants in the medicalization of our experiences as we earnestly seek to resolve and legitimate our suffering."[22] One reason people engage in behaviors that further medicalization and so forth is because the impacts of these "-izations" are transformative.[23]

Diagnosis is a double-edged sword, a metaphor scholars have used and one that some of my interviewees utilized as well. Professor Julie Guthman explained this metaphor through the the concept of obesity: "These days many states of being are medicalized, from attention deficit disorder to chronic fatigue syndrome to anxiety, shyness, and depression. . . . Medicalization is thus a double-edged sword. It can provide access to resources to treat unwanted conditions, and for some people having an official diagnosis and a possibility of treatment brings relief. . . . At the same time, medicalization can turn nonnormative conditions and behaviors into problems in need of biomedical solution, and subject people to medical scrutiny regardless of their desires."[24]

Table 5.1 illustrates the double-edged sword of diagnosis through the eyes of people with OCD, presenting quotes from four people who resided in different countries and belonged to varying age-groups. The two columns of the table depict their perceptions before diagnosis and after they labeled themselves or were professionally diagnosed.

Diagnosis provided a ticket into a world where interviewees were assured that they were not alone and that others shared the same problem, where experts could provide explanations and treatments. It was a ticket they could cash in as they interacted with others in society. Decades ago, Parsons described the "sick role," including how a sick person is relieved from regular work and other social duties until recovered.[25] A diagnosis provides a license of sorts, such as when a child provides a sick note to a teacher or an employee provides documentation justifying a need to take a leave of absence from work. The explanation that comes with diagnosis is not just for the individual being labeled, then, but is an

TABLE 5.1. Perspectives before and after Diagnosis

Before Perceiving Oneself as Having OCD	After Self-Labeling or Being Diagnosed with OCD
Rodney *(US, diagnosed with OCD, depression, and OCPD, although he disagreed with the latter)*	
I kept my OCD a secret for decades.... To be honest I would not have recognized my disease from reading the plethora of literature and media that makes OCD sound like perfectionism or being a "neat freak." [A friend recognized something that I was doing as a compulsion and mentioned that it could be OCD.] ... I never could imagine that even one person in the whole world had what I had. It was so unbelievable that it took me years after learning about OCD to truly believe the disorder existed.	[After I read about OCD in books,] I wanted to run down the street saying, "It's not just me!" It was a revelation.... [I got a professional diagnosis because] I thought if my disease was recognized by the medical community it would be easier to get social service help. Also, if I were observed or caught in some of my compulsive behaviors I would have a better mechanism of explaining.... I felt relieved [after diagnosis] but still skeptical that anyone would believe me ... that the rest of the world would really believe there is such a thing as OCD.... [I feel] somewhat stigmatized, somewhat relieved, yet I also feel morose over the fact that I have to live with this the rest of my life.... [Before] I lived with the delusion that after I finished a particular phase of some compulsive behavior, I would begin life anew, free from all my compulsive behaviors.
Clara *(India, diagnosed with OCD)*	
I knew something was wrong, that I was turning mad. Only later did I realize that it was called OCD.... I was reluctant to go [for professional help] till the end. I thought people will be labeled as mentally disturbed if I went there.... I did not want the society to abandon me as a mentally ill person, so I would hide all my OCD ... but everything went out of control.... I was sixteen years old and my board exams were nearing when I grew really anxious about a thought and used to act like a freak.... I believed in OCD too much.... [My family] got to me to a psychiatrist when I was deeply suffering. I wanted to go to a psychiatrist myself as it was not under my control.	[After the diagnosis] I was feeling very awkward. I thought I had become a mentally sick person and would cry a lot. I would be sad all the time and get depressed.... I felt bad in the beginning but later I thought it was OK, as it reminded me of the other thousands of people who had what I had.... [Not having a diagnosis] would have [bothered me].... The guilt of getting bad sexual thoughts faded in me after knowing that it was just an ailment and that I was not responsible for my thoughts.... I was really extremely worried about my future. I thought I would never achieve all I wanted to do in my life. But now that I am fine, I will do fine.

TABLE 5.1. *(cont.)*

Before Perceiving Oneself as Having OCD	After Self-Labeling or Being Diagnosed with OCD
Jesse *(US, diagnosed with OCD, ADHD, depression, and GAD)*	
My symptoms, prediagnosis, definitely made me feel different and abnormal. I knew something was wrong and that other people didn't seem to struggle with this, but I had no explanation as to what was wrong with me. . . . I was at a loss. . . . I felt very alone because I couldn't find any evidence anywhere of someone with similar experiences.	Since being diagnosed I feel as though I finally have an answer that explains what I struggled with all my life. . . . I take some comfort in this and it has helped me to re-fine my search for help. . . . Being diagnosed was, however, a double-edged sword. On the one hand it was good to know I have a legitimate mental condition. I'm not some kind of "special" outlier who no one knows what to do with. On the other hand, I have a legitimate mental condition. That, I've had to come to terms with. . . . I realized that I might actually be "mentally ill." This had an impact on my self-image and made me feel sick and impaired. . . . It also caused me to think that I have something that although treatable would probably never go away. . . . At the same time, paradoxi-cally, I felt some sadness that I struggled for all those years without knowing what was wrong with me and maybe I could have gotten help much sooner. . . . I suppose I'm a little disappointed that reaching this diagnosis required so much self-advocacy [years of looking up information] and hav-ing the good fortune of being married to a psychiatrist.
Lacy *(UK, diagnosed with OCD, depression, and GAD)*	
I have felt very "fobbed off " by the medical profes-sion. I have been told over the years to "go home and forget about it," "it's your age," "you're not feminine," . . . "it's all on your head." . . . I found this terribly frustrating and upsetting. I didn't feel I was being listened to at all, and felt like a freak.	I finally had an explanation for my weird behavior. I first realized I had OCD when I read an article about it around ten years ago. However, because I had never told my doctors everything about my thoughts/ actions, they first put it down to stress, and then told me I had obsessive traits. I know I had OCD because of what I'd read, but I was too afraid to tell anyone about it because I was afraid of being locked up in prison or in a mental asylum. Finally, last month—after reading a book—I told my doctor about my scary thoughts. . . . It has taken me at least eight years to get a proper diagnosis, and now that I finally have, I hope I can move on with my life. . . . I feel I can now say my behavior is the OCD and not just me! This makes a huge difference, and gives me so much relief.

explanation for others. People who feel sick and unable to fulfill ordinary obligations, but have no diagnosis, sometimes struggle in the face of a hostile social environment.[26] Those around them may feel they are making something up, trying to get out of work, or being lazy. As Jutel wrote, "Being diagnosed gives permission to be ill."[27]

Before Rodney's diagnosis of OCD, he felt he did not have this permission, and people responded to him in condescending and negative ways. He considered his self-diagnosis sufficient for himself, but he sought an official diagnosis from a professional in order to appease society. He thought a professional diagnosis might provide him with more access to social services and also engender more patience and understanding from others.

Gaining information about OCD as a mental disorder expanded the available meanings from which people could draw when conceptualizing what was happening to them. Interviewees sometimes described a feeling of isolation in the last chapter, but once they had the OCD label, they were linked to a whole world of other people. They were not "mad" or "a slow worker" or "lazy." They had OCD. All of the quotes in table 5.1 reveal this. Recently, I attended a conference at which someone used the phrase "diagnostic capital" to try to capture this import, indicating that a diagnosis is a resource. In Barker's book about fibromyalgia, she documented how women hungered for an explanation for their chronic symptoms but were sometimes dismissed by the general public and healthcare professionals, for example, being told it's all in their heads. This questioning of their pain increased "sufferers' social isolation and dark mood."[28]

With diagnosis, interviewees expressed relief in knowing they were not alone. A diagnosis signified that other people experienced the same and that there was public recognition of an explainable problem.[29] Previously, they were struggling. Some, like Lacy, hid, fearing stigma and the reactions of other people.

Diagnoses come with explanations. A diagnosis of OCD meant that people's bizarre and troubling thoughts were not reflective of who they were as people and were not necessarily true. Like Maeve, mentioned at the beginning of this chapter, some people began trying to separate what was them versus what was their OCD. Lacy felt diagnosis gave her permission to separate herself from the OCD.

Bodies have culture and a history.[30] As people with OCD continued to learn about OCD, they sometimes grouped more and more thoughts and behaviors under this heading, even those they had not previously perceived as a problem. This was most obvious when people looked back at their past and perceived that they had perhaps experienced obsessions and compulsions as a child, although not necessarily to a degree they felt would be diagnosable. They reframed their earlier experiences and reconstructed their OCD trajectory.

Importantly, diagnoses indicate there is hope for treatment, if desired. A diagnosis indicates there are professionals studying the sickness and experts to whom one can turn. Jesse regretted not being able to get help sooner; Clara claimed that, with diagnosis and treatment, she will now be fine.

I referred to diagnosis as a ticket, but this ticket does not come cheap.[31] Anyone who has feared the results of a medical test, such as that for cancer, wondering if it will come back positive or negative, knows this. Karp depicted diagnosis as a "double-edged benchmark in the illness career" of those with depression, as it confirms that you have *something*.[32] This is compounded for people with mental disorders because these labels can be associated with stigma. Medical/professional conceptions of disorders as well as public stereotypes of disorders now hang like a coat on those diagnosed. For interviewees, diagnosis meant they had a diagnosable mental disorder, which may or may not lead to remission.

Stigma

Diagnosis brings concerns about being stigmatized for having a mental disorder. Professional conceptions, as well as the whispers, taunts, jabs, compliments, stereotypes, and overall public conceptions of a disorder, become relevant for people with OCD. They are now personal. A joke in the media about someone checking something repeatedly is no longer a joke about someone else, but a joke about *themselves*. Those I interviewed had been socialized into societal views and stereotypes of those with mental disorders. These conceptions affected how the people I interviewed looked at themselves and what they expected when interacting with others. Sometimes interviewees even believed them or acted on them.

Monty said he used to "make fun" of people with symptoms all the time. Meghan said she and her husband still laugh at people with OCD for doing "crazy" things. Generally, although the people I interviewed sometimes believed the stigma surrounding mental disorders had been decreasing over time, they recognized that public perceptions of mental disorders could be negative and stereotypical. This was true despite the diversity in locations of respondents, as is apparent from the following comments:

[In England, people view those with mental illness] as strange and odd. Because we still have old institutions . . . old Victorian mental hospitals, which brings up images of straitjackets and slaver. (Chris, United Kingdom)

Even a couple of years ago I felt that if you had a mental disorder people just thought you were worthless and crazy. And I think some people still do feel that way. . . . [Although] I think society has grown more accustomed to people with mental disorders . . . there is definitely still a stigma placed on people with any mental disorder. I can easily tell my coworkers that I have to leave work early to go to a dentist appointment, because that is "normal." It's not as easy for me to tell my coworkers I'm leaving early for a psychologist appointment. (Maeve, United States)

[Perceptions of people with mental disorders] are really bad, especially here in my country. . . . People laugh at mentally ill people. They don't receive love and affection, which they need the most during that period, [but can be] neglected and abandoned. (Clara, India)

Stigma has a number of definitions, but the sociologist Erving Goffman broke this concept down in a useful way from which many scholars still draw.[33] He argued that as we go through life, we regularly categorize people, and in particular contexts we have certain expectations:

Social settings establish the categories of persons likely to be encountered there. . . . When a stranger comes into our presence, then, first appearances are likely to enable us to anticipate his category and attributes, his "social identity." . . . We lean on these anticipations that we have,

transforming them into normative expectations, into righteously presented demands. Typically, we do not become aware that we have made
these demands or aware of what they are until an active question arises as
to whether or not they will be fulfilled. . . . [This imputation can be called]
a *virtual social identity*. The category and attributes he could in fact be
proved to possess will be called his *actual social identity*.[34]

Stigma exists when there is a negative gap between these two identities
(virtual and actual social identity). In other words, we meet a person and
find out they are not what we assumed. They are different in a negative
way from our presumption.

Stigma is thus a discrediting attribute grounded in societal stereotypes that people use to distinguish groups as different (other than
themselves). Avoidance and discrimination can follow. For researchers Bruce G. Link and Jo C. Phelan, stigma refers to the co-occurrence
of interrelated processes, including the grouping of people into negative stereotypes and the creation of inequality from status loss and
discrimination.[35]

Mental disorders can be stigmatizing, so it is no surprise that the people I interviewed were fearful of stigma. People can anticipate and be
concerned about whether others will primarily view them through stereotypes about mental disorders (stigma consciousness).[36] Researchers
have noted how media have long portrayed people with mental disorders
in stigmatizing ways.[37] Individuals with mental disorders face difficulties
and challenges in everything from securing housing to participating in
the workforce.[38] Communities have protested against housing for those
with mental disorders within their borders. Employers have admitted to
being less likely to hire someone with a mental disorder than they would
someone with a physical illness. There is evidence of a wage gap between
people with and without disorders. Despite popular claims and hopes,
stigma has not radically diminished over time. Bear in mind that we are
not talking only about stigma that might occur as a reaction to a person's
actual thoughts and behaviors. Labels themselves—that is, being diagnosed as having a mental illness—can be stigmatizing and have been
linked to poorer well-being.[39] With respect to self-stigma, people with
mental disorders recognize societal prejudice and discrimination and
can internalize these; stigmatized self-views have been associated with

lowered self-efficacy and self-esteem.[40] In a way, people can discriminate against themselves by, for example, isolating themselves.

The Stigma Hierarchy and Trivialization

While there does appear to be a general stigma that can come with having any "mental disorder," the story is not so simple. Imagine a close friend tells you about a recent diagnosis. Would your feelings vary if they said depression versus schizophrenia? When I was talking with Talia, who lived in the United States and was diagnosed with OCD and depression, she told me there is a "hierarchy" in terms of how people think about mental disorders. She remembered having a conversation with someone who said they would date someone with OCD but not someone with a personality disorder. Not all mental disorders are perceived the same or treated the same by the general public. Some are perceived as less serious than others. Some are perceived as more treatable than others. Still others are conceptualized as more amusing and quirkier than others. These distinctions reveal that there is an acceptance or stigma hierarchy. It captures the way in which some disorders are perceived differently from others at times, leading to particular disorders being less stigmatized. The idea of a stigma hierarchy is an underused concept people have employed in the past to talk about how people, even professionals, rank people's sicknesses and health problems.[41]

The hierarchy was something interviewees applied to themselves.[42] In order to make sense of their diagnosis, some people with OCD compared the disorder to other sicknesses and disorders, physical or otherwise. They ranked disorders based on a variety of factors, including perceived seriousness, prevalence, and ability to be overcome. For instance, if they saw OCD as worse than other illnesses and disorders people might have, they could have more negative perceptions of self. When Jesse was diagnosed with generalized anxiety disorder (GAD), he was able to accept the diagnosis and saw it as fairly commonplace. He thought "a lot of people are anxious (and depressed for that matter) so it didn't seem very unusual." However, when the diagnosis was switched to OCD, his self-conception declined. He appeared to think OCD was perceived by society as more severe, and this affected his self-conception negatively.

On the other hand, if people with OCD saw it as less serious than other disorders, they could have more positive perceptions of self. For instance, Monty said his OCD was "not like hearing voices" and "not like being depressed to the point where you don't want to live anymore." A couple people argued that OCD was more capable of being overcome than other health concerns. One of them explained that people think of mental illness as something serious and requiring hospitalization because the sufferer might be dangerous. They said OCD is different and, from their perspective, is not even a mental illness because it can be overcome.

Generally, the people I interviewed felt that the public perceives OCD as less stigmatizing than other disorders, and they talked about how the disorder is trivialized. According to Phineas, "Unfortunately, in today's world, OCDers are a big joke to people. I hear it all the time. There is even a guy on a local radio show here that cracks jokes about us all the time. They think it's funny when people have to wash their hands over and over again, or can't stop pulling their hair out, or anything else we do. You bring up OCD, and people automatically assume you are afraid of germs. It's sad that more people don't realize the other ways people are affected."

Tangled Web

Overall, I argue that OCD has become increasingly medicalized/psychiatrized/psychologized, as well as treated as typical or everyday. The result is that people with OCD are caught in a tangled web between potential stigma and trivialization.

I have covered how having a mental disorder is potentially stigmatizing, and people with OCD are concerned about this. The effects of trivialization are a bit different but nonetheless problematic to people with OCD. Some interviewees mentioned this, and a host of articles, blog posts, podcasts, videos, and other materials exist online that rail against the trivialization of OCD. They were created by people who have the disorder, as well as by others, including their family members, mental health organizations/advocacy groups (such as the National Alliance on Mental Illness [NAMI] and the International OCD Foundation), and counseling centers and news outlets. I found this out by doing an online search for the phrase "so OCD."

That phrase really bothers some people with OCD when they hear it because it symbolizes the public trivializing of the disorder, for example, when they see someone without a problem acting *so OCD*. I did a google search for the phrase and scrolled through the first fifty results. I analyzed the thirty-one pieces that actually used the phrase (and were not duplicate results).[43] These sources argued that it may be trendy for the general public and the media to throw around the term "OCD." Saying someone is "so OCD" has gotten to the point that it is akin to a "fun fad."[44] However, when this is done, these authors have said OCD is treated as something humorous, and not that serious, like a quirky personality trait. Interestingly, some of these sources claimed, more people may end up believing or saying they have OCD than would really be diagnosed.

Meanwhile, trivialization can make it hard for people who actually have the disorder to perceive themselves as potentially having OCD. As mentioned at the beginning of this chapter, some people I interviewed knew OCD existed and were aware of stereotypical forms the disorder can take. Because these forms did not align with what they were experiencing, they did not perceive themselves as having OCD. Winona lived in the United States and was in her thirties when we spoke. Her best friend was a psychologist and used to tell her, "Girl, you're so OCD," but using that phrase had become so clichéd that Winona thought her friend was joking. Winona was later professionally diagnosed with the disorder.

I argue that trivialization can lead to its own form of stigma. For example, imagine that people have been pleasantly interacting with someone who has OCD. Then one day he tells them that he has OCD and needs to get off work early to visit a therapist or has to cancel their evening plans. Basically, his disorder is debilitating, but they do not realize this. His boss and friends think OCD is just a quirky personality trait. They perceive him as not having a real problem and think that he wants special privileges. As a result, they may start distancing themselves from him. One man I interviewed argued that trivialization had led people to perceive him as lazy because he was unable to hold down a job as a result of his OCD. A study of children with ADHD in the United Kingdom found that some teachers and headmasters did not perceive the disorder as real and therefore did not provide allowances for such children.[45]

One interviewee who worked in the mental health care field felt that stigma resides more in that field than any other, noting the jokes they frequently heard and how professionals "really fail to see the terror/horror/nightmare that it [OCD] causes for those of us who suffer with it." For people with OCD, it can feel as if everything is conspiring against them. As Janet phrased it, "Society does not view people with OCD in the true sense because it is so carefully hidden. When they are forced to look at it, there can be a range of reactions including distaste, fascination, pity or even amusement. . . . Mental health services view the disorder as a low priority because they are busy trying to help those with psychoses, the *real* mental health patients. As the OC [obsessive-compulsive], you are left feeling you lose out on both sides. Society thinks you are 'mad,' but the health service doesn't, so you get the stigma but not the care." Effectively, she said, "You almost feel you have failed to be really 'mentally ill.' You couldn't even do that properly."

Therefore, people with OCD can never quite be sure how people will treat them. They face uncertainty and risk in presenting themselves to others regardless of whether they attempt to reveal or hide their OCD. The disorder already involves uncertainty. Grayson argued that the "intellectual and emotional uncertainty of 'what if' is, I believe, the root of most OCD symptoms."[46] Social interaction compounds the issue.

What is the solution? Many people and organizations believe, as reflected in the comments by Maeve at the start of this chapter, that the public needs more information about OCD. The online pieces I analyzed blamed the general public, media, businesses, and even healthcare professionals for promulgating incorrect stereotypes of OCD. They largely reiterated that OCD is misunderstood and treated information as a weapon to combat such. The belief that more information and mental health literacy provide a solution seems plausible in light of research indicating greater mental health literacy may reduce stigmatizing attitudes.[47]

Yet, I argue that we must be cautious, especially when considering how information is relayed. If you have OCD, it can be easier to tell people that you have the disorder without fearing what people will think because it is trivialized as quirky and not that serious. One woman with OCD described having "mixed feelings" about how much she wanted the public to learn about the disorder. She preferred "safe" representations of OCD in the media that omitted the suffering and ritualizing that can go along with OCD. Will encouraging the public to perceive OCD as more serious lead to increased fear and stigma? Consider an editorial by Tania Louise Gergel in the *Psychiatric Bulletin*, in which she wrote: "Challenges to psychiatric stigma fall between a rock and a hard place. Decreasing one prejudice may inadvertently increase another. Emphasizing similarities between mental illness and 'ordinary' experience to escape the fear-related prejudices associated with the imagined 'otherness' of persons with mental illness risks conclusions that mental illness indicates moral weakness and the loss of any benefits of a medical model. An emphasis on illness and difference from normal experience risks a response of fear of the alien."[48]

In one study, researchers provided people with information about a hypothetical person who experienced violent thoughts of hurting a relative. Participants in the study who believed the vignette was about OCD versus schizophrenia expressed less stigmatizing attitudes.[49] For this reason, I am concerned that while greater public understanding of OCD may reduce trivialization, it could potentially fuel negative misperceptions; reducing one problem may further another.

Considering the Impact of Increased Mental Health Literacy

To explore the issue of whether greater knowledge of OCD may reduce trivialization and/or foment stigma, I surveyed students enrolled in introductory sociology classes between the years 2016 and 2018 at a university in the southern United States about their knowledge and perceptions of different forms of OCD.[50] I surveyed 556 students whose mean age was 21 (SD = 4.965, range of 18–54). Table 5.2 presents the demographics of this group of students. I presented them with written vignettes depicting different forms of OCD that involved obsessions about *inadvertent harm; sexual orientation; blasphemy (religious/scrupulosity OCD); contamination; order/symmetry; harm; sexual thoughts about children ("pedophilia OCD")*; or *relationships*. Vignettes also depicted responses to the obsessions such as compulsions or avoidance. After each vignette, I asked the survey respondents to tell me what illness/disorder/disability, if any, they thought the person in the vignette had.[51] Then I asked them questions designed to tap into stigma, asking if they

TABLE 5.2. Descriptive Information about the Sample of Students Responding

Variable	% (frequency)
Sex, $n = 556$	
Female	77.7 (432)
Male	21.8 (121)
Other	0.5 (3)
Race, $n = 548$	
White or Caucasian	61.9 (339)
Black or African American	32.1 (176)
Asian	1.6 (9)
Other	0.4 (2)
Self-identified as more than one race	4.0 (22)
Ethnicity, $n = 553$	
Hispanic, Latino, or Spanish origin	5.4 (30)
Yearly Income Bracket, $n = 554$	
$0–15,000	82.7 (458)
$15,001–30,000	6.7 (37)
$30,001–45,000	4.0 (22)
$45,001–60,000	2.2 (12)
$60,001 and above	4.5 (25)
Religious, $n = 555$	
Very religious	38.7 (215)
Somewhat religious	52.6 (292)
Not religious at all	8.6 (48)
Yourself, a Family Member, or Close Friend Ever Been Diagnosed or Labeled with a Mental Disorder, $n = 556$	
Yes	44.6 (248)
No	54.0 (300)
Rather not answer	1.4 (8)

would be willing to work closely with the person on a job, have them as a friend, have them as a neighbor, and go on a date with them. I also asked if they would support work or school accommodations for the person, hoping that would help me see if they were treating the problem in the vignette as serious or trivializing it. Finally, I told them that all the vignettes were about OCD and asked them if that changed their perceptions of the disorder and people with the disorder. The survey contained closed-ended and open-ended questions.

The surveys confirmed that there is a knowledge hierarchy based on type of OCD. Just as occurred in surveys of healthcare professionals, the students were more likely to recognize certain thoughts/behaviors as OCD more than others (table 5.3). (Note that if they mentioned "OCD" or terms such as "obsession," "compulsion," or "intrusive thought," I grouped that into the category labeled *OCD*. For the contamination vignette, I grouped responses such as "germaphobia," "phobia," and "mysophobia" into the category labeled *germaphobia*.) Students were better able to identify stereotypical representations of OCD but had trouble identifying other forms of obsessions and compulsions. More specifically, 81.8 percent of those who read about a fictional person with obsessions and compulsions related to order/symmetry were able to identify the problem as potentially related to OCD; 73.7 percent of respondents marked the vignette depicting contamination concerns as potentially related to OCD or germaphobia. Less than half (44.4 percent) were able to identify the vignette depicting someone worrying and checking for inadvertent harm as related to OCD. Very few could identify vignettes about sexual orientation (2.5 percent), relationships (3.7 percent), blasphemy (6.5 percent), harm (6.4 percent), or sexual thoughts involving children (4.0 percent).

The students found the "normal" in or downplayed some of the content of these vignettes. A large proportion of students felt that concerns about relationships (45.8 percent) and blasphemy (31.3 percent) were not illustrative of an illness/disorder/disability. For instance, a number of students indicated the individual described in the vignette about blasphemy might just be highly religious. One person wrote, "No mental illness there, seen a lot of those down here in the South." Another said, "I'm not quite sure about this one either, but I am going to say none because a very religious person would probably pray constantly anyway."

112 | STIGMA AND TRIVIALIZATION

TABLE 5.3. Identification of Vignettes by Respondents: Percent (Frequency)

Label Given by Respondents	Vignette							
	Sexual Orientation	Order/ Symmetry	Relation-ship	Contami-nation	Inadver-tent Harm	Blasphemy	Harm	Child Sexual
	$n = 552$	$n = 555$	$n = 542$	$n = 555$	$n = 554$	$n = 553$	$n = 551$	$n = 546$
OCD	2.5 (14)	81.8 (454)	3.7 (20)	38.2 (212)	44.4 (246)	6.5 (36)	6.4 (35)	4.0 (22)
Germa-phobia	—	—	—	35.5 (197)	—	—	—	—
Anxiety	0.9 (5)	0.2 (1)	4.6 (25)	1.1 (6)	15.7 (87)	8.5 (47)	3.6 (20)	1.3 (7)
Other type of illness/ disorder/ disability	6.0 (33)	3.2 (18)	5.0 (27)	5.4 (30)	14.6 (81)	7.6 (42)	23 (127)	28.8 (157)
No illness/ disorder/ disability depicted	45.8 (253)	4.7 (26)	45.8 (248)	5.2 (29)	2.2 (12)	31.3 (173)	4.7 (26)	5.7 (31)
Don't know/ unclear response	44.7 (247)	10.1 (56)	41.0 (222)	14.6 (81)	23.1 (128)	46.1 (255)	62.3 (343)	60.3 (329)

Similarly, some respondents thought the vignette about sexual orientation might depict someone who was confused about their sexuality or was gay or bisexual.[52]

One concern I share with researchers as well with individuals with OCD is that the public may misinterpret people's thoughts as reflective of their deepest desires and/or future actions. I found this occurred with my students. As already mentioned, some students labeled the vignette about a person with obsessions about their sexuality as being bi-curious or gay. I am also concerned that people might misperceive taboo thoughts, such as those about harm, as reflective of future actions, when in actuality having these thoughts does not mean one is at a higher risk of acting violently compared with the general population.[53] Student responses indicated a level of confusion over how to interpret vignettes with content related to fears of causing harm and pedophilia. A number of students misinterpreted the vignettes as depicting people who wanted to cause harm to others, sometimes labeling them as "crazy," or "bad." More than a quarter of students reading the vignette about fears related to pedophilia inaccurately labeled the person as having pedophilia or being a child molester, a rapist, a sexual predator, or something similar.

Students' views on accommodations were a bit hard to interpret but did vary by type of OCD (table 5.4). Students chose from the following options regarding whether a person should be able to receive accommodations at work and/or school: 1 = "definitely should"; 2 = "probably should"; 3 = "probably should not"; and 4 = "definitely should not."[54] Vignettes involving obsessions about inadvertent harm and causing harm received the most support for accommodations. Concerns about one's sexual preference and love for one's partner generated relatively little support for accommodations, which may be related to how students sometimes interpreted these concerns as within the bounds of social norms or reflective of people's true desires.

Students' interpretations of the vignettes impacted their stated willingness to interact with people who had these worries, leading to a stigma hierarchy based on form of OCD. Table 5.4 provides information about student answers by type of OCD, and at this point students did not yet know the vignettes depicted OCD. Students chose from the following responses: 1 = "definitely willing"; 2 = "probably willing"; 3 = "probably unwilling"; and 4 = "definitely unwilling." At one end of this hierarchy, some students claimed they were always willing to support and help people with OCD. I found that many students said they were willing to interact with people with various types of obsessions and compulsions as a neighbor, friend, and work colleague. However, for taboo thoughts about harm and pedophilia, students exhibited more hesitation, sometimes with even willingness to have such a person as a neighbor giving them pause. To explain, some students said that vignettes involving obsessions regarding harm/sexual molestation were more stigmatizing because these thoughts were about illegal activities that had the potential to affect others (including children who cannot protect themselves). This was different relative to problems they felt had little impact on an individual's functioning, especially their impact on

TABLE 5.4. Social Distance Ratings and Accommodation Perceptions by Vignette: Mean, (SD), and Mode; Chi-Square

	Sexual Orientation	Order/ Symmetry	Inadvertent Harm	Contamination	Relationship	Blasphemy	Harm Thoughts	Child Sexual	Chi-Square ($df = 7$)
Social Distance									
Willingness to have as a neighbor (1 = definitely willing to 4 = definitely unwilling)	n = 553 1.57 (.715) 1	n = 555 1.69 (.742) 1	n = 554 1.75 (.758) 2	n = 556 1.78 (.738) 2	n = 541 1.79 (.766) 2	n = 553 1.81 (.765) 2	n = 553 2.93 (.999) 4	n = 547 3.21 (.915) 4	n = 532 1681.59*
Willingness to work closely with on a job (1 = definitely willing to 4 = definitely unwilling)	n = 553 1.63 (.756) 1	n = 556 1.82 (.796) 2	n = 553 1.95 (.780) 2	n = 556 1.97 (.816) 2	n = 544 1.81 (.779) 2	n = 555 1.93 (.831) 2	n = 553 2.93 (.965) 3	n = 549 3.02 (.972) 4	n = 538 1360.87*
Willingness to have as a friend (1 = definitely willing to 4 = definitely unwilling)	n = 554 1.65 (.763) 1	n = 554 1.77 (.730) 2	n = 555 1.75 (.731) 2	n = 556 1.93 (.814) 2	n = 543 1.82 (.779) 2	n = 555 2.06 (.869) 2	n = 553 2.91 (.983) 3	n = 548 3.17 (.923) 4	n = 536 1520.45*
Willingness to go on a date (1 = definitely willing to 4 = definitely unwilling)	n = 554 2.98 (1.001) 4	n = 554 2.43 (.935) 2	n = 553 2.68 (.929) 3	n = 555 2.70 (.921) 3	n = 542 2.75 (.974) 3	n = 553 2.74 (.984) 3	n = 549 3.30 (.865) 4	n = 547 3.55 (.733) 4	n = 533 818.63*
Accommodations									
Agreement should receive accommodations (1 = definitely should to 4 = definitely should not)	n = 556 2.82 (1.068) 3	n = 552 2.39 (.971) 2	n = 556 1.81 (.753) 2	n = 555 2.46 (.969) 2	n = 544 2.92 (1.008) 4	n = 554 2.67 (1.008) 3	n = 552 2.06 (.998) 1	n = 548 2.52 (1.124) 4	n = 535 812.03*

* $p < .0005$.

others' lives. One respondent wrote: "Some [symptoms] only affect them like leaving the house or germs, while others such as inappropriately touching a kid or pushing a lady deals with other people and can lead to them one day possibly acting upon these thoughts." Students also put up more barriers in the dating realm. The most common response (i.e., mode) for almost all of the forms of OCD in this study was that that students were "probably unwilling" to date a person with such fears.[55] This relates to previous research that indicates people's stigmatizing attitudes vary depending on how disruptive or dangerous they perceive an attribute or condition to be.[56]

Importantly, students' views were subject to some change once students were told that the vignettes depicted OCD and they learned that not all thoughts are windows into people's true desires—more specifically, that having thoughts about harm is not correlated with engaging in harmful deeds and that these are things a person with OCD fears. This was reflected in comments in which respondents said that they learned OCD is more complex and involves a wider variety of symptoms than they originally believed, and some became more empathetic and understanding. One person wrote, "I learned there are many forms of OCD and I am willing to interact and help someone with the disorder." Another said, "I understand what OCD is and I am willing to interact with someone with OCD and try to be understanding of their situation." Therefore, information has the potential to reduce stigma and misunderstanding. Despite this, not all students' views shifted. There was a proportion of students whose perceptions of OCD seemingly changed for the worse as a result of completing the survey. One student explained how some of the forms of OCD described still made them uncomfortable and indicated they would feel "unsafe around such individuals."

Therefore, my results provide support for the hypothesis that more information may encourage the public's recognition that OCD can take many forms, and also may reduce stigmatizing attitudes and trivialization. However, the difficulty lies in helping the public understand that these forms of OCD exist without leading people to become afraid of those with OCD or alternatively leading them to think individuals with OCD are exaggerating their problems. My results showed that increasing people's knowledge of OCD can encourage empathy but can also trigger stigma and fears based on misunderstanding. Further, considering the students who felt some of the thoughts/behaviors described were expected (i.e., religious obsessions typical for a religious person), this survey unexpectedly revealed how greater public recognition of OCD could possibly increase rather than diminish trivialization.

6

Coping and Treatment

[Journal Entry] I really laughed a lot in the group [at the treatment program for OCD] because the therapist is really cool and the . . . other patients were just really nice. Then came the part that I was dreading: exposures. I had to rank my obsessions and compulsions. Then the doctor spent some time with me asking questions about my not so severe ones. Apparently, I do not have an extreme problem with order and symmetry because he tried moving the chairs around and moved some papers and it did not bother me. Next was my need to check doors, lights, and windows. I told him that I am afraid that there will be a fire if a light is left on. . . . My homework for tonight is to not check any doors or windows. . . . So far so good with my homework. Some other things that I had to do was on my way home from the hospital I had to say that I am going to kill a person while driving over and over again to see that saying this will not cause an accident. I did not run over anyone so that is good. I am still not entirely confident about this, but I am going to keep saying it while I drive for a while so I can see that nothing will happen. . . .

[Entry Four Days Later] Today was a really hard day for me. . . . [In OCD group] some patient talked about fire . . . [and apparently] I looked anxious! Another therapist called me out on this. Dang, it is like these people are inside my brain, haha (it is good though that they are so attentive!). Exposure time came and today it was really anxiety-provoking. . . . [The therapist] knew what was causing me great anxiety today: God. I refuse to say the number after 5, the opposite of God, and the opposite of Heaven. [For treatment purposes I] had to stare at a whiteboard that said "God hates (the name of the therapist)."
—Kelcie

Once individuals perceived themselves as having OCD, a world opened up in which they were not alone, and people like Kelcie could seek targeted professional help, the next stage of the OCD "career." The epigraphs to this chapter are two excerpts from Kelcie's journal written four days apart, documenting her journey with OCD. When she first contacted me, Kelcie was in her early twenties and had graduated from college. Before learning about the disorder, she thought she was a "bad person" for her rituals such as checking the lights to make sure there was not a fire. She told me, "I am Catholic and one time for Lent I tried to give up doing my quirky behaviors. That did not last long, haha." Kelcie was bright and articulate, and her journal documented her valiant efforts to challenge her obsessions and compulsions. It revealed what treatment can look like for those with the disorder.

Although we commonly hear that OCD is chronic and there is no magic cure-all,[1] it is heartening to know that more than half of people with OCD may achieve a level of recovery and potentially remission, and even more can experience improvement. Regardless, a significant proportion of people do not respond as well as they would like to contemporary treatments.[2] (See chapter 3 for a description of available treatments.) Perhaps 10 to 20 percent of people with OCD may be "refractory to all available pharmacological and psychological treatments," potentially leading them to choose more invasive treatments.[3] It is true that some people's obsessions and compulsions spontaneously improve, but one cannot count on that happening.

Over the years, I checked in with Kelcie and read her journal entries. I observed her try multiple treatments, including medication, an intensive outpatient program for OCD, and a residential program tailored to helping people with OCD, the latter of which regularly have waiting lists. She went through numerous highs and lows. Regardless, she managed to complete a master's degree and get married. At times she made progress. There were journal entries where she depicted herself as eager and hopeful, such as one in which she wrote, "I will be back to myself (although I do not even remember my normal self anymore because it has been so long) soon (I hope). Grr (good grr, the grr that makes me seem like I am going to fight OCD down)!" In another she said OCD was trying to change her: "I will, however, not let OCD overcome me. I am who I am and nothing is going to change it."

It can be a herculean task for people with OCD to confront and go against thoughts that are coming from their own minds and that seem very real and important. Researchers looking at the experiences of those with health concerns have found that the help-seeking stage involves people looking at themselves anew.[4] Obviously, treatment can play havoc with one's sense of self, for instance, when one undergoes chemotherapy and loses their hair or has breast removal surgery. Those are pieces of one's body that shape identity. Interviewees became cognizant earlier in the OCD trajectory that they could not take the mind for granted. At this stage, they tried to change how they responded to thoughts and their own mental processes. Consider Kelcie's fear of germs and contamination. She and some other interviewees compared OCD to an addiction, with Kelcie saying in her journal, "I am addicted to washing my hands and keeping myself and belongings perfectly clean." She continued, "I cannot stop myself from doing it. I think about it constantly, and when I am not doing it, I am anxious."

Aspects of treatment made her feel that her religion was being belittled, and contamination concerns led her to keep washing her hands and using hand sanitizer. She wrote about going outside without a coat and feeling cold and sick, rather than wear a dirty jacket, which for her was one that had gone longer than a day without being washed. One day, therapists asked Kelcie to wear some of the same clothes two days in a row as part of her therapy. Kelcie wore the clothes and managed to hold off washing them in the washer. However, she washed them by hand.

In one journal entry she wrote that the program responded by getting stricter. "If I am going to go to the bathroom a therapist has to come with me. The therapist is going to have to time the amount of time it takes for me to wash my hands and if it is longer than 30 seconds, the therapist would knock on the door. If it is longer than 1 minute the therapist is going to come into the bathroom. This freaks me out so much because the bathroom is my safe place, but I guess not anymore."

It is fruitful to perceive the people I interviewed as being in a metaphorical relationship or marriage with their OCD. Over time, OCD became intertwined in many of their lives. Karp likened starting medication for depression to getting "married."[5] I am borrowing from this metaphor but altering it a bit. People with OCD have formed certain patterns of thinking and ways of responding to their thoughts and coping, what I refer to as the daily grind. I am suggesting that at this stage people with OCD consider if and how they want to reimagine this by doing things like ingesting medications or going to a therapist. At times, Kelcie even questioned whether she wanted to get rid of her OCD. She explained in her journal, "As much as I hate having it this severe, I really do like some of the aspects of OCD. Will I not be a neat freak anymore, but be a slob? . . . I do not want to be seen as just another normal person. I take pride in being quirky."

We must also not forget that people's use of conventional treatments is circumscribed by larger structural factors. Interviewees were affected by factors such as the cost and availability of qualified and knowledge-able therapists. For instance, the price of visiting a knowledgeable provider in the United States was sometimes prohibitive for persons I interviewed, and in the United Kingdom people sometimes had to wait to see healthcare professionals. These factors in combination with the daily grind help explain what is behind what researchers refer to as gaps between symptom onset and enrollment in effective treatments. In one study of a sample of patients in Italy, approximately six years passed between onset of symptoms and disorder onset, then seven years between disorder onset and help-seeking; finally, approximately a couple years passed between seeking help and receiving adequate treatment.[6] (There is evidence that some people who do *not* meet the criteria for diagnosis of a mental disorder routinely seek help, though.)[7]

Healthcare professionals currently consider medications and cognitive behavior therapy as the first-line treatments for OCD. These treatments require different investments. Swallowing a prescribed pill is very different from one popular form of treatment called ERP that falls under the umbrella of CBT and that Kelcie described in her journal. This form of therapy "consists of facing your feared situation."[8] Part of the difficulty, as Kelcie demonstrated, is that treatment for OCD can involve going against commonsense strategies. What many people with and without OCD do not realize is how the basic strategies we use to understand and cope with our thoughts do not necessarily work the way we assume. It is at this help-seeking stage that many people and those close to them reassess their strategies in light of the available evidence-based professional knowledge about the disorder. That, from my perspective, is one of the largest impacts of the medicalization/psychiatrization/psychologization of OCD.

People with OCD do not live in a vacuum, and those around them also have a relationship with the OCD. The OCD therapist Shapiro told me that in some cases, whole households have been controlled by the disorder. Kelcie's OCD was even part of her interactions with friends. For instance, as she described in an email to me, "When my friends call me at night to do something I usually say no. I need to know earlier in the day so I can have the time to get my OCD rituals done. This of course does not coincide with the college lifestyle, haha." When speaking of her life with her husband, one woman said the OCD was "part of everything that we do." People may get a reprieve from certain social expectations when they are sick, but others may expect them to seek treatment and conform to therapists' guidance.[9] Loved ones can help people with OCD continue their old strategies or form new ones, even becoming part of the treatment process.

Kelcie's family worked hard to get her treatment approved by insurance, and at times Kelcie was told that insurance was dependent on how well she did in therapy. When she was not making enough progress, therapists asked Kelcie's mother to assist. Kelcie explained in her journal, "My parents and I have to come up with a behavioral contract or something which basically means that my mom is going to have to watch over my every move and punish or reward me for doing or not doing anything OCD. I really do not like this idea at all because this would make me seem like a little kid having his/her mommy watch his/her every action! I also think that this would put a lot of stress on my mom."

The experiences of interviewees and their loved ones in coping with the disorder and utilizing conventional treatments are the focus of this chapter. I continue my discussion of the help-seeking stage in the next chapter, in which I examine how people with OCD used information and social support to their advantage.

The Daily Grind

When we were discussing medications, Jeff, who was in his thirties, said, "I have a lifetime of thoughts and habits and learned responses keeping me from getting to 100 percent normal even if there is such a thing. Besides, how would I measure normal?" His words address what

I mean by the daily grind. People with OCD can spend years with their thoughts and behaviors, coping in their own (sometimes unique) ways. People's attempts to manage and salve their OCD were complex, and so any examination of these attempts cannot be limited to conventional treatments. Interviewees developed patterns of noticing their thoughts, for instance, and responding to them. They formed a type of relationship or marriage with their obsessions/compulsions and their coping techniques. Healthcare professionals would consider these coping techniques helpful in some cases but hurtful (e.g., reinforcing the OCD) in others.

Kelcie demonstrated how ERP therapy involves minimizing and eliminating compulsions, but some interviewees got used to their compulsions or thought they could utilize them as coping techniques. For instance, Mick was willing to get help for the obsessions but found his compulsions relatively functional.[10] As he explained, "I feel that my compulsions are a shield against chaos and obsessions, a structure I can cling to when confused or overwhelmed." He told me that compulsions work for him as long as he does not let them get out of control: "I was a biology major, you remember. We learned that one must be very careful before concluding that any trait in biology exists without conferring some advantage to its organism. Compulsions are an inefficient and sometimes embarrassing way of dealing with life's problems, a technique—to speak loosely—with many undesirable side effects, but as the singer declaimed, 'I know that drinking makes my thinking hazy / but at least [it allows me to] think.'" Mick has taken medication when times were bad. Mick referenced biological adaptations, and researchers have questioned whether some mental disorders are evolutionary adaptations, and if they might have served a beneficial function at some point in the past. For instance, the psychiatrist Joseph Polimeni, along with Jeffrey P. Reiss and Jitender Sareen, asked if OCD "could be a vestigial phenotype once advantageous to ancient hunting and gathering tribes. Symptoms such as checking, hoarding or adhering to excessive hygiene could have conferred benefits to an entire tribe."[11]

Interviewees tried out a vast number of coping techniques before and after diagnosis in attempts to minimize their obsessions and compulsions or make themselves feel better. They did so in more ways than I had the creativity to imagine, and these became part of the daily grind.

Chance regaled me with stories, saying that he was the happiest while sitting on his couch in the buff, smoking weed with his wife. While we spoke, he confessed that his thoughts were taking him other places: "It will make you crazy because it almost hurts sometimes, having so many thoughts go on and it constantly racing. It makes you tired without ever moving. And when I smoke marijuana they stop." (Note that some people have reported to professionals that marijuana has no effect or makes their symptoms worse.)[12] Aiten even moved to live in a greener part of the city to improve his mood.[13]

Many people tried to minimize their anxiety and stress and distract themselves. They reported doing everything from spending time in creative activities, to getting out of the house and interacting with others socially, working long hours, journaling, crying, exercising, trying to have a positive attitude, using self-hypnosis, and changing their diets. One thing Patrick did after being diagnosed, in addition to taking medications and a vitamin B supplement, was to create a routine: "What I am trying to work on is a routine of physical exercise and mindfulness based on self-therapy. I have experienced some bright spots from both, most notably an increased ability to relax during high-anxiety thoughts." Missy, who was taking medications and had just found a new doctor who was teaching her CBT and breathing techniques, talked to me about eliminating caffeine from her diet: "I think that OCD is made worse by additional stress, anxiety, etc. So my feeling is that if diet helps those, it will also help OCD. . . . I think that so much of our mental makeup is what we put in our bodies, both mentally and physically." Some people talked to me about the role of religion in their lives and how it served as a salve. Janet wrote, "I find it comforting to believe that I was created this way for a purpose and that God loves me as I am, OCD and all."

Still others became preternaturally creative in their coping. Nancy had not been diagnosed when we spoke, but when her rituals started taking up hours of her day, she tried to make not doing a ritual into its own ritual, in other words, attempted to use the OCD *on* the OCD. She said, "Any time I feel an obsessive thought entering my head, I try to refuse it. I promise myself that by allowing it to pervade my thoughts and actions that bad things will happen—that by ignoring them and not acting upon them will mean good luck." One might wonder why she and others with OCD did not just stop their thoughts (and thought suppression was an early form of professional treatment).[14] Researchers pointed out that "it is almost impossible to achieve perfect suppression of any unwanted thought, image, or impulse even for a few minutes,"[15] and attempting to do so may lead to their increase.[16]

At times people wanted to shut or slow down their minds, so they turned to strategies such as sleeping and consuming alcohol. In Sarah's words, "[During an episode I] feel incredibly depressed, sometimes buy a bottle of wine, sleep more to avoid the thoughts." When she told me this, she was also partaking of conventional treatments. She lived in the United Kingdom, was in her thirties, and had been diagnosed with OCD and depression.

Without effective coping and/or treatment, situations could become devastating. Sixteen people I interviewed said that at times they had suicidal thoughts or attempted suicide, although all of them perceived themselves as having comorbid disorders such as depression, which sometimes they associated with the suicidal thoughts rather than OCD. My heart hurt when Janet said, "At its very worst, OCD can be life-threatening. This may sound dramatic, but I have been reduced to alcoholism in trying to control the symptoms, years ago when I didn't even know what it was. I once took an overdose because I couldn't face living with it any longer."

A More Comprehensive Picture

My point is that we need to look at people's help-seeking in a more comprehensive way than simply the use of conventional treatments—that is, one that incorporates people's divergent ways of perceiving their obsessions/compulsions, as well as their coping and use of complementary and alternative practices. For instance, at times the daily grind was linked to interviewees being hesitant to change. In other cases, people felt coping techniques and complementary and alternative medicine helped them function after they had tried conventional treatments that were not 100 percent effective.

Consider Phineas, who told me that he has had OCD since age four. I was struck by the imagery he used to describe a breakthrough he had in therapy at a residential program for OCD. After two months he was getting breaks in which he felt as if he was in the present versus obsessing and caught up in his mind: "For the first time in my life, the outside world held meaning . . . everything that usually goes on in my head was in the background." I assumed Phineas had always been eager to participate, as he had gone through a lot before making it to the program (including trying other professional treatments). He told me the opposite was true: "I kind of fought the whole concept and ideas that they were trying to feed me. You have to understand that growing up and knowing nothing but obsessing, it has become who I am and what I believe about myself." After his doctor asked him to consider how his life had been going following that path, Phineas became more receptive. He explained, "From that moment, I started doing the therapy and what they asked. I had no clue if it would actually work, but he was right." Another interviewee described being "afraid" to give up compulsions, fearing she might "forget to do something, or something might happen if I don't, or I will be less organized and ruin something or be less efficient at my job, and it starts all over again."

Some interviewees weighed the costs and benefits of trying a treatment against how well they were coping as part of the daily grind, as well as their past attempts at conventional help-seeking. When I interviewed her, Joanie, who lived in the United States and was in her forties, referred to herself as "functional" and able to work. She said that if she were not, she might try taking medications for OCD. Years prior to us communicating, Joanie saw a counselor who diagnosed her with OCD, PTSD, and dysthymic disorder and helped her with her stress. She had also seen someone who promoted what she termed a "wacky type of therapy." Still earlier, Joanie had seen a therapist who "was saying she didn't think I was crazy and there's not much more she could do for me."

One interviewee experienced side effects from medications and said he believed alternative medicine and therapy should be tried first: "I am a bit touchy on this subject because I trusted this psychiatrist when he gave me Effexor at age nineteen and never told me anything about the side effects." This interviewee felt he overcame the OCD after visiting professionals (one an MD and the other who worked with an MD) who prescribed complementary and alternative treatments such as nutrient therapy. He argued that OCD needs to be treated on "all fronts," including CBT, nutrition, mindfulness, and lifestyle.

There are overlaps among coping techniques, conventional treatments, and complementary and alternative medicine—such as the use of mindfulness as presented in self-help books, religion, and conventional therapies (see chapter 3). Complementary and alternative approaches were incorporated into the daily grind by interviewees themselves as well as recommended formally by healthcare professionals. Overall, people's feelings about complementary and alternative approaches were extremely mixed. Compared with conventional treatments, some interviewees perceived CAM as potentially more empowering (giving them more control over their health), more natural (associated with fewer side effects), and faster acting (e.g., an on-the-spot relaxation technique). However, most people I interviewed at least tried conventional treatments, and I did not find widespread aversion to conventional treatments.

Me, My OCD, and Medication

The people I interviewed sometimes hesitated (both before and after believing they had OCD) to seek help from professionals or to share everything they were experiencing. Going to a healthcare professional could feel risky. Maeve would only tell her therapist everything when she was having what she called a "breakdown" during which she could not work or function well. Fear and embarrassment prevented her from saying more. At times interviewees lacked faith in professionals; were afraid that telling a therapist all their thoughts might lead to their being judged or "locked up"; feared stigma (including that from just visiting a professional); expressed concern that seeking professional help would make the problem more real and/or confirm OCD as part of their identity; or were embarrassed or ashamed of their thoughts/behaviors. Researchers have cautioned us to consider the complexities of the OCD career for ethnoracial minorities. For instance, to avoid stereotypes based on race, African Americans might not disclose obsessions with aggressive or sexual content and may face increased anxiety in encounters with professionals.[17]

Trying to divorce your OCD using medications is different from taking it to therapy. These approaches require different time investments and mental fortitude, leading to dissimilar impacts on the self.

I assumed incorrectly that if people with OCD took medications, they might be able to avoid the difficult work of confronting their thoughts. Medications generally did not erase the OCD for interviewees, although they added to the existing questions about self and identity that those with OCD were already facing. Karp pointed out that medicalization and pharmaceuticalization come with changes to people's identities.[18] In his studies of people with depression, people could be reluctant to take medications for a host of reasons surrounding who they would become if they did so. They might be stigmatized. Ingesting pills works on the mind and feelings and might change their personality, raising uncomfortable questions about their identity. They sometimes encountered side effects like sexual problems which would affect them and the people close to them. As a result, Karp's interviewees exhibited some hesitancy to take the proffered hand that medicine offered them when they visited psychiatrists and doctors.

Those I interviewed asked themselves if they were ready to replace their relationship with OCD with medications, and they exhibited some of the same types of concerns and hesitations described by Karp.[19] Miles told me, "[I] didn't like (and still don't) the idea of taking something that makes changes in your brain. I worry that I'm not 'real' anymore because the drugs affect how your head works." Some people saw themselves as inferior or were worried that others might see them as inferior for having to take medications. Maeve said, "When I first started taking it . . . I felt like I was crazy, like I have to take medicine and I shouldn't have to be dependent on medicine to live my life." Some people critiqued professionals (e.g., for prescribing too little or too much), the pharmaceutical industry, and social structures. "I think that drug companies make an incredible amount of money off of convincing people that they are helpless victims of a disease and can only deal with it through drugs," said Errol, who lived in the United States and had been diagnosed with OCD. Joanie told me: "I don't like to be a government experiment. . . . [It's] a fear about what the medication actually does and the lack of studies out there for long-term use and what it actually does chemically in your head."

If interviewees got past their trepidation and took medications, it was more likely that they ended up in a relationship with the medication and their OCD rather than filing divorce papers. Swallowing pills almost never led to their obsessive thoughts or urges to engage in compulsions magically disappearing. One common effect reported by interviewees who talked positively about medications was that they made it easier to cope with OCD. "Prozac makes the OCD easier to live with," Miles said. For instance, some people felt that certain medications helped by indirectly reducing their anxiety. Clara messaged me to say, "I was on all kinds of medications, one after another. . . . [None] worked and I had to solely depend on behavior therapy, but the medicines decreased my anxiety."

When medications worked more directly on their obsessions and compulsions, interviewees tended to explain the effect as dulling or slowing their obsessive thoughts and urges to engage in compulsions, giving them an opening to change. Janet wrote: "I became aware that the 'sharp edges' of my compulsive thought patterns were slowly softening. It became possible to leave some of the rituals alone. I was like a dog who has always been tied on a short leash being given a longer one. The boundaries were still there but further away. . . . I began to believe it might be possible to get free altogether." Mick said he could more easily "shrug off" compulsions because they didn't seem to matter as much. One man said that the medications took care of 40 to 50 percent of the problem, and he took care of 40 to 50 percent. Bella had a more overwhelmingly positive response when she referred to medication as a "savior" that allowed her to learn what "normal" was for the first time. Bella was over sixty years old when we spoke; she lived in the United States and had been diagnosed with OCD, chronic post-traumatic stress, and GAD. She described herself as having been depressed in the past and was once told by a psychiatrist that she sounded manic-depressive (but she did not feel he listened to her, and so she dismissed that diagnosis).

Some medications presented interviewees with a new problem in the form of side effects. The people I interviewed reported taking a range of medications (not just SSRIs) and experiencing everything from sexual dysfunction to weight gain. Consider what Janet experienced with an SSRI:

At first, it was more difficult to eat and sleep. . . . But gradually . . . I entered a phase of feeling "better than well." . . . I could feel energized, electrified, bubbling over with ideas and self-confidence. . . . The downside to this came when I discovered I could not grieve for one of my dead patients. It felt like rubber walls had been placed around my emotions and you try to punch through to get to the bad feelings but it just wasn't worth the effort, so you bounce back. This seemed glorious after years of self-conscious, uncertain introspection but I sometimes wondered if things were going too far. . . . You are distracted and bedazzled by what is around you. . . . Getting lost in the supermarket and stepping out in front of traffic were two major difficulties in the early days.

Taking medication and then getting off of it is associated with the risk of relapse, according to research.[20] Jesse said that if he missed a dose or two of his prescribed SSRI, he felt "terrible, dizzy, and electric shock–like feelings in my head when I move it suddenly. They go away about an hour after taking the missed dose." Further, interviewees sometimes reported trying a variety of medications and dosages until they found one that worked and that did not have a lot of side effects. Or, sometimes they experienced a medication that worked for a period of time, and then they had to switch again. This process of trial and error and finding the right medication "cocktail" could be trying. (Genetic tests have been proposed as a tool to assist people in targeting which medications would be most effective for them.)

Their perspectives on medications and side effects affected their cost-benefit analyses of whether to continue taking medication, helping to explain why even those who took medications sometimes tried to get off them, whether on their own or with the help of a professional. Researchers and professionals regularly talk about the noncompliance of consumers and try to figure out how to make them more compliant. However, compliance "suggests that an objective is clear and can be met if the patient does what the doctor orders,"[21] but as we have seen, people with OCD can have various goals. Importantly, some people I interviewed said medication made engaging in CBT easier, as well as participating in other activities such as meditation.[22]

Taking OCD to Therapy

Destin talked to me about how treating OCD with CBT can be empowering. It can be disempowering to believe that one has a "disease" and to recognize that consuming medications changes aspects of your identity. For instance, Karp pointed out how some people went through changes after taking medications that led them to question if their authentic self was the one on the medication or off.[23] In contrast, CBT can show people they are the ones in control over their relationship with OCD. Destin offered the following description:

> Medication definitely helps but you also need that psychological realization you can take control, that you're not reliant necessarily on the medication, although in part you know you kind of are. But the CBT really reinforces or enforces the notion that you can and you are in control. It's you who gives in to the symptoms. It's you that can also not give in to those symptoms. And the more and more you don't give in to them, the more and more you gain control, the more and more you feel better and it becomes, it becomes a roller coaster to keep going up and up and up. The difficulty in that, again, is that you have to face it every day, and some days you just feel exhausted by it all. And you know once you give in to that one . . . the whole stack of dominoes falls.

After interviewees started to see themselves as people with OCD, they began labeling thoughts/behaviors as "obsessions" or "compulsions"; through CBT, people further distinguished the thoughts/behaviors from their selves. For instance, Maeve appreciated the book *Brain Lock*, which outlines a four-step program that coaches readers into separating their OCD from reality and talking back to it. This included recognizing that the brain can send out false messages.[24] Maeve said, "Every time I thought about something and I was obsessing, I'd stop myself and I'd be like, 'This is OCD. This is not a real issue. Stop thinking about it.' And it worked. It was the first thing that had ever worked that I ever tried that actually cognitively did that, fixed it. It wasn't just medicine. It was actually me stopping it." More recently, Jeffrey Schwartz and Rebecca Gladding argued that similar steps can be used by anyone, with or without OCD, to change "deceptive brain messages."[25]

Often those people I interviewed who tried CBT, either with a professional or self-guided, reported that they were able to understand their selves better and create distance between themselves and the OCD. Chris wrote, "I realized that before CBT I had turned into someone who had little contact with the outside world because I was scared of what I was going to do to them." When Chris and I first interacted, he described having obsessive thoughts constantly. Five years later he was doing quite well and felt he no longer needed to actively see a therapist or take medication. "The *only* positive thing to come out of it [having OCD] is that I have a better understanding of how people work. . . . I feel sad looking back and seeing how much of my life was wasted checking things and ultimately being scared of—me."

To get to this point, people learned that some of their primary ways of coping as part of the everyday grind were problematic. Certainly, some of their coping strategies or use of CAM provided people with distraction or calm and worked to break apart the relationship between them and their OCD. For instance, creative outlets and mindfulness can provide useful complements to conventional treatments, as they do in the McLean Hospital residential program for OCD.[26] Other approaches people tried reinforced the obsessions and compulsions, sometimes inadvertently. Cleaning when they felt dirty, avoiding things when they were afraid, or checking when they were unsure—such strategies appear to be actions anyone might take. However, existing research has indicated ways in which these tactics are problematic for people with OCD.[27] In their book about children and OCD, March and Benton wrote to parents that they and their children have probably "found that sensible measures don't work too well against nonsensical OCD."[28]

More specifically, performing compulsions might seem like a useful approach (i.e., washing if someone feels dirty), and it appears that people can experience at least some temporary relief from anxiety by engaging in compulsions or neutralization.[29] One interviewee referred to some of her cleaning and organizing routines as "soothing." (Like compulsions, neutralization can be seen as an attempt to minimize anxiety; compared with overt compulsions, neutralization is usually covert, and largely intended to cancel out "the effects of a person's own thought or action."[30] An example would be a person with fears of harm coming to a particular person attempting to neutralize violent images by replacing them with images of the person as happy and healthy.)

However, researchers have argued that not engaging in compulsions and neutralization is central. They have written that people with OCD may not realize that their discomfort would have declined anyway if they had not participated in such compulsive behaviors and neutraliza-tion.[31] Instead, doing so can reinforce participation in such behaviors. For instance, Rachman, a psychologist, theorized that people engage in checking rituals because they believe "they have a special, elevated responsibility for preventing harm [and] feel unsure that a perceived threat has been adequately reduced or removed. In their attempts to achieve certainty . . . people with high responsibility repeatedly check for safety."[32] Paradoxically, checking itself may increase one's perceived responsibility for preventing harm.[33] Compulsive checking may encour-age distrust in memory confidence in people with or without OCD.[34] Checking repeatedly may also lead to feelings that something is "not just right."[35] Note that people with OCD sometimes try to check and "test" if their thoughts are true. For instance, people with sexual obsessions might try to assess if they get aroused by them; sometimes they might even feel they notice a groinal response. However, "attending to one's groin actually causes sensations to occur there," and groinal sensations can occur for no reason; therefore, noticing a groinal response does not equate to a person's fears being true.[36] This checking can just fuel the OCD.

Avoidance can fuel the OCD as well. Rather than challenging people's false ideas, it can reinforce them. One researcher explained this using the example of a woman with obsessions involving fears of harming someone, saying her attempts at avoidance, neutralization, or having others with her "in turn increase her doubts and prevent her from dis-confirming her fears, and the vicious circle continues."[37]

The therapist Penzel wrote:

> When it comes to controlling OCD, I think the single most important thing to understand is this: "The problem is not the anxiety—the problem is the compulsions." If you think that the problem is the anxiety, then you will most likely keep doing compulsions as a way of relieving it. This is of course wrong, as the compulsions only keep things going and convince sufferers that the thoughts really are important and should be acted upon. In actuality, when you stop doing the compulsions the anxiety eventually subsides when nothing bad occurs. It is also important to realize and accept that you cannot block the thoughts out, switch to a different set of thoughts, argue with them, or reason them away. You need to see that

when it comes to escaping the thoughts, you have lost this particular battle and that it is one you will never win. Once you understand this, you
can then get down to the business of confronting and overcoming your
frightening thoughts. . . . Some have suggested that having people carry
out such therapy work is cruel or mean in some way, but thirty-five years
of research contradicts this. . . . If the therapy ultimately relieves people
of their suffering in the quickest and most efficient way, and enables them
to function as parents again, I would label it as kind. Besides, as I tell my
patients, "You know what I would really do if I wanted to be mean? I'd
leave you the way you are."[38]

Because confronting one's fears is obviously not easy, some forms of
CBT can be difficult for people with the disorder to implement, much
less understand how they work. One issue was the amount of time and
work involved. Winona told me she wanted a "quick fix" and that "everything that I read is such a turnoff to me. It's so intimidating. It seems
like so much work." To bring this type of therapy to life, consider how
Kirstyn said ERP was the "hardest thing I have ever done in my entire
life" but also the "best thing I ever did because I got better."

What is actually involved in an exposure might seem odd to someone without OCD, Kirstyn told me. She described how she was anxious
about the color green, so her therapist brought over a cloth that was
green. Kirstyn had to sit there with the material as her first exposure.
When you tell someone who does not understand the disorder, she said,
it sounds "almost ludicrous." "Like how hard can that be to sit with a
piece of material for 90 minutes? . . . That's what ERP is. Not doing what
your OCD tells you to do, but it really does work."

ERP involves exposing yourself to your fears. As the therapist Shapiro explained to me, this leads to anxiety, and you wait until it reaches
its peak (which is typically when people turn to rituals) but you do
not perform the rituals. The anxiety runs its course and passes. This,
Shapiro continued, requires a person to trust the process and give up
some control for uncertainty, which is difficult considering the connections I have pointed out between OCD and control. Some behaviors
people described being asked to do as part of their therapy included
yelling profanities at a grave site; reading a book without counting syllables; wearing clothing that incorporated LGBTQ symbols; saying and

writing a feared number; touching feared or contaminated items, including knives; having premarital sex and then going to communion; having sex without rituals; and driving a vehicle close to the curb (as the person was avoiding being near the curb in fear of running someone over). In Phineas's view, you are performing the exposure to prove your brain wrong: "Inside of our heads is what feels real. You can actually 'see' yourself doing the things you fear. . . . Doing the exposures shows your brain the falsehood of its thinking. It retrains your brain to show it that what you fear is actually silly. . . . I would break out in a sweat and my brain would literally start to hurt, because it's a muscle and you are retraining it."

Winona told me that she knows "what needs to be done" to break up with her OCD and has "read studies of what works," yet she struggled to put it into practice. She described trying to stop a ritual in which she looked behind the shower curtain five to thirty times a day. She told me that she cannot urinate until she has looked, so if she does not look, then she finds she does not use the restroom either. Finally, she said she just gives in and looks.

When people struggle with some thoughts/behaviors, such as those about harm and sexuality, therapists may recommend utilizing imaginal exposures or scripts.[39] According to one source, "A person with scrupulosity might avoid certain activities, like going to the pool, because the activities come with the risk of touching another person in a bathing suit inappropriately, which might be regarded as a sin. . . . He might be instructed to imagine brushing up against another person in a bathing suit and be asked to experience those levels of anxiety without doing anything to alleviate the anxiety."[40] According to the therapist Grayson, a person who has hit-and-run OCD might be directed by a therapist to listen to a recorded "imaginal exposure script" while driving that emphasizes how they may never know whether they hit anyone or not.[41] Grayson said we all live with uncertainty, and we can see how this challenges the intolerance of uncertainty in people with OCD.

Maeve had obsessions regarding whether she should be with her boyfriend because he is not as religious as she is. In response to this, a therapist told her that rather than wrestling with these thoughts, she should tell herself, "Maybe I shouldn't be with him." Maeve explained further:

It's hard for me to even tell myself that because every other counselor or therapist I've ever went to has always used like a positive reassurance method like just keep telling yourself, "This is just OCD. This isn't real." And with him, instead of doing that, I can't reassure myself. I can't ask for reassurance from my boyfriend. Whatever I'm OCD'ing about I just have to tell myself [how it might come true].

Grayson explained that fears should not be put into statements that they will definitely come true but that they might come true.[42] Such treatments might seem a bit deviant unto themselves, but therapists have indicated that they are training people to respond as people without OCD would. However, an article published in a neuropsychiatry journal argued that exposure through scripts has not yet been well validated by studies and is sometimes performed in an ethically questionable manner.[43]

It was not always easy for interviewees to understand what techniques would help versus hurt them. As one therapist told me, this can be complicated because a lot of supposedly "positive" coping techniques can become unhealthy if used excessively or in the wrong context, such as cleaning and exercising. Some people I talked to were not even sure what method their therapist was using with them. Perhaps it would reduce some of the confusion I saw in my interviewees if they knew what type of treatment protocol they were participating in and were provided with data supporting its use. Some clients might also benefit from therapists who inform them of the wide variety of ways OCD can manifest, from intrusive doubts about past events (false memory OCD) to the urge to compulsively urinate, in case clients are hiding something. Some interviewees were unsure which thoughts/behaviors were OCD and should be reported.

Note that even behaviors that can be problematic may potentially be useful in moderation. For instance, a few prominent OCD researchers have argued that safety behaviors (e.g., avoidance) can be used judiciously to help people when they are new to treatment.[44] It may also be useful to allow people to engage in a compulsion like checking something once rather than not at all. According to an article in the Journal of Behavior Therapy and Experimental Psychiatry, "Given that ritual is a very normal behavior . . . perhaps people with OCD can be given permission to engage in it within reasonable parameters."[45] Therapists have to work with what people with OCD are willing to try. Jeff said:

> My therapist and I were going to do straightforward behavior therapy using ERP worksheets, like those in Bruce Hyman and Cherry Pedrick's workbook. But I found out that I would have to do imaginal exposure to my fear of committing the crime [one that he was too uncomfortable to discuss with me] and I wasn't willing to try even imagining that. So we decided to do cognitive therapy instead and a limited ERP at a relaxed pace. . . . I thought it would be wrong to fantasize about doing something so bad. I also had obsessions about being humiliated, or going to hell, and nobody wants to sit around thinking about negative experiences.

The therapist Shapiro told me about how people with obsessions about harm may not be willing to let such thoughts sit in their minds because they feel other people's lives might be at stake or that to do so would be uncaring of them.

I also saw online comments from people who worked hard to let troubling thoughts pass through their minds without obsessing, but then turned around and questioned why they were no longer bothered by such thoughts and began to fear and obsess that they did not have enough feeling. (Therapists refer to this as a "backdoor spike.")[46]

Friends and Family: Their Relationship with the OCD

A couple interviewees surprised me by telling me about how they largely hid their rituals and managed to put a stop to them alone when they were young. Such a story was not typical among those I interviewed. The sociologist Kathy Charmaz referred to friends and family as audiences to chronic illness,[47] but since people with OCD can metaphorically be seen as married to the OCD, I perceive those closest to them as forming their own relationship to the disorder. One family member I spoke to compared it to a merry-go-round. Sometimes you are watching the loved one seemingly going in circles with their obsessions and compulsions without moving forward. At other times it can feel as if you are on the ride with them as you try to help.

In one of the extreme cases I heard, Savannah said her life with her husband, Sam, changed completely because of his OCD. He would follow her around the house asking for reassurance constantly, and finally she desired space. "We used to sleep together [and now don't]. . . . He has his own bathroom. I clean about every day almost and make sure everything is how he needs it to be. . . . I am somebody who is probably more of his friend than anybody else. . . . You love the person. . . . [But it's] no longer the emotion you would have toward a spouse." The burden of OCD on the family can be the same as it is for other disorders like schizophrenia.[48]

Overall, confidants such as friends and loved ones can traverse the same stages of the OCD "career" as those who have the disorder and can try to alter their own relationship to the OCD at this help-seeking stage. For example, confidants may help those with OCD decide if their thoughts/behaviors seem problematic; provide them with potential explanations for the problem or financial resources to seek professional help; become part of professional treatment plans; and learn to live with people who might have long-term OCD.

Consider how Lucinda's daughter Becky had OCD and initially Lucinda was frustrated and confused by Becky's behavior. When Lucinda first noticed Becky flipping lights on and off "like a hundred times," she searched for a way to explain what was occurring. She told me, "Her dad and I, we thought she was just being ornery. . . . I said, 'If you turn that light on one more time you are going to sleep in the hallway.' I go back to my bedroom. The light goes on. . . . I made her lay on the carpet in the hallway and we made her sleep on the floor. And when she was still crying at four in the morning I decided this was more than just being stubborn." After defining the behavior as a problem, they sought to figure out the nature of the problem. In this way, Lucinda traversed the first two stages of the OCD career with her daughter.

They lived in the United States, and after a psychiatrist labeled the problem OCD, this changed how Lucinda perceived and treated her daughter. Just as people with the disorder began to separate their "selves" from the OCD, so did Lucinda. Previous research has shown that families can struggle with how to conceptualize the disorder, including being unsure of which behaviors are part of the disorder versus part of the person's personality, leading to conflict.[49] As Lucinda explained, "I realized it's not all her fault. It's, you know, a feeling that they have to do something to even get through the day. . . . [I went from blaming to] understanding. . . . It made me understand mental illness better. . . . Made me not be that kind of a person who thought 'Oh, they're just weak or crazy,' and just write them off." Lucinda moved heaven and earth to try to get her daughter treatment and help after this, visiting many therapists. It took a toll on their emotions as well as their finances. Lucinda told me how her husband was ready to retire but they no longer had any savings, leading to arguments. The whole family had to find a way to live with the disorder (the last stage of the OCD "career").

A few interviewees talked to me about how others cannot get well for you. Although this is true, other people can certainly play a role in this process and be affected. One critical but difficult aspect of being around people with OCD is determining how to demonstrate care without accommodating the OCD. While the people I interviewed utilized many strategies to keep their thoughts/behaviors from impacting others, in many cases the OCD seeped into their lives, with confidants forming relationships with the OCD as part of their daily grind. Sometimes interviewees had their families participate in their rituals, such as having family members wash, check, clean, organize, and avoid. Even if others did not participate in specific rituals, they could be impacted. For instance, some families were not able to travel or engage in certain activities because the person with OCD had difficulties doing so. After graduating from college, Becky had trouble working, got caught up in her OCD, and became reclusive. Her mother said, "She couldn't eat with us or be around us. She was scared of everything, not socializing and barely leaving the house. . . . [After she left for a job] it was OK for a few weeks but then the OCD took over again. She could barely function and called me crying she couldn't eat and felt like fainting (OCD had convinced her the food was contaminated). She was stick thin and dehydrated." Family and friends might be asked to provide empathy and reassurance.

People with OCD can be desperate for reassurance that they aren't going "crazy," that they are not really child molesters, that they are not gay, and on and on. They turn to therapists, self-help groups, online forums and communities, friends, family, significant others, and more in order to find answers. Their requests for reassurance can be unending.

Mick's older brother remembered him asking his mother for reassurance, for instance, to confirm that the door was locked. Mick's mother responded as many people would respond. She wanted to make her son feel better so she checked and reassured him. Mick's brother told me that he would get frustrated but mostly thought to himself that this stuff really bothers his brother, and it is easy enough for him to do what his brother wanted.

However, OCD specialists have argued that there are problems with family "accommodation" to OCD, such as helping with rituals, waiting for people with OCD to complete these, or providing reassurance; OCD may become the "head of the household."[50] Accommodation has been associated with poorer relationship functioning, symptom severity and impairment, worse treatment outcomes for the person with the disorder, distress on the part of the one doing the accommodating, and reduced quality of life in the family.[51] One study of pediatric OCD found that accommodation behaviors by parents were a predictor of severity of OCD symptoms.[52]

For people with OCD, receiving reassurance can feel better than not having it, so healthcare professionals can help the family figure out alternative strategies.[53] I asked two therapists how they deal with this conundrum of being empathetic without providing reassurance. Shapiro said what occurs is that you tell them something once, and then do not continue to provide reassurance. Patrick McGrath described how he teaches therapists "how we can give facts once and then after that we don't give them again . . . although I often tell the patients if I'm going to give them some facts to get a notebook out and write this down because we're not going to talk about it again. And of course that's what people with OCD would like to do is to constantly talk about things, over and over again, just to make sure that they got it right, or they heard it right, or to see if maybe the facts have changed from yesterday to today."

People with OCD and those around them are placed in a difficult position. Imagine how the following feels for someone with OCD. Their mind is feeding them negative thoughts. They want the thoughts to go away, and when this does not occur, they want to analyze the obsessions to tell themselves that they are wrong. As part of treatment, they may be trying to confront their fears or even be utilizing imaginal exposures where they are trying to accept uncertainty about topics on which they very much want certainty, for example, that they are a good person. Now imagine you are a family member or close friend of someone with OCD. You do not want to see them in pain, and you likely want them to just believe they are fine. You want to comfort and reassure them, but how can you do this when you know this may make the OCD worse? Yet, if you withhold the reassurance, your closeness and relationship may suffer as well. What works for the therapist does not always easily translate to the home unless the person with OCD and those around them are in agreement about how they should respond.

Winona discussed family interactions with me. Early in her relationship with her husband, she tried to hide her OCD, but it came out.

> It became easier to do things in front of him [as a result of him knowing I had OCD]. But . . . part of me wishes I'd kept it in just because some things I do are just so stupid and so embarrassing and so crazy. . . . I wish that no one saw me do those things. . . . [But] there's another part of me that, it's amazing to feel so comfortable in my own skin with another human being and in spite of all the stupid-ass things that I do and he loves me anyway.

Her husband tried to put limitations on what he would do for her at times. He would say, "I'm not locking the car door again. I've locked it already." Before Winona had a baby, her husband asked her to get more professional help and show that she was trying to work on the OCD, but nonetheless at times he enabled. She reported that her husband sometimes accommodated her when she got really stuck on something, or when he wanted to do something. Winona told me a story about how her OCD kept them from traveling, much to her husband's frustration. When she did book a trip, her husband was so excited that he did whatever it took to get her there, even assisting with rituals. Her symptoms worsened with pregnancy. She told me, "Everyone is sort of in the mindset of let's just get her through this . . . to the other side, and [then] we'll worry about not enabling." Note that research has shown that while criticism can be acceptable, when people with OCD feel household interactions are negative (e.g., they face hostile criticism and anger from family), they do not experience the same successes in treatment.[54] One therapist I interviewed also argued that it does not pay for families to pressure people into treatment.

Just as there can be a gap between the inner and outer worlds of those with OCD, the same is true for families. Despite how happy Lucinda's family may have looked on the outside, things were difficult behind the scenes. We often think of stigma as clinging to a lone deviant individual or a group of people, yet stigma (and fears of stigma) can pass over to those around the stigmatized, something theorists refer to as "courtesy stigma."[55] This situation is illustrated by the following comments from Lucinda:

> LUCINDA: I can't tell anybody at work. . . . I just tell them she has anxiety. We don't say OCD and that we are all contaminated because I would feel crazy. [At that point, her daughter viewed the family as contaminated and could not live with them.]
>
> ME: So you think anxiety sounds better?
>
> LUCINDA: Uh-huh. It sounds more accepting to society.
>
> ME: How do you think society views OCD?
>
> LUCINDA: As crackpots, as silly crazy people who just won't stop what they are doing, like they are nuts like my husband does.

Lucina brought the stigma hierarchy into play by labeling her daughter as having anxiety rather than OCD because she felt this would be less stigmatizing. She worried not only about how people would view her daughter but also about how they might view her. She thought people might not perceive her as a good mother if they knew.

Overall, OCD had complicated impacts on those close to people with the disorder. Because OCD can be chronic, it can be taxing on friends and family. It has spoiled some relationships. However, OCD could bring people together. A couple of people I interviewed described seeking intensive treatment to improve their family lives. One woman successfully completed this treatment and at the time we spoke was working to improve the lives of others with OCD through volunteering with an organization supporting those with mental disorders. At first her husband did not tell people about his wife's disorder for fear of stigma; but the year I spoke to her, they decided to share. They asked his coworkers

Figure 6.1. JangandFox's *When It's Too Heavy* by Jang

to sponsor her for a walk to raise money for the organization where she was volunteering. She described the response as fantastic. Two or three families even contacted her husband to say that they had loved ones diagnosed with mental illnesses and asked for resources. She told me, "Now they have someone they can ask. So it's wonderful."

Research indicates that caregivers experiencing depressive symptoms is associated with feeling higher levels of caregiver burden.[56] However, Chance talked to me about how his relationship with his second wife, who was diagnosed with bipolar disorder, worked for them: "She picks on me about, you know, my nuttiness, and I pick on her about hers. We're a perfect couple."

Mick's mom told me that as adults she and Mick are "extremely close. We can often joke about OCD. I am slightly OCD . . . although it affects us differently. We have enjoyed watching *Monk* together. We can often laugh at ourselves."

Clyde and his wife regularly worked with their son to help him with tools to address his OCD and tics; Clyde's other young children stepped up to try to help as well. Clyde said his son is "kind of my hero," being brave in how he dealt with the OCD: "I expect him to do great things" when he grows up. I spoke to Clyde last week and his son was graduating with a high school and an associate's degree that month. Chris asked his girlfriend to be part of his treatment plan. Previously he had asked her for reassurance and used her to help him check that he had not caused harm. Although she never went to the therapist with him, Chris said he and his therapist planned what the girlfriend should do to help: "I tried to do everything the psychologist said exactly. I told her [my girlfriend] that if I ever asked something like 'Did I run that guy over?' she was to say 'I don't know' or something similar. Basically she was not to justify my actions and I was supposed to do it myself." He said that OCD has made their relationship "stronger because she knows something no one else [does]." The recipe for someone whose partner has OCD, according to one husband I interviewed, is "patience and understanding."

7

The Power of Knowledge

> Worst moments were those when I gave in to OCD, not knowing how to
> fight it. I knew something was wrong, and I felt very alone in this world
> without anyone to talk to. . . . Internet and books saved me, and also
> talking to sufferers online. Internet came into the picture maybe when
> I was sixteen going on seventeen. Then I read everything I could get my
> hands on about this subject. . . . I found a large amount of information,
> resources, chat rooms, and message boards where I could talk with other
> sufferers around the world and compare thoughts, experiences. . . . Via
> the internet you can communicate with people anonymously. I could
> talk to a sufferer from Australia, let's say, without any fear of opening
> up to that person. . . . I needed to reach out for people, because I did
> not tell anyone about my OCD (family, friends) but I did need to talk
> to someone. . . . [The books I read] were books written for sufferers like
> myself. . . . I got them at the library. . . . I figured this: OCD has overtaken
> my mind, and only I can overcome it.
> —Justine

Justine's narrative brings into sharp relief the centrality of information
and social networks for people with OCD. This was true for interviewees whether or not they sought professional care. Previous research has
shown how information helps people with chronic problems assess the
nature of their problem and make choices about treatment and coping.[1] Because OCD is not widely understood, and is both trivialized and
potentially stigmatizing, information and social support were especially
useful for people with the disorder when navigating the help-seeking
stage of the OCD career. Information and social networks served as
resources for interviewees or operated as forms of "capital" in the game
of life.[2] When Adler and Adler studied people who self-injure, they
found that those who were interviewed at the start of their research

operated as "loners," isolated from others.[3] After the growth of the internet and cyber-communication, they encountered interviewees who built bridges to others online, forming a cyber-community where they were not so alone.

Justine and I communicated online while she lived in Canada. She was nineteen and had avoided seeking professional help in person due to fears of stigma. She felt her OCD started when she was thirteen. She told me, "The therapist would have told my family about my problem. I did not feel like my parents would understand that OCD is a disorder and not a mental illness . . . and that they would spread it to other people/family/friends who would diagnose me in their own way as 'crazy.'" Yet, in her first message to me, Justine said that she no longer had OCD but had suffered from it for four years. While it impacted her life in many ways, she diagnosed herself and effectively crafted her own self-help program based on conventional theories/treatments, in large part due to online resources.

Justine explained how this played out in her life. Before learning about contemporary treatments for OCD and communicating with others who had the disorder, she felt alone and depicted herself as languishing in the quicksand of obsessive thoughts and compulsions (for more than a year after diagnosing herself). She experienced a number of thoughts/behaviors she would now identify as OCD that took up at least two to three hours of each day. These included reopening envelopes before sending them due to fears that she wrote something incorrectly; using extra commas when writing sentences (which hurt her grades in school); avoiding the number 3 or any number with 3 in it or that was divisible by 3; and checking if the alarm clock was set for the correct hour a certain number of times before going to bed. In her words, "My mind always felt tired, exhausted, trapped. . . . OCD made me very self-conscious . . . but also very responsible (since I always checked things numerous times, I never forgot anything, never was late, etc.)." She knew something was "wrong" and recalled, "I did fear it would drive me to insanity. . . . I gave in to OCD because I did not know how to fight it, did not even know what 'it' was."

Then one day Justine saw a Q and A section in a teen magazine and diagnosed herself with the disorder, realizing "that I am not alone in this." She was unclear about what to do next, other than seek professional help, which she was trying to avoid. At that point, she was about fifteen years old and did not have access to the internet or books, so she said that she "just gave in to it."

Online social networks and information turned things around and helped her craft an approach for treating the OCD and receive social support while avoiding stigma. Researcher Tania Lewis explained that in contemporary society "the ideal enterprising citizen . . . is one who actively monitors, regulates and manages their own health (with the help of appropriate expert advice and knowledge)."[4] Justine made herself into such a citizen:

> What helped me was a sufferer [online] would mention how he/she was treated in therapy by a doctor. . . . I figured I could do it myself. . . . I simply willed myself to go against the compulsions, forced myself to overcome them. . . . If the need came to check whether a door is locked, I would sit tight on the chair and force myself to stay put. It was extremely difficult and painful, but after a few times the compulsion simply went away. And I realized it was worth all the pain and effort. I did the same with certain other compulsions, and once I started this self-therapy certain compulsions disappeared on their own. With obsessions it was different because they are in your head (horrible, nonrealistic thoughts), but they too disappeared one by one once the compulsions started fading away. . . . I no longer have the disorder, because now I am in control and OCD is not. . . . I also turn to religion/God.

Justine's experience reiterates how health knowledge is "not an individual property" but is "shared and co-produced" in interaction with others.[5]

The healthcare industry is powerful, and doctors/therapists are experts. They tell us how to understand what is happening to us and our minds and bodies, but medical discourse does not truly reflect people's everyday experiences with illness. One theme in sociological research in the United States and the United Kingdom during the 1960s, 1970s, and 1980s was "medical dominance."[6] Sociologists have been concerned that medicalization gives more power to experts and individualizes social problems, shifting attention away from social forces.[7] Many studies discuss how medicalization and labels have been placed on people, sometimes to their surprise and dismay.

In contrast to medical dominance, researchers in multiple fields as well as the healthcare industry have been buzzing more recently about the existence of informed and active patients/consumers/clients, as well as shared or collaborative decision-making between patients/consumers and doctors/practitioners. The reason for this shift is multiple. Medical dominance was challenged by a variety of societal developments, including the growth of the internet, increasing interest in complementary and alternative medicine (CAM), the understanding that medical knowledge is not all-encompassing, decreasing trust in the profession, the idea that laypeople may be able to have a greater share in decision-making, and more.[8] An article in a psychiatry journal argued that instead of a paternalistic model for mental health services, some consumers and professionals have generated a recovery movement "based on a model of recovery and health care that emphasizes hope, respect, and consumer control of their lives and mental health services."[9]

In this chapter, I look at the ways in which interviewees gathered and utilized capital and were powerful actors in their own right. Justine was one of only two people I interviewed who felt they tackled and conquered OCD on their own without telling family, friends, or a healthcare professional. For those who sought professional care, information and social networks helped them advocate for themselves, for instance, amid larger structural impediments such as the cost of and lack of access to qualified treatment. These factors affect some groups more than others, such as minority groups with relatively lower incomes, reinforcing disparities.[10] Herein, I discuss what interviewees wanted out of their relationships with healthcare professionals, and the ways in which they were active consumers.

They were active consumers but sometimes in ways that affirmed contemporary professional views of OCD rather than challenged them. This contrasts with how groups can be resistant to medicalization, such as those who have built a pro-anorexia community that goes against medical conceptions of anorexia nervosa as a mental illness. One of the primary benefits of finding information and connecting with others with the same health concern online would appear to be that you are able to discuss commonalities in your experiences.[11] However, people with OCD limited their attempts to do so at times in order to minimize what might be perceived as asking for reassurance (which contemporary theories perceive as problematic). Their concern with contemporary theories and treatments for OCD is not unsurprising, because the healthcare industry itself has encouraged patients to get informed—that is, feeding the public messages that they need to be vigilant against risk, monitor their health, and ask their providers about medical tests and medications.[12] As I wrote this chapter, an ad came on the television advertising an app for tracking one's health. Self-monitoring and self-treatment in line with medicalization/psychologization may perhaps increase in the future, as researchers have suggested that "the treatment of mental health problems is expected to change considerably over the next few decades as a result of the widespread availability of Internet and mobile-device applications, and their use to deliver psychological interventions."[13] Growth in apps for mental health may reduce barriers to treatment,[14] presumably increasing the number of people in treatment.

Cultural Capital

In life, financial resources obviously matter but do not tell the whole story. Money shapes the type of housing, food, healthcare, and more that people can afford to purchase—all of which has implications for one's health. However, other resources or forms of capital exist that help people improve their health.[15] According to the sociologist William C. Cockerham, "American studies typically show that education is the strongest single predictor of good health."[16] This is in part due to the way in which people with education have more knowledge about health. Sadly, practitioners in their interactions with patients can foster this inequality. There is evidence that "doctors give more information, more explanations, more (emotional) support and adapt more often a shared decision making style with higher SES [socioeconomic status] participants."[17] At least some of this is due to how "patients" act: "Patients with a high SES tend to ask more questions, ask for explanations, [and] are more expressive . . . than their lower SES counterparts."[18] Receiving less information from doctors than expected can be a source of dissatisfaction for patients.[19]

The information-seeking of people with OCD increased their cultural capital. Drawing from the sociologist Pierre Bourdieu's ideas on capital,[20] we can view society as being composed of different spaces where having certain types of resources may be more or less important.[21] It is akin to a card game: "Players are dealt different cards (e.g. social and cultural capital), but the outcome is dependent on not only the cards (and the rules of the game) but the skills with which individuals play their cards. Depending on their 'investment patterns' individuals can realize different amounts of social profits from relatively similar social and cultural resources."[22]

More specifically, people can have cultural knowledge that they utilize to improve their health. Cultural capital includes "the operational skills, linguistic styles, values and norms that one accrues through education and lifelong socialization."[23] For instance, we can speak of people's understanding of and ability to use the healthcare system, and their comfortableness in interacting with and asking questions of their doctors as cultural capital, or even cultural health capital.[24] The opposite of such comfortableness would include feeling oneself as inferior in this relationship and following the doctor's instructions dutifully. Studies show that gaining a small but important piece of knowledge about how the healthcare system works, such as how and when a person can ask for a specialist and have the care covered by insurance, can improve a person's health.[25]

People with OCD did face particular impediments in their hunt for information. They indicated that obsessions and compulsions could keep them from effective searching. As one example, Sam was unable to type answers to his questions to me because he was concerned he might "contaminate" the computer. Riley spent so much time on his OCD rituals that he had little time for anything else. Other persons were hesitant to look for information or interact with others who had OCD. They felt that they might take on new obsessions/compulsions based on what they encountered, or they found that information-seeking itself could become a compulsion. Patrick conceptualized the internet as a "two-edged sword" that has "been helpful in allowing me to learn more about OCD," but also served as "a source of compulsive reassurance from everything from religion to philosophy." Percy told me, "With OCD, you're always trying to find a definite answer. . . . You look and look."

Regardless, interviewees relayed many stories about how information sources and experience helped them create opportunities. One sentiment I heard expressed a number of times was regret—that is, if they only knew at the start of the help-seeking process what they knew at the point at which we chatted, they would have gone about things differently. On their paths to treatment, I talked to people who described not knowing how to go about finding help, not realizing there were OCD specialists or professionals with more knowledge in treating OCD, not recognizing there were a diversity of treatments for OCD (including specialized residential treatment programs), and initially paying professionals who lacked knowledge of OCD or followed outmoded methods of treating the disorder. As a result, some interviewees spent years mired in this stage, struggling to find qualified help, while others happened upon experienced, caring professionals. Stephen Smith, founder of the app NOCD, argued that unlike medical issues for which people encounter a good screening and diagnostic process, essentially a solid infrastructure; he told me, with OCD "the challenge is how do you not only get somebody to treatment. It's how do you get them diagnosed right, out of the ineffective system."

Leveraging Information and Experience

The people I interviewed could not always do much to counter economic hurdles, but with information and experience they could better direct the resources they did have to create treatment and coping techniques to perform on their own, or else better navigate the healthcare system. This allowed people a chance to flex their consumer muscles, for instance. Consumers purchase services, so one aspect of their power in their relationships with healthcare professionals comes from this ability to hire and fire, to doctor-shop. This is not always viewed as a positive thing from the provider's perspective, and some nations make it harder for patients to do this than others. However, doctor-shopping can assist service users in getting their symptoms recognized and finding a provider they perceive as considerate of their needs.[26]

For instance, Nellie scrutinized which therapists were knowledgeable of contemporary treatments and should be trusted. We spoke in 2010, at which time she was twenty-one years old; she lived in the United States and had been diagnosed with OCD and depression. She told me one of her therapists had used the wrong names for current treatments or described them incorrectly. She continued, "By this time my mom and I had already read up on a lot of this stuff that we could find on the internet and in bookstores and with psychiatrists. . . . After we found out about that stuff we were like, well, we need to find a new one." Percy used information and experience in a similar fashion. As he told me, "I eventually found a counselor who realized I had a form of OCD and at first we made progress. I began to question her skills after contacting the OC Foundation and reading OCD behavior books. Soon I knew more than she did." He went on to get information from books and help himself. Kelcie told me positive things about her psychologist at one point. Later she said, "When I look back, I am quite frustrated that she [my psychologist] never told me that she was not very knowledgeable on OCD and that perhaps I should see a different therapist." Kelcie looked up information on her own to find specialized programs for the disorder. She also learned what professional behavior is expected of a psychologist in her psychology classes at school. Before this, she tolerated when her therapist swore at her, came late, and talked about people on the phone during therapy sessions. Kirstyn, who volunteered with a mental health organization, pointed me toward an online article written to help people determine if their therapist was trained in ERP. Martin invited me to call up medical professionals and ask them pointed questions, pretending I was a potential patient, to test their knowledge (something he has done himself). Therefore, I talked to people with OCD who questioned, tested, and checked up on their providers. They sometimes cross-checked the information from one medical professional with another, even contacting OCD specialists online, or asking other persons with OCD for their perceptions. Online forums and groups provide examples of the latter.

Flexing one's consumer muscles requires not only knowledge of treatments and providers but also knowledge of how the healthcare system works. As one example, Jesse discussed parity laws in the United States. He thought that insurance programs sometimes tried to play with the law. He told me, "I was denied more coverage by my HMO when I reached twenty visits. I told my therapist about the parity law (i.e., Timothy's Law),[27] and he called the HMO. The HMO claimed my employer had not purchased the parity 'rider.' " Jesse knew this was not true and got the HMO to change its position.

Relationships with Doctors/Therapists

The people I interviewed leveraged their capital and experience not only to find qualified therapists and healthcare professionals but also to get what they wanted out of relationships with these practitioners. It behooves us to consider what people with particular illnesses seek from healthcare professionals, something researchers are currently doing for a variety of health concerns. Writing for a journal published by the American Psychological Association, Irving Kirsch and colleagues advocated that we find ways to improve relationships as part of improving the effectiveness of treatment: "Positive expectations and the therapeutic alliance [cooperative relationship between patient and therapist] have been shown to be significant predictors of outcome for both psychotherapy and medication. . . . Therefore, although new and potentially more effective psychotherapy techniques should continue to be developed and tested, it may be even more profitable to focus research efforts on how to maximize the effects of positive expectations and the therapeutic alliance in psychotherapy—and in medical treatment."[28]

Beyond the effect of a particular treatment, we are affected by various factors, including the color of the pills that doctors prescribe, how professionals present themselves, how they deliver information about health, and the environment in which they do so. The effectiveness of treatment is related to our expectations regarding treatment.[29] Anthropologist Daniel E. Moerman and physician Wayne B. Jonas elucidated how "most elements of medicine *are* meaningful, even if practitioners do not intend them to be so. The physician's costume (the white coat with stethoscope hanging out of the pocket), manner (enthusiastic or not), style (therapeutic or experimental), and language are all meaningful and can be shown to affect the outcome."[30]

In many cases, the people with whom I communicated wanted a shared relationship with doctors/therapists. Bella said, "I interview them . . . as they interview me. And if I don't feel like they're a good fit . . . I fire them." She continued, "I just make an appointment with someone else. I just feel like I'm worth it. . . . I'm seeking, I'm buying, someone's position of power . . . to honor my wishes." The persons I talked to wanted someone who was knowledgeable in treating OCD and comorbid conditions and who was familiar with contemporary treatment options, but they also wanted more. When interviewing people with depression, Karp asked what people wanted most from a therapist; they described a relationship akin to a close friendship, although he admitted that if they were asked directly, most clients and consumers would probably not phrase it as such.[31] Years ago, Parsons described situations where healthcare professionals felt a pull to turn patients into friends, but they felt this was problematic with respect to maintaining objectivity.[32] More recently, new questions regarding boundaries and ethics between practitioners and patients have arisen as a result of social media, such as whether professionals and clients should be "friends" on social media.[33] However, some therapists have decided to use social media platforms to promote tips for mental health; this may be a gray area with respect to professional boundaries as I have seen some such therapists wonder how licensing boards may view their humorous content that attracts viewers.

The type of professionals that my interviewees sought included those who were caring and empathetic but provided an objective perspective, were nonjudgmental and explained things, listened to them, and treated what they said seriously rather than perceived them as lacking knowledge. They did not agree, however, on how formal or strict professionals should be. Perhaps most of all, they desired a healthcare professional who responded promptly to them. This is notable, as in one study, professionals sometimes admitted that they perceived people with OCD as time-consuming and making them feel as if they needed more time and patience.[34] Research has indicated how even clinicians can stigmatize people with OCD.[35] However, a good provider-consumer relationship can foster healing. When I reflected on what the people I interviewed said about these relationships, I realized that they were at heart looking for someone to trust. Shapiro brought this to my attention, describing how from the provider's perspective, it is critical that people with OCD trust their therapist.

Technology is being harnessed in new ways for OCD that can affect these dynamics. For instance, computer-based therapy, telephone-based support, and digital applications have formed the basis of or been incorporated into treatment programs. One app called Liberate was designed by fourteen-to-twenty-year-old students in India to help people better track their obsessions and compulsions, and to provide tools and exercises to follow. A group of researchers published an article in 2016 about an app that was developed for a patient who spent so much time checking that he did not make it to treatment on time and struggled with daily activities; the app warned him when he had not physically moved much over a period of time, as he might have been involved in checking behaviors.[36] I can imagine a future in which apps could be created or modified for particular clients. The trick will be to see if these technologies improve standards of care and provider-consumer relationships or end up being used as a stand-in that costs less money.

Certainly these approaches can minimize barriers to treatment and reduce stigma. However, one question that has already arisen is to what degree therapist-client interactions are needed versus patients interacting with the technology. Even unguided internet-based therapy technology can improve outcomes for people with OCD, although there is evidence that technology cannot completely supplant interactions between therapists and clients.[37] One characteristic that would be difficult for technology alone to provide would be detecting when someone is obsessing, engaging in rituals, or trying to manipulate the therapist. As described in the previous chapter, Kelcie did not always follow her therapists' instructions, and they had to monitor her more closely. Winona told me that she asks the therapist for sixty-minute appointments because the number 45 feels wrong to her (and is part of her OCD). She tried to tell him that it is because she needs extra time to warm up, but he called her out on her deception. One interviewee talked to me about the early days of a residential program she attended:

> They had only been open a year the day I checked in and almost all of the people there had been there almost seven months or a year. . . . They [staff] were still learning what to do. They [patients] had been there a long time. They all knew each other and each others' rituals. . . . They enabled each other. I come in and I'm totally the opposite. . . . It made me angry because I had to wait six months to get there and I found out half of these people weren't telling their therapist all of their symptoms and

they were still doing their rituals when their therapist wasn't looking and they weren't trying. . . . I graduated in [a shorter period of time].

Since then, the program has changed.

Yet, there is potential for applications to improve relationships between practitioners and consumers. The app NOCD, brainchild of Smith, who has OCD, was designed to reduce structural gaps in access to affordable care. According to my conversation with Smith, "The problem with OCD is it is 24/7, 365 [days a week] and the problem with therapy is you see your provider once a week, so what happens in between? That's when you need help the most. . . . You can use a mobile app to do that pretty well. . . . Our mission is to make sure people can access care no matter where they live in their state and no matter how much money they make and that's our big vision." He explained that in the United States many therapists who specialize in treatments for OCD are out-of-network, which is costly for those who want treatment. Therefore, his company hires and trains clinicians to treat people with OCD using ERP, credentialing them in-network with various health insurance providers. Therapy sessions are digital and take place over video. Therapists are accessible in that patients can contact them in between sessions, and therapists will respond at least once per day. McGrath, who at the time we spoke was serving as the head of clinical services for NOCD, told me that this type of therapy brings the therapist into the home of the person with OCD. If the client has had issues related to something within the home or out on the street, the therapist can do the exposures with them without having to physically travel there. As McGrath explained, "My hope is that we'll see that this actually makes exposure therapy even better, by now always being able to be with the patient in the experience."

Therefore, while the practitioner-client relationship can be based on opposition, people with OCD described to me ways in which the relationship can be more collaborative. Sometimes the push for this came from therapists, especially those who provide CBT. Kelcie realized therapy is "a shared process" in her psychology classes at school and through her interactions with her therapists. CBT requires that patients take a more active role in their therapy because the goal is for the patient to eventually be their own coach.[38] The psychologist Grayson said, "We want clients to understand the treatment process as opposed to simply following our directions because we are the doctors. . . . We believe that helping the patient understand his or her OCD increases compliance."[39]

Sometimes it was the consumers who demanded a shared relationship, for example, when people with OCD brought information they had read to providers' offices. Information included details about OCD itself, as well as treatments they had read about. They used this information as a springboard from which to ask their provider questions and start a dialogue, or to advocate for their provider to let them try a new treatment, such as a particular medication. Interviewees were not always successful in their bid for a shared relationship, and sometimes this kept them from continuing with professional treatment:

> I have . . . mutual respect . . . with all my doctors, and if I don't then they are not my doctors. . . . Maybe I just read a study where they're trying this new drug for whatever. . . . I might want to go to my doctor and say, "Can you put me on this and let me try it?" . . . I need somebody who will work with me. I'm not saying they should do everything you want like Michael Jackson (Kirstyn)

> I dumped Dr. Medicine [a psychiatrist who said she should take medications]. I guess it hit me that no one is responsible for me getting the best treatment for my condition but me. . . . Since that time I found a new psych. . . . I didn't feel a connection. I felt rushed. I think my insurance pays for me to be seen for an hour but after twenty to thirty minutes she takes out her plan book and gives me a date and time. She just assumes that this is convenient. . . . I feel that I am just another patient to her but to me—I take this quest to get better very seriously. . . . I have been reading the OCD handbook [a self-help book] and have been learning about exposure response. I wrote down the things that scare me the most but am afraid to do the ERP without clinical assistance, but it is taking so long to find someone I feel comfortable with. Looking for the right psych is like looking for a house. . . . I feel like some reality show now, some girl's quest to find help for her OCD. I guess I would call the show "Top Nut." (Monica, self-diagnosed with OCD and diagnosed with depression)

One tricky issue when considering relationships with professionals for treating OCD is religion. Differentiating what constitutes OCD from what a religion expects in a person's thoughts/behaviors is not easy. Some religions may expect followers to engage in patterns of thinking or acting that a therapist might misperceive as cognitive distortions or problematic. Therefore, an additional characteristic some interviewees looked for in a healthcare professional was someone of the same religion, or at least someone who respected their religion. At other times, they sought outside advice from a religious authority. Kelcie discussed her views:

> I had a hard time working with [some therapists at the OCD program because they] . . . did not believe in God. . . . I am so thankful [to have the OCD specialist I do]. . . . I feel more at ease talking to her about my religious obsessions knowing that she believes in God. The reason why I feel this way is because when she says that, for example, doing the sign of the cross five times after I hear an ambulance is OCD and unnecessary, I believe her because she is Catholic and believes in the same practice as I do. . . . I have no problem seeing a therapist who does not believe in God to work on the majority of my OCD stuff . . . but for this particular aspect of my OCD it is important to me that I see someone who does.

Kelcie's argument is supported by research that suggests it can be important for a healthcare professional to understand religious ideas or collaborate with religious clergy/professionals to best ascertain if something a person is thinking and/or doing is best classified as OCD or part of their religion.[40] Kelcie exhibited sincere confusion over whether some of her religious ideas and activities were "symptoms" of OCD or accepted for her religion; she even considered whether having OCD was part of God's plan for her and that she deserved to suffer.

Flexibility of the Internet

The people I interviewed obviously gained knowledge through experience, but they took it upon themselves to seek out information using a variety of sources as well. They benefited in particular from the flexibility of online sources, with those who recall a time before the growth of the internet especially cognizant of this. When we communicated in 2004, Clara said OCD was not well known in India, making it hard to find information outside of the internet. In 2019, I chatted with the moderator of an online support group begun for people with OCD in Europe who commented on how the group attracted people from across the world: "For some, reaching out through a group like this is the only communication they may have about their situations, as a source of comfort and potentially help at times." The internet has helped turn illness into a public experience and no longer a private one.[41]

People with OCD used levels of interaction to their advantage to minimize the potential for stigmatizing responses. Adler and Adler explained how the internet has "modes" of use, which include viewing without active participation and active participation.[42] The internet allows people with OCD to take steps to avoid stigma and not have to "haul" themselves somewhere, to use one interviewee's phrasing, to get information. To provide a comparison, Monica likened having to look for information about OCD in a public bookstore to buying a condom: "I was embarrassed to ask where I could find the book and kept my head down when I purchased it."

The internet has provided people with a bird's-eye view into others' thoughts and conversations, enabling them to reap some of the benefits of being part of a community without being forced to actively contribute. For instance, Maeve told me, "The great thing about the internet thing is that you can be anonymous and you can get help. . . . It's a lot more embarrassing to be in person, and have people look you in the face and tell people what's going on with your life. It's so much easier to hide behind a computer screen." Kira was able to use the computer in her own home and avoid going to an in-person support group. She got inspiration from online materials by researching ways that hoarding behaviors impact people's lives, reasons why people hoard, and treatments. This helped her keep on track with the self-treatment program she created, which itself was based partly on online research. She lived in the United States, was over age sixty, was professionally diagnosed with depression, and diagnosed herself with OCD and some other issues.

Those who wanted to share but were hesitant could take steps to manage how much personal information they provided. Maeve explained: "For a long time I didn't even participate [in online discussions]. I just read what other people were writing. . . . Then I got brave enough to actually create an account and join. I didn't have to put my real name, put a picture up. . . . But I still felt like I was vulnerable. . . . When I actually joined I kind of got over that fear." She went on to make an online friend off that board. She never met anyone in person, but some interviewees eventually felt comfortable enough to do this.

Therefore, many interviewees took advantage of the flexibility of the internet. Some of them took an active role in online conversations and communities, while others lurked. However, the flexibility that was a boon for people with OCD, giving them a certain leeway in protecting how much they shared about their identities, was something they feared in the hands of others. For instance, some interviewees were concerned that people online could be pretending to be one thing but really be a stalker or out to harm them.

It does pay to be critical of the information that one consumes, as people with OCD have to wade through information that can be misleading or trivializing. For instance, perusing the interactive digital applications available on the topic of OCD in 2019, I found informational apps explicitly designed to inform and guide consumers in contemporary medicalized/psychologized ways of understanding obsessions and compulsions and treating them. However, I also found apps that seemingly reinforced stereotypes, despite their claims that they would help you recognize how aware you are of disorganization and help you relax. A few entertainment apps took the form of games in which players were supposed to detect inaccuracies and disorganization (for instance, in patterns) and correct them. In some cases I wondered if these entertainment apps could reinforce compulsive behavior. Most surprising to me was the app that allowed the user to pretend to be a character with OCD and try to engage in rituals as fast as possible.

Social Capital

Social capital is another element in the card game of life. Interviewees' attendance at support groups and their use of technology connecting them to others with OCD led to increases in their social capital or connections to others, as well as information. Bourdieu defined social capital as "the sum of the resources, actual or virtual, that accrue to an individual or a group by virtue of possessing a durable network of more or less institutionalized relationships of mutual acquaintance and recognition."[43] I even ran across a dating application specifically for people with mental disorders. The ties we have with others can put us under additional strain, but they also can provide us with resources such as emotional support, information, and advice.[44]

The internet has allowed people increased access to others with OCD beyond face-to-face support groups, building their social capital. When Missy discovered how many other people had issues similar to hers, she became more open about her own, at times even offering advice to others. She told me, "For a long time, I didn't have support, so it was very meaningful for me to be able to share experiences." Family members and OCD specialists could be found participating in some groups online. "That's the beauty of the internet, which has just changed society in general. You could never find these people [OCD specialists] before, no less write to them," said Kirstyn.

Online groups made up of people with OCD are sometimes moderated in ways to inhibit stigma and trivialization. For instance, some groups screened those who entered, such as one online group that asked people whether they had OCD or knew someone with OCD before allowing them to enter. Participants monitored groups as well as moderators, for instance, posting trigger warnings on topics that might aggravate another person's OCD.

Interviewees relayed many positive aspects about connecting with others online. However, some interviewees felt that one downside to developing social networks online was that the actual bonds formed with others online did not measure up to those formed in person. Individuals with OCD sometimes saw online communication as less intimate, real, captivating, active, or apt to hold the possibility for further development. Macvc told me about a site she visited where "there were so many people that it was almost overwhelming. There were so many issues, so many people talking about different things . . . somebody posted something and then there were like two hundred responses." In other situations, I have seen posts in which someone bared their soul and then received no responses.

Researchers have questioned whether people compare themselves to others online, leading to negative self-evaluations or depression. However, two authors of an article published in a cyberpsychology journal claimed that comparisons do not have to be negative.[45] I found this as well. People with OCD compared themselves with others in support groups and online groups, and this sometimes made them feel more "normal" (e.g., feeling that other people had problems similar to theirs). One woman confessed to me that hearing about how bad other people's problems are made hers seem much smaller in comparison. Clara argued it made her less depressed: "The Internet is a treasure house of information. It tells us about people like us and assures us that we too can live our life in a nice way. . . . It told me about other patients and how they struggled. . . . It gave me the hope to continue with my life."

To better assess the functions of online groups, I took a sample of about 150 posts on one forum and analyzed the content of people's responses to each other. A core component of the responses involved helping people feel that they were not alone. Posters commented on how they have faced similar situations, even monitoring each other's progress. Another important element of responses was acknowledging how hard it can be to fight OCD. People regularly commiserated about how OCD can feel devastating and unfair, and that improvement does not always happen quickly. They supported each other, for instance, congratulating others on hanging in there, going to therapy, staying strong, and showing OCD who is boss. Much advice was given regarding separating OCD from one's "self." People told each other how OCD can distort and manipulate. They encouraged each other to live their lives in spite of OCD, to have relationships, to enjoy activities, and be nice to themselves. They told each other that they deserve a nice life and that OCD can take a hike. Some conversations dealt with social issues, such as how to manage OCD and personal and work relationships. For example, a number of posters had relationship obsessions that made them question whether they had legitimate relationship doubts or if it was just their OCD, and these became important topics for discussion.

Many conversations focused on strategies for dealing with the OCD. As I noted in previous chapters, conversations in support groups can include nontraditional ways to deal with obsessions and compulsions or critiques of the healthcare system. However, conversations regularly medicalized/psychologized/psychiatrized the disorder. On this board, people shared articles written by OCD specialists as well as advice from their own therapists. This is similar to what can happen in groups for other illnesses or issues, where people socialize each other into medicalized views.[46]

In the previous chapter I discussed how friends and family of those with OCD sometimes struggled to find ways to help those with the disorder (such as providing emotional support) without doing things that healthcare professionals say might exacerbate the OCD (such as providing reassurance). Those with OCD engaged in the same struggle while attempting to help themselves and each other in support groups. For example, a person might ask for reassurance while saying they know they should not. I recently observed a person say that they were having a rough day and hoped the group could help them through, unless, they asked, are they not supposed to do that? While at times people provided each other with reassurance, in other cases they informed each other that this type of behavior was harmful, or that they were posting repeatedly and should seek professional help. More recently, some sites appear to have gotten stricter: upon opening NOCD, visitors are welcomed into a community of people with the disorder, where they are informed that this is a reassurance-free zone. Groups that follow these norms encourage people with OCD to police each other, reinforcing contemporary theories and professional viewpoints.

8

Life Goes On

I do not want my epitaph to read "He survived OCD." . . . I do not just want to endure OCD but do something productive with my talents for God and humanity. . . . I want to tell you the immense difficulty that an OCD person has in securing and holding a job. . . . When a person gets older there is the additional problem of not having a work history. . . . Of course I cannot apply for highly skilled jobs, but when I applied to more menial positions I am often thought strange. . . . They often ply me with questions like: "If you are not going to school why are you working here? Can't you find a better job?" . . . First I get castigated for not being humble enough to take any position (this usually happens when I ask for money) and then when I do take "anything" I get chastised. . . .

Now that I have my OCD under control I am trying to make up what I missed all of my life. . . . I am now applying to a prestigious MBA program. . . . Here is my dilemma: I have to show that I have the abilities . . . but I do have to cover for those unproductive years of my life dominated by OCD. . . . An admissions interview is no time to enlighten your interviewers about OCD. I usually say I have had depression (which is related, even biologically to OCD) and perhaps I add I have an anxiety disorder.
—Rodney

Rodney, who resided in the United States, provided me with vivid descriptions of the impacts of OCD on his life. Rodney first contacted me in 2004, when he was in his fifties. We converse periodically, where he updates me on events in his life. It was a few years after we first "met" online that he wrote about applying to an MBA program. Through his experiences such as this, I gained a better understanding of the impacts OCD can have on one's career and personal interactions over time. I am able to report that Rodney successfully applied and completed that graduate degree. He is currently retired and on disability for OCD, as he

told me that after age fifty-five it was easier to qualify for disability benefits; he also explained that an organization helped him with this process.
Rodney's words point to another stage in the "career" of having OCD.

This stage in the OCD trajectory involves learning to live with the
disorder in the longer term. The degree to which interviewees wrestled
with obsessions and compulsions was highly variable, as some struggled
for years while others felt they had conquered their OCD. Even for those
whose OCD was in remission, however, there could be a chronicity to
having had the disorder. This included managing the impacts of the past
and watching to make sure the OCD did not come back, putting people
in a liminal state between illness and wellness.[1] A few interviewees utilized words like "recovery," "relapse," and "remission." Rodney asked us
to consider the difficulties of going to school and securing a job when
one has gaps in their work history, itself a result of having debilitating
OCD. He regularly talked about his trials and tribulations when engaging with the "normal" world.

For instance, Rodney considered if, when, and how to tell others
about his OCD over the years, often worrying about being discovered. Eventually he told some of his friends in staggered groups. As he
recalled:

> I first told a few and waited some time, maybe several years to see if they
> would still accept me. When I was assured they did not reject me, I would
> proceed to enlighten another group. . . . [I don't worry about telling peo-
> ple] as much as I used to since I realized none of my former friends aban-
> doned me. [My advice to someone with OCD:] "You have more friends
> than you know. God loves you."

Akin to Rodney, the people I interviewed were worried about experiencing stigma, yet they did not encounter as much stigma as they had
feared. (Of course, some of this was because they were hiding!) What
people with OCD appeared to desire the most from others was understanding. Over time, people's perceptions of themselves could change as
well. Sometimes self-stigma declined, and the descriptions and metaphors they used to describe their interactions with OCD became less
adversarial. Janet, who spent much of her life blaming herself, wrote to
me, "But I am beginning to see that *the most important person you need*

to communicate with re: the disorder is yourself. This may sound strange but I think you can actually be failing to do that, to your detriment. *For years I was saying to myself things like, 'there's something wrong with you' and 'you can't cope like other people, don't take on any kind of pressure, you aren't up to it' and 'I despise you for being this way.' Now I need to find better things to say to myself."* People's attitudes toward themselves can have deep impacts beyond any impairment.

While Janet focused on her personal relationship to OCD, Rodney saw OCD in more political terms:[2]

> As an OCD person the word "lazy" [is akin to a racial slur]. . . . This town is known for its progressive, liberal, and tolerant views for certain groups, yet it can be very bigoted against people like me. . . . The dichotomy I am speaking of is . . . groups with political lobbies versus those who are unconnected. Political groups can include immigrants, workers' rights, gender, sexual orientation, and groups for the environment—even animals (as in animal rights) get more attention than OCDers. . . . I always felt ashamed to ask for help—very ashamed. But when I see all the "Safe Zones" stickers—the ones that offer safe places for gay, lesbian, and transgender people to feel at home—I get so angry that I have no one to go to. . . . I have always wanted to be self-sufficient but after fifty years I just have to throw in the towel, swallow my pride, and just cry out "Could I have at least some assistance?" . . . I'm not asking for reparations, special recognitions, affirmative action for OCDers, an openly acknowledged OCD person in some high position on campus, an "OCD Studies" department, [or] sensitivity training. . . . Why can't I have a safe zone to talk about OCD? I can't even go to people who are psychologists or psychiatrists or social workers. I don't even have a safe zone there. . . . There's political correctness in this town, but it's open season for OCD.

Although those I interviewed, like Rodney, certainly sought to improve society's knowledge of OCD, and I spoke to many people about desires to reduce stigma and trivialization, they were not united in other ways on how they felt people with OCD should ideally be treated or how to improve the lives of those with the disorder. Rodney viewed himself as part of a larger group of people with OCD who are disadvantaged in society. He told me how there "should be an effort to inform the public of the unique sufferings that OCDers endure." However, other interviewees exhibited some hesitancy in identifying too closely with the OCD label. Even Rodney did not advocate that "OCDers organize their own political lobby," but he claimed a need for greater social justice for individuals, saying, "I would rather that society focus on helping individuals as individuals instead of only helping those disadvantaged who belong to well-recognized and well-publicized groups." One reason for this was because Rodney felt many people with OCD hide their thoughts/behaviors and experience internalized guilt for having OCD, and therefore would not avail themselves of public services.

In this chapter, I explore the dynamics of this stage of learning to live with OCD, from stigma and social interactions, to interviewees' views on how to move forward into the future. The way in which interviewees commonly medicalized/psychologized the disorder and viewed it as a problem they needed to handle set them apart from the disability rights movement. However, some interviewees provided glimmers of a path forward based on being more flexible and tolerant of individuals' diverse problems in contemporary society.

Chronicity and Identity

Chronicity was an important theme in the interviews, and one way it manifested was through people's discussion of vigilance. Justine, who felt she had tackled her obsessions and compulsions, told me that she was now in control but nonetheless watched out in case the OCD tried to reemerge. Kirstyn explained that she could go a year without thinking about OCD, but "then one morning I can wake up and be doing the dishes and I look down and I'm doing a ritual with the plates. . . . Then I stop and I think 'OK, what's stressful in my life right now that is making me do this?' . . . That's what OCD likes to do, creep right back in . . . so you have to fight it. You have to use your skills that you learned."

In contemporary society, we are often on the lookout; the physical body could be at risk without us being aware of it, for instance, with cancer or heart disease.[3] The same is true of the mind and emotions. Certain symptoms might go away or decrease but could potentially recur or increase. Other symptoms might appear in their place. Maeve told me that the obsessions she had in the past were different. "I go through one and I conquer it and I'm like 'Yes! That was the worst thing ever and now I'm done with it.' . . . But then [sort of laughs] something else pops up like out of nowhere." Sarah told me that she had a successful life, but "it is difficult for me to plan a future as I don't know how I'll be emotionally."

People's sense of the disorder came into being over time, and the ways that they envisioned their future were multiple. Some people had hope the OCD would go away. Others felt they had conquered their OCD. Then there were those who felt as if OCD (or treating it with something like medications) would be a chronic part of their life and who worked to adjust to this. As people became more accepting of the OCD as a part of their lives, I saw shifts in how some interviewees described their identities and the metaphors they used to depict the disorder. In chapter 2, I described how one common way people referred to their OCD was as a negative outside force. Contrast this to how Missy began to perceive OCD:

> I think that was the biggest turning point for me, was accepting that it was a part of who I am and I'm just going to have to learn ways to deal with it. Because I spent twenty years trying to cure it. And make it go away. Or take a bunch of medications just to block it out. It doesn't work long term. . . . As I've gotten older, I've given myself a little bit more slack. . . . I feel like once I accepted that . . . I moved so much more quickly down the chain of being able to understand, to analyze, react, and deal with these problems than before. . . . I'm not battling my thoughts and compulsions as much. Does that make sense?

Some interviewees found less antagonistic ways to view OCD, such as viewing it as a part of themselves or as a friend. Two sentiments associated with this shift were a greater acceptance of oneself and caring less about the thoughts and perceptions of others. Talia's depiction of her OCD as a stuffed animal stuck with me after our interview. As she had told me, "Sometimes when I meet somebody . . . it's so much a part of who I am and stuff that I say 'Oh and I told you I have OCD, right?' . . . It's like a little stuffed bear [that I drag along]. It's like, 'Oh, what, you didn't see my stuffed bear?'"

Figure 8.1. *Ten Years Ago-Now* by Hannah Hillam

Destin came to have a "symbiotic relationship" with the OCD, and Bella came to view her OCD as a friend. She described realizing OCD was a defense mechanism her body had put in place to survive some abusive situations: "Rather than see it as an enemy, I see it as a friend. I see it as a condition. I thank my body—whatever it took at the time to help me survive, whatever it did to my brain chemistry. I'm sorry my body had to do all that."

Chance stopped perceiving his OCD as a problem when the people around him became more supportive. As a child, he grew up with an abusive relative who punished him physically for things she felt were silly or wrong. As an adult, he said: "It doesn't affect my life as much and

I think that's only because of my situation, because of the fact that I have somebody else [a wife] who understands it who lives with it. I'm not an outcast to my kids because they have the same thing."

Another aspect of chronicity centered on children. Those considering having children sometimes raised questions about whether they might pass the disorder down to them. Leanne lived in the United States, was in her twenties, and had been diagnosed with OCD, depression, and premenstrual dysphoric disorder. She told me:

> [Passing the OCD down] was definitely a concern, and something my husband and I talked about extensively with each other and my doctors. . . . First, I was concerned that I might have to stop my meds while pregnant. If that was going to be the case, then I knew it wouldn't be a good idea, and we could pretty much squash the kid talks. Secondly, we were concerned she might inherit it. My doctors seemed to think that even though there is a chance, that at least I'd be able to recognize the symptoms early and get her the help she might need. . . . [My husband] mostly wanted to make sure the baby was safe during pregnancy with my medications. . . . I think knowing that I can recognize symptoms and get her help if, God forbid, she needs it, makes him feel better. . . . I still hope and pray every day that she's OCD free.

Families with children might watch for signs of the disorder, their vigilance extending beyond themselves. Monty recounted a story about something that happened when his son was three or four years old. His son told him, "Dad I'm scared of the thunder." Monty was distressed because his own OCD had started with him being afraid of thunderstorms. Monty told his wife, "Oh my God, he's got OCD." He ended up telling his son to stand up to the bully of thunderstorms and showed him that there was nothing to be afraid of. Monty viewed the situation with a sense of humor as he realized that he was helping his son in ways he had not been able to do for himself. I spoke to one woman who was concerned children might learn OCD behaviors from watching her, but research does not suggest that OCD is primarily learned from parents in that way.[4]

Although there was some chronicity to having OCD, this did not necessitate defeat or being mired in despair. Time, knowledge, coping, and treatments earned many people a sense that they had more control over their OCD, or they had hope for such in the future. Various people I interviewed taught me the importance of hard work and hope. Kirstyn wanted people to know that "you can live life in recovery from OCD. . . . You can live a totally normal life."

Impacts on Functioning

I know that more than anything, some people with OCD want the public to realize how the disorder can affect their lives in fundamental ways. It is difficult to depict the impact of OCD on people's functioning across the life course because it varied so much. The lives of people with OCD looked very different because each person had their particular obsessions and compulsions, and navigated different institutions and social networks. Some people's obsessions/compulsions were viewed as beneficial at work, such as when coworkers appreciated meticulousness and checking, while in other cases they led them to being mocked. Chance provided one example: "I had one boss in the past who actually liked it. I worked as an [auto] technician for several years. . . . The reason I did so well at it was everything had to be perfect. . . . You could rest assured that if I was working on your vehicle that there was no such thing as good enough." In school settings, some people received accommodations, while others felt ostracized.

The end result was that I interviewed people who managed stressful and skilled jobs, such as a pediatric nurse, doctor, and research scientist. I also talked to people who struggled to support themselves financially and relied on assistance from others (including the government). One article indicated that "approximately 25% of OCD adult patients will still be living with their parents."[5] Rodney talked about OCD-produced poverty.

Remember that regardless of how successful people with OCD appeared on the outside, this could hide the hurdles they overcame. Sarah said, "It has been a very hard struggle to get this far in life, but I now have my own home, a job in cancer research, and a dog! However, my life is much harder and stressful than it appears to other people." Inner worlds were easier to hide at work than within intimate relationships. People can have obsessions and compulsions that relate to intimacy, or they may ask for reassurance regularly, as described in earlier chapters. Although OCD can be hard on relationships, people with the disorder can, and many do, have typical family lives with marriages and children. People with the disorder have a relatively low divorce rate, and communication within families in which someone has the disorder is not necessarily worse.[6]

Yet, there were a few people in my study who curtailed romantic liaisons, and extant research has suggested that people with OCD, especially men, have higher rates of celibacy and lower rates of marriage than the general population.[7] Mick explained how this could occur:

> I am forty-five years old. I never married. Never dated. Never had sexual intercourse, if you'll pardon its mention; and never had a passionate kiss. I have been attracted to women; there was even a long phase in my life during which I felt that romance and relationship were worthy, indeed imperative, goals. But whenever I came close, I found some way to destroy the very possibility. . . . When I imagine myself in that kind of a relationship, it just feels wrong, kind of like I don't belong there or do not deserve it. . . . It is perennially, occasionally easy for me to lament my lack of romance and blame circumstances or decisions I've made. "If I had only said 'yes' to [names a woman] when she'd asked me to lunch" or "if it would not mean abandoning my mother." . . . That is really all bullshit. . . . I just don't function reliably. I am self-employed because I dislike working for anyone else; but I don't earn enough to live independently, much less support a family. I keep piles of useless junk because it hurts me to part with it; but that does not mean I want to find a way to do so. . . . The very thought of romance makes my OCD worse; because even though I need some interaction with people, I find it much harder to do many things when I'm not alone; and because I'm smart enough to know there are not nearly enough compensatory mechanisms in place to render any attempt worthwhile.

People with OCD were not oblivious to the effect their disorder might have on others, and their expectations of themselves and what they felt they deserved added to the complexity of the impact of OCD on their lives. Psychologists have noted that people with OCD can have obsessions in areas where they lack confidence; have fears about their self and who they might become; experience obsessive guilt; and feel an inflated sense of responsibility.[8] I believe this leads people with OCD to face extra hurdles in interpersonal relationships. Mick was clearly intelligent, had earned a graduate degree, and had good friends. However, Mick was not the only person I interviewed who hesitated to get close to people, as they did not want to make others' lives difficult. On a more positive note, some interviewees shared with me that they became sensitized to the needs of others.

Dance of Hiding and Revealing

The impacts of OCD on interviewees' lives were affected by their decisions to hide their obsessions and compulsions or not, and how successful they were in these endeavors. People with mental disorders and chronic illnesses struggle with how and whether to tell others about their diagnoses and personal experiences, but they are not the only ones. We can imagine people with largely hidden problems at one end of a spectrum, and at the other end are those whose issues are visible on all occasions.[9] Honestly, everyone likely has some partly hidden challenge. If we take the sociologist Goffman's words to heart, life is similar to a stage performance. As we move through life, people are observing what we are doing and saying and making inferences. This gives them a sense of who we are. For our part, we try to engage in impression management. When we are at work with colleagues, when we are at home with family, when we are at school with professors, we can try to manage how people view us. This includes managing our emotions in interactions with others.[10] Impression management is not only about getting people to view us in a particular way but is often about looking as if one is performing a task well.[11] We commonly work in cooperation with others to present a certain image of an organization or workplace, or some larger group or entity.[12] It would be nice if there were a set of simple rules for people with relatively less visible mental disorders regarding if, when, and how to disclose such. A group of researchers published an article in which they developed and initially tested a decision aid for mental health service users to help them with disclosure decisions in the workplace.[13] However, social life can be extraordinarily complex. Communication studies professor Catherine Francis Brooks has OCD; she wrote that her public performance was so "believable that before my therapy and for a period during my treatment, I doubted that I had OCD."[14]

When I first tried to craft a model outlining interviewees' reasons for telling others about their OCD versus hiding, I had trouble drawing a strict line between behaviors that constituted "concealing" versus "disclosing." For instance, people who engaged in OCD rituals in front of others sometimes were attempting to hide that it was OCD, whereas others felt they were disclosing. Sometimes interviewees told me they verbally revealed they had OCD to others in an effort to disclose, while others used it as subterfuge for their real thoughts, feelings, and behaviors.

Therefore, I decided to consider the overall impression people with OCD were trying to give others in particular contexts. From this vantage point, I perceived a typology of ways in which people with OCD interact with others. First, *concealing* involves people with OCD giving off an impression of themselves as something other than a person with OCD or a mental disorder, reinforcing a gap between their inner and outer worlds. One way in which interviewees did so was by shaping what they said and did publicly to hide their obsessions/compulsions— that is, keeping thoughts to themselves and doing rituals when others were not around. For those who hoard, this might mean keeping visitors from their homes. This helped people continue to maintain whatever impression they were already aiming for at work, at home, and in other contexts.

Stigmatizing attributes can be obvious as well as hidden; for this reason, Goffman referred to people as being "discredited" or "discreditable."[15] Having OCD places people somewhere in the middle, as people with OCD are not universally able to remove their OCD-related thoughts and behaviors from the view of others. Nor do they always desire to hide. However, at times these people still wanted to avoid giving the impression they had OCD or were doing anything out of the ordinary for a context, creating a second type of interactional strategy: *hiding in plain sight*. The people I interviewed employed a variety of tactics to achieve this. For instance, Maeve found that at work people noticed her panicking and obsessing, but she played it off as if she were really upset about something. As another example, Nellie had obsessions related to babies and contamination, and she sometimes tried to avoid being near them. When eating out with friends, if they were seated in a booth next to a baby, she might get her friends to move by saying, "Oh, well, this table's dirty," or "The lighting's better, let's go move over here." They used these techniques to give their behaviors a meaning befitting the context rather than OCD. Importantly, as shown in Nellie's example, sometimes other people were included in avoidance/rituals even while interviewees were hiding their disorder. When people noticed his behaviors, Chris tried to gloss things over with a joke.

A third type of interaction occurred when interviewees engaged in or talked about OCD-related behaviors in front of others without physically concealing them or trying to hide them behind alternative explanations. Thoughts/behaviors could appear outside of the "social norms," but interviewees did not refer to them as OCD. For example, Jesse described what his interactions were like with girlfriends before he knew he had the disorder: "It was simply obvious to them that I spent a lot of time distressed over their past relationships and my behavior wasn't normal. I don't think they understood it, but they knew something was wrong and clearly had never encountered this with other boyfriends." In this example, he did not give off the impression that he had OCD, but neither were his behaviors construed as "normal." Jesse's approach was affected by his lack of knowledge of the disorder. However, Kira, who diagnosed herself with OCD, sought social support by telling friends about her struggles but purposefully did not use the term "OCD." She did this to reduce stigma, or negative judgments she assumed people held about the disorder. People with OCD, as well as observers, shaped the meanings given to thoughts/behaviors. For instance, it was observers who gave meaning to the ritual Joanie did when food packages got stuck in vending machines; this included hitting the machine a certain number of times. People noticed, but they did not label her as having a mental disorder. They just saw her as physically aggressive.

Next were interactions where interviewees specifically wanted to (or were willing to) give off the impression they had OCD: *revealing*. They could do this piecemeal, for instance, telling certain people that they had OCD but providing little detail or only talking about particular obsessions. Winona cautioned me with the advice "you don't put all your eggs in one basket," so she did not let any one person know too much. "My friend in Chicago knows different stuff than my husband knows, and

I don't like to keep it all in one place. . . . I think it's just too much crazy for me to put out on any one person."[16]

Disclosure decisions are part of all stages of the OCD career but can vary by stage. At the start of the career, people did not necessarily associate the thoughts/behaviors with the label OCD. Further, just as some people became more accepting of themselves and having the disorder, a number of people I interviewed became more open about their OCD over time.[17] Bella began to see mental illness from a totally different angle and became more open about its impact on her life. She told me that she could "sort of understand gay people who come out. It's a huge relief." Destin felt that there was a connection between how you perceive yourself and how others view you: "I feel like I can be myself now which also means that I'm not as willing to hide. . . . If you accept yourself, it follows most of the time, that other people will accept you as well."

When being most open, interviewees confided to others that they had OCD and provided confidants with general information about the disorder.[18] They discussed their own symptoms, talked about how it affected them, related how it impacted their lives, did not hide their OCD-related behaviors, and sometimes asked for help in dealing with the disorder. However, that does not mean those in whom they confided necessarily "got it." We take much for granted in everyday interaction. Friends may not explicitly tell you the meaning of every one of their actions. You nonetheless give meaning to their actions, and social life marches on.[19] In other words, OCD-related thoughts and behaviors do not always jump up and scream, "Hi, this is OCD!" Therefore, sometimes even when a person with OCD has divulged to others that they have the disorder, people can misinterpret the thoughts/behaviors as something else entirely or not even notice them. On the flip side, interviewees' non-OCD thoughts/behaviors sometimes got mistakenly labeled as such, which could be frustrating.[20] For example, Miles told me about an instance where he was going through a project for work. The file was neat and organized, and his girlfriend asked if this was the result of his OCD. He told me, "I just think I'm organized."

One way in which interviewees addressed the potential for misunderstanding was by using the label of OCD more often or explaining details about their OCD. For instance, Nellie said she tells her best friend, "I'm having an OCD moment," or an "OCD problem," when needed.

In her conversations with people with chronic illnesses, Charmaz learned about some benefits to organized strategic announcing. She argued that while illness can take power and control away from people, strategic announcing is one way for people to gain some measure of control. This is especially useful for people with invisible illnesses.[21] However, not everyone I interviewed wanted to keep announcing. Delia told me that her need to have things clean, and activities done in certain ways within her house, led to arguments. I asked Delia if she thought her husband saw her behaviors, and thereby their arguments, as tied to her OCD. Her response was, "He's not thinking about the disorder. . . . [I don't try to explain] because he knows that's how I am. . . . I've never really thought about sitting down and . . . talk[ing] like 'Baby, I'm sorry. Can you try to help me with this?' I look at it like he's been married to me twenty years. He knows I'm this way. Get over it."

Finally, I want to point out that people with OCD at times leveraged the way the disorder is trivialized and stereotyped by the public, exploiting this to their own advantage.[22] Leanne explained:[23]

OCD has become more popular to talk about in the media, so people *think* they know what it is, and I usually just let them think whatever. Like I said, it's tiring to tell people what it really means, and that it's more than what they think it is. . . . I really have never told anyone *everything*, not in any great detail anyway . . . because the thoughts were so bad. I thought they might think I was crazy or perverted or something. I wind up being plagued by a lot of incestuous thoughts, and thoughts of being raped, as well as other people having sex. Most people would be horrified to know that, and when they think it's something you can control, obviously they think you should be on some kind of list in the neighborhood. . . . A lot of times, too, the thoughts (even nonsexual) are hard to explain to people because they are just flashes in your head. . . . A while back I would tell people how I felt without mentioning OCD per se. They usually reacted badly then. They'd want to argue with me, and make me see things their way. Some people got so mad they stopped talking to me almost altogether. Now I try to at least mention OCD to people when I'm discussing my views, even if they don't understand it.

Leanne believed people had stereotypical understandings about the disorder, and she did not bother to correct them. Other people took a similar approach, leading to a subtype of revealing interactions that I call *stereotypical revealing*, as they are revealing they have OCD but relying on people's relatively innocuous stereotypes of OCD.

For instance, Chance told people he had OCD but said it in a joking manner so they would not treat it seriously. Once he perceived himself as having OCD, he said he was more attentive to his actions and attempted to hide them. When others noticed them, he would make a joke. Chance explained that his personality was to make jokes. If he did something silly (and unrelated to OCD), he might say something like, "God, I need to get off this crack." Therefore, when his OCD was noticed by others, he might say, "Oh, there's my OCD kicking in again," and laugh about it. The result was that people kind of brushed it off, he said, and he found a way to hide it. Note that there were times people preferred to label themselves with some other type of issue such as anxiety or depression. They gave different reasons for this, including thinking OCD might be more stigmatizing or less understandable to people.

Rodney wanted people to know that those with OCD can get into awkward situations as a result of the disorder. Goffman noted that the impressions we are trying to sustain can be fragile and fall apart.[24] At times Rodney desired to hide his compulsions but was unable to give off a favorable impression. If people said something negative toward him or teased him at school when he was younger, he worried that this would act as a curse and come true. He therefore tried to get them to take their words back or make a positive statement (that he felt counteracted the negative) a particular number of times. Rodney tried to work it into the conversation so they would not pick up on any compulsive/ritualistic aspects, but he sometimes ended up vexing people and increasing their hostility. He told me, "I do not have time to tell you all the situations where I appeared to have some negative personality characteristic that was really the result of having to cover up some OCD ritual." He pondered what authority figures such as the police might think if he admitted why he did things such as checking a library shelf over and over—that is, because he believed that if a book he read was not lined up perfectly, the knowledge would disappear from his brain.

He feared they would think he was lying to cover up criminal behaviors such as stealing from the library.

The Struggle for Acceptance

The philosopher Axel Honneth talked about the "struggle for recognition" as the cornerstone of conflict. I asked interviewees how they would like to be treated if they lived in a perfect world. What people with OCD often wanted from others was their acceptance, their willingness to listen, their understanding, and sometimes their help. As Clara told me:

> [People with OCD need] words of courage. They definitely do not want to yield to OCD but still they are not able to come out of it. It's because they believe in their OCD. They need lots of love while suffering which mostly they don't get. This leads them to become very sad and depressed. They also need a little criticism from time to time. It should be perceived by others with respect. Respect is what declines when a person gets a mental illness. They should understand the needs of mentally ill people and should not ridicule them behind their backs.

As a whole, the people I interviewed had significant fears regarding stigma. Research tells us that just the anticipation of stigma can have negative effects on people's health.[25] In their everyday lives, while they encountered some instances of stigma, the degree of stigma interviewees anticipated did not come to pass in reality. By and large, those with whom I communicated were able to find core people in their lives, or connect with people online, who accepted what they told them about their obsessions and compulsions without judgment, tried to understand their OCD, or provided some social support. Compared with those with other chronic mental disorders, people with OCD largely do not need regular supervision and help with basic self-care activities like bathing.[26] Therefore, some common responses that interviewees received from others were listening to them, attempting to understand them, asking questions and being curious, and providing support.

Leanne said, "[My husband] has come to understand more. I've opened up more about it and explained things better, too. He will

LIFE GOES ON | 179

never 'get it' all, but he's come a long way in the six years we've been to-gether. . . . [For example, one troublesome] 'obsession' did resolve some thanks to my supportive husband. If he wasn't someone I could com-pletely trust, and someone who was so understanding to a fault, I don't think it would have improved as much as it has."

Laveda told me about how her husband tried to understand and help as they began dating:

> My husband and I started dating in high school. On our first date we were walking to my house and [this person walked up that I felt was contami-nated]. I made up an excuse to have to turn around, but it seemed weird and I did tell him I had OCD at that time. A couple weeks later some sce-nario happened and he told me he had something to help me with it. . . . I went to his house and he had a grapefruit in water and told me that would help with the germs. A valiant effort, but of course it did not work with OCD, but probably helped me fall in love with him.

Monty conveyed that while he still stigmatizes himself, those around him have told him his disorder is no big deal. "I still to this day feel that I'm broken. . . . I've told others. They're like 'What's the big deal?' . . . because people have always said, 'OK, you have OCD, what's the problem?'"

Nellie had a supportive mother and friends. She said, "I tell my friends straight up I'm having an OCD moment . . . and pretty much all of them just go, 'Oh OK is there anything we can do?' and you know most of the time I don't really have anything they can do." She described her mom as being so supportive that she could almost understand what it feels like to have the disorder. When Nellie went to therapy, her mom would be in the waiting room, and often they would get in the car afterward and discuss what the therapist said. Her mom and another therapist even tried to start an adult OCD support group.

Although family members, coworkers, friends, and loved ones of those with OCD may not always understand everything there is to know about the disorder, they could still provide support, humor, and love. Those who were supportive did such things as listen to those with OCD, help find information and therapists, pay for treatment, coach, challenge negative thoughts (e.g., that people with OCD are crazy or perverted), provide a shoulder to cry on, or contribute a sense of humor. Just as confidants could struggle with how much to accommodate the OCD, for their part, the people I interviewed also struggled with how much they hoped someone close to them would do things like reassure them and adjust to their rituals versus challenge them. Obviously, they did not want to lose friends because they took too long getting ready to go out. But they appreciated people who were supportive of treatment as well. Winona told me: "I don't think I want anyone to respond in any way because I think the activity itself is a giant catch-22, like of course I want all my friends to . . . do everything that I want them to do to make me comfortable. But I also know that it kind of exacerbates the problem because they're all enabling me."

What types of negative reactions or stigma did people with obsessions and compulsions face? Sometimes others responded by hoping the person with OCD could just stop or overcome the OCD. Poor responses included people who called them names, disappeared from their lives, denied the disorder and trivialized their experiences, did not try to understand what they were going through, or mocked them. In a few instances, interviewees were perceived as making up their OCD or using it to get out of things. Destin told me how his father "is a very two dimensional kind of guy when it comes to certain things so for him . . . he's not a big talker but this is basically what he says, he implies, 'Why can't you control this? Why are you doing this? Why do you need me to help you out and do this, blah blah blah.'"

Maeve described her family's emotional abuse:

> When I was younger my mom would take my sisters shopping while I was at counseling and buy them clothes and all kinds of stuff and she said that . . . I didn't deserve any of the other stuff that my sisters were getting because I was basically being a burden on them by making them pay for counseling. . . . She did call me crazy a lot after I did go talk to a psychologist. She was very emotionally abusive to me and my sisters at that time in our lives . . . which may have actually led to, or increased the severity of, my OCD.

Family members could get frustrated or angry, putting a strain on relationships.[27] In two cases, interviewees reported that family members physically abused them while they were children because of OCD-related

behaviors. Even supportive people could find it difficult to be supportive all the time. Laveda, who spent time describing her caring husband
to me, has feared he might leave her. One interviewee and his current
wife both had been diagnosed with OCD. He said, "While we understand
each other's 'issues,' it places strains on our relationship that others do not
experience." He said that previously, "I lost a thirty-year marriage and I
believe that a good deal of the divorce was due to my OCD."

Importantly, Kirstyn indicated family members could express frustration in a way that did not hurt the person with OCD. She referred to her
husband as the most "patient and kind" man she knew. When her OCD
got bad and she had a breakdown, her husband and daughter stepped up
to take care of the family. As Kirstyn told me:

> They were doing all the work and then he [my husband] would come in
> my room and he would try to get me to come out sit with them and watch
> one television show you know just to get me out of the bedroom and with
> them. But I would always say no because there were too many rituals that
> could take me an hour just to get out there doing all the rituals on the
> way, and then another hour to get back so it wasn't worth it. But he would
> never give up trying. And of course he didn't know what to say or what
> to do. . . . Well one night he came in and he sat down and said the same
> thing he always did. And this time I didn't even respond at all. And he
> got up and he walked out into the hall. And he took his fist and he put it
> through the wall and he said "I hate your OCD" which is really the kind-
> est thing he could have ever said because he didn't say he hated me. He
> said he hated my OCD, and most people can't separate them.

Discrimination was harder to pinpoint, for instance, because an employer was unlikely to come out and say, "I am firing you because of
your OCD." A few people felt their OCD contributed to unfair or problematic treatment at school, work, church, and other organizations. For
example, one woman said that the daycare where she worked fired her
because she had entered a psychiatric ward of a hospital in the past. Nellie told me about her struggles to receive accommodations in school:

> I was really, really into scrupulosity and getting things perfect. And one of
> my things was writing letters perfectly . . . so I would literally . . . write the

word and if the letter wasn't perfect, I'd erase the whole word and then try again and then erase the whole word. I did that so much I would have rips in my paper, and I had one of those moments. My teacher interrupted me. . . . She was like, "Nellie you need to turn this in right now." . . . Part of my OCD is that I'm a perfectionist so I take a little bit more time and still to this day I have accommodations in college for extra time and a distraction-reduced environment just because with my OCD I get really overwhelmed. . . . I said hold on just a second . . . and she kept bugging me about it so finally I said, "Just leave me alone." She was like, "I'll give you two minutes," so she came back after the two minutes and I just completely blew up in her face. "I was like, you don't get it. You don't get how I'm feeling and I can't get this into you. It's not perfect." And she just flipped out, she was, "How dare you talk to me that way. You need to hand in your test. You know I should really be giving you an F for this." . . . By the time I reached sixth grade they were the kind of school who said we accept everybody, you know everybody who was unique and different, but . . . they didn't really care about my OCD or how it affected my learning. And so my mom . . . [switched my school]. It ended up being a great thing because I met my best friend and I got the accommodations that I needed and we didn't have to pay thousands of dollars for a private school that wouldn't accommodate me.

In one study of young people with OCD, most of the participants perceived schools as lacking knowledge of OCD, regularly misinterpreting their actions as misbehavior.[28] This highlights the importance of institutions in understanding and supporting those with mental health concerns such as OCD. A repeated issue for people was access to quality healthcare, including having health insurance that treated mental disorders on a par with physical problems.

Group Identification and Power

Responses such as Nellie's made me curious about the degree to which interviewees felt aligned with other people with the disorder. I began to wonder if people with OCD ever perceived themselves as being part of a minority group, especially after considering Rodney's words at the beginning of this chapter. (Note that for sociologists like me, minority groups need not be small in number but instead lack power and resources.) This is important because stigma relates to issues of power, civil liberties, and human rights but has not always been linked to them in research.[29] Sarah told me that as a society we had managed to address "subjects from sexual orientation to racism and religion," but "mental illness appears to be the last taboo in society." I asked questions about social support, stigma, and online connections in my initial interviews; after topics related to power and inequality manifested in various ways in my interviews, I began to ask more questions about these topics explicitly.

There were definitely times when interviewees connected with others who had OCD and saw themselves as part of a group of "people with OCD" (or people with mental disorders). In other chapters I discussed how people sought out and interacted with others who had OCD online, in support groups, and at conferences, for instance. If you have the disorder, others with OCD might be the only people who can truly understand what you are going through, according to Janet.

There were ways in which the people I interviewed were part of advocacy for those with OCD. They were interested in changing society in order to minimize stigma and trivialization, increasing the public's understanding of OCD, furthering social support resources for those with OCD, and improving access to treatment. For instance, Aiten built a website for a popular OCD organization and started setting up an in-person support group. As another example, Martin went into the field of mental health and started building a practice around OCD. Martin and Karla even attempted to challenge what they felt were negligent and misguided professionals in their efforts to advocate for others with mental disorders. Some interviewees wanted to facilitate knowledge of OCD to improve treatment, and they (and their family members) participated in research studies. Notably, they all shared their stories with me and contributed to society's knowledge of what OCD is really like. One motivation they gave for doing this was to help others who might be going through similar experiences. It seems the most prominent way in which the people I interviewed sought to improve the lives of those with OCD and to challenge stereotypes and stigma was through the dissemination of information.

Yet, developing a group identity, or a sense of themselves as part of a larger group of people with OCD, met with a few impediments. Meeting and forming connections with others with OCD presented difficulties because these people are not generally around the corner wearing an obvious sign. Even if you connect with others with OCD online or in person, they may not have the same type of OCD, said Jeff, who explained, "Everybody's OCD symptoms are a little different, and change over time. . . . So it can be like being a minority of one. That's extra isolating because there is no 'Chinatown' or 'Little Italy' or anything like that where you could go and be with other people 'like you.'"

Looking at the interviews as a whole, there were ways in which people explicitly hesitated and rebelled against such a group identity. OCD is a potentially stigmatizing condition, and embracing this identity could mean taking on this stigma. Jeff felt that taking on this identity might mean one is giving up on getting better. He elaborated, "But one disadvantage of thinking of OCD as part of your identity—as I guess I do sometimes—is that it seems to involve admitting that you'll never get better. . . . [This is different from some other discriminated groups.] It wouldn't sound right if you heard an African American say, 'Well, I am still kind of Black but I'm trying to get whiter.'" Further, because OCD is associated with ego-dystonic symptoms, or symptoms people do not desire, Jeff argued this can isolate people rather than facilitate community building.

Rodney said that he didn't want to "revel in my identity of a person with a disability. It is not my goal to wallow in people's sympathy—I am not looking to be a poster child for OCD, but I would like to have close relationships, do something useful with my life, contribute something to the world, and live with self-respect and dignity." The pride and purpose in Rodney's retort are worth noting. One barrier to people with obsessions and compulsions forming a social movement advocating for changes in the name of OCD was what I perceive as their sense of responsibility. This included the way in which some people expressed a philosophy where they held themselves accountable for getting better, or where they felt they had to have their obsessions and compulsions under control before allowing themselves to engage in particular activities (such as starting a romantic relationship). "It's *my* problem," Meghan reiterated. Janet told me that "no one else can really help you overcome them [rituals]. You have to do that yourself." Patrick said that people "who feel sorry for themselves don't recognize an important part of their life, which is that they are unique, special even." Kelcie said she "never" compares having OCD to being in a minority group. "I believe that if you treat mental illness as a minority group then you are also giving mentally ill people the right to feel victimized" (although she admitted that she might feel otherwise if she had a different mental disorder). Yet, Kelcie herself needed extra assistance at times, such as when she took a semester off from college to get treatment for OCD. I wonder if perhaps one reason people with OCD view the disorder this way is due to how they can experience feelings of obsessive guilt.[30] Based on what a couple of interviewees said, their views on this topic may also be related to the way in which people with OCD learn how accommodations by family and friends can be detrimental to their recovery.

Therefore, Destin, like some of the others quoted earlier, vacillated between identifying with and distancing himself from an OCD-based identity. He thoughtfully depicted the tension a person can face over feeling a need to acknowledge that one has OCD but not wanting to identify with the label:

> One of my psychiatrists . . . told me pretty early on that maybe I'll just "grow out of it [having OCD]." And so I always kept that desire in my mind and that reinforced my urge to want to try to push it to the side of my thoughts of who I was. I didn't try to identify with it. But now it's changed [and I'm not bothered by talking about the OCD like I was] because I have identified with it. I understand that it's going to be a part of my life. . . . And just like feminism, it's just like any kind of identity movement. You kind of want to come out and say, "Yeah that's me and I'm not ashamed of it. This is who I am." . . . But I don't. To me, the label—because I don't have to deal with OCD severely . . . it's different. And I don't mind the perfectionism. So I tend to see a lot of the good qualities, I *like* to see a lot of the good qualities in OCD. Even though it negatively affects me in a number of ways and really disrupts my life more than I would like. . . .
>
> It's part of who I am, as my identity, if you will. . . . [But] don't try to label me with it. . . . I'm me. I'm not my OCD. I would just prefer to think of myself as a quirky individual who is obsessed about certain things and has some compulsions. . . . I want to fight with all of who I am the idea that I can be nothing but this, and that I should be labeled with for the rest of my life. I don't want to be one of these people who go out and

protest for their legal rights as someone with this or that disorder. . . . I'm a very individualistic kind of person and I believe in everyone taking personal responsibility for their actions. And OCD kind of takes away from that. If you have OCD, some people will use that as an excuse for their inappropriate actions in one way or another. And we can't tolerate that as a society. And I think it doesn't help at all for those with OCD as far as finding them a better way to cope with their OCD. It might even exasperate [*sic*] it. . . . [Also] once institutions are created, for "OCD" or "bipolarity," these things, they tend to . . . grow into living, breathing institutions that change and that kind of reinforce maybe some of the consequences that groups who originally formed these institutions, organizations, and so forth try to alleviate.

Notably, Destin saw potential for OCD to form the basis for an identity-based movement. However, he and others I interviewed expressed some hesitancy to move in this direction, which set them on a different track from the disability rights movement.

To explain, there have been people with physical impairments or who are disabled who have been vocal in fighting for social justice. Internationally, they have pushed us to question how we think of able bodies and disability and turned some of our common conceptions on their head. As we age, it is possible we will suffer declines in our hearing, eyesight, and more. Compared with racism, sexism, and other -isms, "handicapism" or "ableism" "is the only 'ism' to which *all* human beings are susceptible."[31] Instead of seeing disability as something from which an individual suffers, the social model of disability suggests disability has to do with how people are treated in society. The social model of disability was popularized in the 1980s and 1990s, and prior to this a medical perspective was dominant.[32] The medical model treats disability as a medical problem that needs solving, one that a person must deal with in concert with a healthcare professional. In contrast, the social model proposes that people can face a variety of impairments—but it is the context in which they live, their surrounding physical and social environment, that makes these impairments into disability. The Union of the Physically Impaired Against Segregation representatives indicated: "In our view, it is society which disables physically impaired people. Disability is something imposed on top of our impairments, by the way we are unnecessarily isolated and excluded from full participation in society. Disabled people are therefore an oppressed group in society."[33]

From this perspective, one solution to disablism, or the discrimination or inequality people with disabilities face, is to change society.[34] The social model of disability has had an impact on policy and how we see disability at the international level. For example, legislation has been passed in the past few decades in the United Kingdom and the United States prohibiting discrimination and furthering equal opportunity to jobs, housing, and more. In the United States today, the changes are obvious (although more can be done). Where the needs of those with impairments were once ignored, today buildings are designed with regulations in mind.

Mental disorders can be a considered a type of disability,[35] but the disability movement (including disability studies) and the mental health service users' or survivors' movement (referring to people's survival of the psychiatric system) have proceeded apace with somewhat different perspectives.[36] Mental health service users have reacted against a psychiatric system that sometimes treats them as passive, and they have repudiated being defined in terms of their medical diagnosis. They have also spoken out against stigmatization by the public and sought to repurpose terms such as "madness" as positive. Both the disability movement and the mental health user/survivor movement challenge the medical model, then, but the latter has not generated a cohesive framework akin to the social model. Moreover, some researchers have noted that "the medicalized individual model of 'mental illness' continues to dominate mental health policy and practice internationally."[37] The media sometimes particularly promote a medical framing,[38] and even sociologists have tended to frame disability along "'individual' lines, that is by focusing on limitations, medicalization, diagnoses, individual adjustment, etc."[39]

The medical model played an important part in how those I interviewed talked about their experiences and viewed their lives. They were not necessarily sure of the causes of the disorder, and they attributed it to biological as well as environmental and social causes. However, they often viewed their obsessions and compulsions through a personal lens. Their thoughts and behaviors were regularly seen as an impediment or problem they wanted solved, commonly a problem requiring a medical/psychological solution, versus an impairment that became a disability through society's treatment of them. For instance, the advice some people would give to others with the disorder would be to seek professional help, and those with children sometimes talked about how they would seek this type of help if their child exhibited signs of the disorder. When I looked at the websites of two prominent organizations for OCD (OCD Action and the International OCD Foundation), both had missions/visions that incorporated improving access to treatment for those with the disorder.

There was some mention of alternative perspectives, but not a cohesive one promoted by the majority of interviewees. Mona argued that she only has a problem insofar as other people let her behaviors get to them: "I like things to be done a very specific way and almost to the point where I like don't even want to let anybody do it. . . . That is irritating to them. . . . I don't see it as a problem besides the fact that it irritates other people. Which maybe that's their problem. Maybe they should do it right." Chance promoted a perspective that had some overlaps with the social model of disability: "We have this problem that we deal with and some of us don't see it as a problem, you know. Do left-handed people see that as a problem? I'm sorry this world is set up for right-handed [people]. . . . Should people who are left-handed be put into a special group?" A few people I interviewed disliked terms such as "mental illness," "mental disorder," and "mental disability," as they felt the terms insinuate something is "broken" in people. Clyde said his son just "processes things differently," and they have learned how to "navigate" this. Jeff pondered if it is "better to aim at thinking of myself as different but not necessarily in a bad way (rather like the X-Men), or as so not very different at all."

Overall, then, interviewees' perceptions of how people with OCD should ideally be treated in society were complex, and they did not share a single uniform perspective. They did perceive society as shaping the public's responses to people with OCD, and thereby the ability of those with the disorder to maneuver in society. Interviewees used this as a basis from which to make claims about the need for society to better understand the disorder. However, as I have said, interviewees exhibited some hesitation in identifying with the label "OCD," inhibiting a social justice movement in the name of OCD. They were not united in advocating for particular societal changes for OCD. Clyde argued that people with the disorder deserve to be treated equitably; that means leveling the playing field, for instance, perhaps giving a child with OCD extra time on a test. Yet, Mick said, "It's almost as bad for America to dictate that you get to play by different rules if you're a member of a marginalized group as it was to say that you could not vote because you were."

A few people, including Rodney, who was described at the start of the chapter, expressed that society should be cognizant and respectful of individuals' needs. For instance, Janet said, "I don't believe people with OCD deserve special treatment but that, in the workplace, everyone should be open-minded and supportive of each other's disabilities." Intriguingly, in some cases this meant advocating for social change by arguing that we need to shift our perspective on what we view as "normal" in society. Perhaps we need more "tolerance," to borrow a term from one interviewee. There is a neurodiversity movement that grew out of advocacy from people diagnosed with autism; it incorporates more groups now and argues that "neurological diversity should be celebrated and appreciated."[40] Those I interviewed did not reference this movement, but some suggested that society is made up of people with a spectrum of problems, and perhaps we could have greater respect and tolerance for this in society. Arguably, a downside to this approach is that it may neglect group inequities.[41] However, the progressive aspect of this view is that it disrupts the way we stereotype groups of people and indicates that many of us face bumps in the road in our mental health or physical well-being. The question, then, said Bella, is how to create community from this diverse group:

> In an ideal world I think it, the actual mental illness, would just be considered as normal as any other activity or any other way of living. And then there are degrees . . . [gives example of her mom who is schizophrenic]. . . . What I'm looking at is how do we fit together, and to make ourselves known, and to go where we need to go? Or have community. How does community work when you've got variations in thinking? I don't know. I'm working on that myself every day.

Conclusion

Where Do We Go from Here?

I don't know if you ever saw *As Good as It Gets* with Jack Nicholson. The whole studio audience is sitting there laughing and I'm sitting there crying my eyes out. . . . [My family teasing me does not bother me, but] my friend kind of hurt my feelings when she was like, "Well, obviously, this is your OCD because this is just not normal." Those kind of comments have hurt. Because no one's normal, so why should I feel any different. . . . I'm definitely more sensitive to others because having something like OCD makes you realize that everyone has their own shit no matter how much they look like they've got it all together. . . . We've all got issues and we're all a lot more than that.

—Zelda

I decided to write this book for people like Zelda, who was introduced earlier in the book. She depicted how society has constructed a version of OCD that is at odds with what many people with the disorder experience. We now recognize OCD as affecting millions of people worldwide. "OCD," "obsessions," and "compulsions" are terms that have entered our lexicon but are arguably stereotyped and misunderstood. Within this book, I provided a view into the inner worlds of people with OCD that they often hide from the public and that extend beyond the therapist's office. My hope is that this book will help the public better understand OCD, especially its diverse manifestations, as well as show people with the disorder that they are not alone. For researchers, the book adds to our understanding of the lived experience of OCD, which has been minimally studied. It provides useful data on the problems of not just stigma but also the trivialization of mental illness, which has been relatively neglected in research.

OCD Career

The experience of having OCD can, like other health concerns or roles, be likened to a "career." The chapters of this book traced the following stages of the lived experience of OCD: coming to see oneself as having a problem, defining it as OCD, seeking help, and learning to live with the disorder. Numerous stories have been written about the power of medicalization, of professional labels, and the technology of medicine that looks deep into our bodies and finds problems that we previously might not have recognized as such. The narratives of people with OCD in this book iterated aspects of this. Certainly, psychological/psychiatric labels shaped their experiences. Gaining information about OCD, even learning about it through a news story, was enough to create a significant change in people's lives, as they began to redefine what they were experiencing. It was the double-edged sword of diagnosis that people with other illnesses have faced. For instance, diagnosis indicates that there might be help, and that others are going through the same experience. On the other hand, it confirms that there is a problem and one that is potentially stigmatizing. Within online forums and groups, people with OCD are regularly seen monitoring each other so they do not violate what contemporary doctors and therapists say is beneficial for the disorder, reinforcing psychological/psychiatric perspectives.

However, for those people I interviewed, the "OCD career" often began before diagnosis. Most of them noticed, questioned, and/or judged some of their thoughts/behaviors as problematic before perceiving themselves as having the disorder. They drew from the knowledge they had to decide their thoughts/behaviors were outside of social norms and assign a host of explanations, including religious ones, to simply having a problem unique unto themselves. At times, those with whom I communicated also encountered healthcare professionals who lacked knowledge about the disorder or the most effective ways to treat it. Such are the implications of OCD not being widely recognized in society.

My research reinforces more recent conceptualizations of the illness career and the impacts of illness on identity as shifting rather than linear.[1] Indeed, people sometimes went through stages of the career again as they encountered different forms of obsessions and/or compulsions. My data support how managing a diagnosis can involve resistance as well as acceptance of the illness. Interviewees commonly accepted the diagnosis but regularly demonstrated reflexivity as they searched for information, made decisions about treatment as active consumers, and altered how they presented themselves to others. They used knowledge and experience as capital to assist them in getting what they wanted out of practitioner-client relationships, for instance.

Overall, the picture interviewees drew of what it meant to live with the disorder was complex. This is partly the result of how the OCD career posed uncomfortable questions about identity and what makes us who we are. People with OCD considered what thoughts and behaviors were theirs versus "OCD." From their viewpoint, OCD could be a monster or something attacking them. In rarer cases, the disorder was seen more positively. Over time, some people perceived it as more of a companion. At the end of our interviews, some people believed they had conquered the OCD, while others were still in a fight to claim their authentic self, and still others came to see the OCD as part of themselves.

Interestingly, those I interviewed sometimes shied away from perceiving OCD in political terms. Much about the disorder can feel personalized and individualized to someone with OCD, but there are many aspects of the OCD career that are rooted in society. The people I interviewed made choices about what to try to hide or share about the disorder in part based on public conceptions of the disorder and how they imagined others would perceive them. This affected their social relationships. Both stigma and trivialization are grounded in public stereotypes, so how do we move forward in improving lives of people with OCD and others diagnosed with mental disorders by minimizing these?

Trivialization and Stigma

While the OCD career has overlaps with the experiences of other disorders, public conceptions that feed trivialization and stigma loomed over the lives of people with OCD in a way that made their experiences relatively unique. In everyday conversation, you might hear someone refer to themselves as being "so OCD," much to Zelda's chagrin. Upon telling people that I was studying OCD, a common refrain I heard was, "Oh, I have a little OCD" or something similar.

As a result, OCD is often stereotyped as relatively benign and humorous compared with other mental disorders. However, it is a diagnosable mental disorder that can be just as debilitating as other disorders in some respects, can take up hours of a person's day, can involve rituals that are illogical, and may including having taboo thoughts. Attention to stigma matters, as studies have indicated stigma may be more difficult to deal with than physical impacts for those with long-term illnesses.[2] Many interviewees, such as Zelda, feared stigma from others and engaged in some self-stigma. She told me, "I wouldn't tell [my workplace about my OCD] because that's the part of me that feels a little freakish. It's a very strange thing because you can be so intelligent and so smart and have your life together in so many other areas but yet you're this intelligent person who has graduated college with honors and yet you're sitting there touching a doorknob twenty times." At the same time, people with OCD can be angered and frustrated by more innocuous public perceptions of the disorder, as well as benefit from them when avoiding stigma. Ideally, OCD would not be trivialized or stigmatized, but I have shown how improving people's mental health literacy can potentially come with a hidden cost—an increase in stigma as people perceive the disorder more seriously or mistakenly take people's thoughts as indicative of future actions.

In order to improve the public's mental health literacy while reducing stigma and minimizing trivialization for OCD or any other social issue, let us contrast how stigma and trivialization operate. Link and Phelan conceptualized the inception of stigma in people's recognition of certain differences.[3] There are a host of things on which we can distinguish people. However, society picks certain ones as important and ignores others. I like to tell my students to imagine a world where we ranked people according to the length of their pinky toes. Once society picks a particular difference as worth noticing and labeling, it may be linked to stereotypes, specifically negative ones. This is the second component of their model of stigma. The third component occurs when people use labels to separate *those* people from themselves. The fourth component involves emotional responses, for example, irritation and fear from the stigmatizer, and shame from the stigmatized. Finally, Link and Phelan discussed the status loss and discrimination that can occur, resulting in inequality. Their model includes consideration of power; stigma occurs because some groups have the power to label and separate.

A wide swath of research exists on stigma, but much less on trivialization.[4] I theorize that the seed of trivialization arises in people's recognition of differences as well. These differences are also associated with stereotypes, just not necessarily negative ones. For instance, OCD is simplified and stereotyped as being extraconcerned with cleanliness and order. From here, trivialization is like a coin as it has two sides. On one side, oversimplification can lead society to perceive symptoms positively, diminishing separations between "us" and "them," and thereby discrimination. On the other side, however, oversimplification can also lead to reactions that feel like microaggressions for people with the disorder. For example, Zelda depicted how those experiencing OCD may watch a movie about someone with OCD and see it through the prism of their own painful experiences, while others without the disorder may see it as a joke. Further, what happens when the more complex and serious sides of OCD arise?

Trivialization can be such a mismatch with reality that it may lead to misunderstanding and stigma. Myrick and Pavelko argued that trivialization could potentially lead people "to be less likely to seek help or less likely to support policy-related efforts."[5] I imagine that a gap could arise between what audiences expect and what they encounter, leading to problems. For instance, those holding more benign stereotypes of the disorder may not understand why people with OCD want or need particular accommodations in school or specialized therapy. As one interviewee who worked in the healthcare industry told me, "I hear professionals joke about OCD all of the time. . . . OCD is a big joke." When I asked him what it was like being in the industry and also having OCD, he said, "Scary, because I know how discriminated against 'we' are by my peers." Audiences may think someone with OCD is overexaggerating their need for help. Alternatively, they may become concerned about symptoms of OCD that are different and more serious than they expected. For instance, they may mistakenly assume people's thoughts are direct reflections of future actions.

Mental Continuum

I suggest that we strive to increase public knowledge of OCD while humanizing the disorder and indicating shared lines between those with the disorder and without, in an effort to reduce both trivialization and stigma. Contact with those with mental disorders is important in reducing stigma because it puts a human face on mental illness.[6] In 2007, England began a countrywide initiative called Time to Change, which included goals such as changing attitudes toward those with mental health problems, reducing discrimination, and improving the social capital of those with mental disorders.[7] Other countries have formed their own initiatives. People with OCD also regularly advocate for educating the public. McGrath, who trains therapists to help those with OCD, told me that when he tells people that he works for an OCD company, "a very typical response is 'Oh, I have a little OCD.' . . . I don't know why people think they have a little OCD but they don't think they have a little of everything else [like schizophrenia] and so part of our goal is to really work on changing that in people and get them to recognize that OCD is a very serious diagnosis." I certainly understand the import of what McGrath and others with OCD are saying, including the truly devastating impact the disorder can have on a person's life. However, I believe education campaigns about OCD can be accurate and include the serious aspects of OCD, while still showing connections that exist between those who have the disorder and those who do not.

Recently, some researchers have been considering whether we may reduce the stigma of mental disorders by showing the public how mental illness lies on a continuum.[8] Previously, government agencies, researchers, and advocates have sometimes argued that if more of the public perceives the cause of mental disorders as neurobiological and genetic, stigma would be reduced; the idea was that mental disorders would be perceived as akin to physical illnesses and less blame would be placed on individuals.[9] Rather than "*disorders* of the *mind*," we would see them as "*diseases* of the *brain*."[10] However, a group of researchers who studied people's knowledge of mental disorders in sixteen countries wrote in 2013: "The majority of the public has received, and at least tacitly endorses, ideas about the severity of mental illness and accepts its underlying causes as located in the same realm as other illnesses."[11] Regrettably, while blame may decrease, viewing mental disorders in this way can be associated with views that people cannot get better, increases in perceptions of perceived dangerousness, and increases in stigma.[12]

Currently studies have found that continuum beliefs, or the perspective that what people with mental disorders are going through is similar to what others face, except for how pronounced it is, may increase social acceptance, reduce stereotypes, and foster more positive emotional reactions.[13] This is because stigma thrives on differentness, on people distinguishing those with mental illness as different from themselves. Perceiving mental health and illness on a continuum highlights connections among people. The continuum perspective incorporates "the perception that a person with mental illness is someone like us, and that to a certain degree his/her experiences resemble experiences of myself. This attitude is supported by epidemiological studies on the prevalence of psychiatric symptoms among the general population. . . . Many persons who do not fulfil criteria for a mental disorder nevertheless experience various psychiatric symptoms to different degrees."[14] With a continuum perspective, we have to be careful that people do not perceive those with mental concerns as weak and able to easily get better, though.[15] "Antistigma advocates need to cultivate empathy that leads to parity, not to condescension and exaggeration of difference."[16]

A continuum model fits people's experiences with intrusive thoughts and OCD.[17] At one end of the continuum I imagine people who experience an occasional intrusive thought and ignore it. Research supports this: "Studies have shown that between 80 and 99% of people experience intrusive thoughts . . . and the content of thoughts is not all that different between nonclinical and clinical populations. . . . It is theorized that the interpretation of the thoughts as meaningless helps individuals without OCD stay lower on the continuum and not develop OCD in response to the thoughts."[18] Sometimes I wonder whether, if those I interviewed had known this sooner—if they knew they were not so alone, and that they should not give their thoughts any merit—their lives might have been different. (Conscientiousness has even been associated with obsessive-compulsive behavior.)[19]

Along the continuum are people who have potential risk factors for developing OCD (such as family members with OCD), but who do not currently have the disorder. Next on the continuum are people who experience obsessions and compulsions but not at a level where they would be diagnosed with OCD. When looking back upon their lives before being diagnosed, or considering their status as in remission, some people I interviewed depicted themselves as having a little bit of OCD. Those I interviewed did not always find their thoughts/behaviors bothersome enough to be a problem. However, research has confirmed that there are people who have obsessions and compulsions and who do not reach the threshold for being diagnosed with OCD, but who find that these inhibit their functioning and lead to distress.[20] Next on the continuum are people who experience OCD. However, we can distinguish those who experience mild forms of the disorder from those who face more severe symptoms, reaching the end of the continuum. Also, remember that people's experiences with the disorder were not wholly negative. For instance, some "obsessions" and "compulsions" went unnoticed until interviewees learned about the disorder, did not particularly bother people, or were viewed as beneficial (e.g., perceived by others as useful at work).

Viewing obsessions and compulsions along a continuum is not just useful for public outreach. Researchers have proposed using a model akin to the one just outlined to generate more targeted strategies for people at different places along the continuum (i.e., a clinical staging model).[21] For instance, those with subthreshold OCD symptoms could participate in programs involving mindfulness or lifestyle programs to minimize stress, because theoretically it is possible that risk factors such as stress may precipitate the occurrence of OCD for them. As another example, those with OCD might be subdivided based on recurrence of symptoms and therapeutic response, with different treatment protocols. However, I believe that we should ensure that people are not overly monitored and labeled, especially people who do not meet the threshold for a diagnosis of OCD.

OCD in Our Times

The concerns that people with OCD have are ones that many of us have in contemporary society, as the content of people's obsessions varies by culture and is related to the disquiets of that era. This was especially noticeable when the world began facing a pandemic in 2019.

More specifically, people with OCD experience problems accepting uncertainty and seek control, and numerous sociologists and other scholars have come to see risk and uncertainty as central issues of our times.[22] Interviewees grappled with questions of control throughout the career of OCD, including how much they could or should control the risks of everyday living (such as germs). Large-scale changes have occurred historically in society, leading to the existence of anxieties that those both with and without OCD must manage. The social theorist Ulrich Beck used the phrase "risk society."[23] We live in a global society where we constantly have to assess the risks of various actions we take, as well as live with risks we may feel we have little control over (e.g., climate change, oil spills, problems at nuclear power plants, catching a virus). As the sociologist Anthony Giddens wrote about society, "Every human individual could (in principle) be overwhelmed by anxieties about risks which are implied by the very business of living."[24] The sociologist Iain Wilkinson wrote that we are "becoming more vulnerable to experiencing our world as a place of threatening uncertainty."[25] While many of us may be able to push some of these concerns to the back of our mind, they nonetheless exist, and I believe that to some degree this is what people with OCD are struggling with. At least some people with OCD are trying to control their lives and avoid unnecessary risk to themselves and loved ones—goals that many of us share.

Destin, who I interviewed, remarked upon this. He proposed that some people have difficulty adjusting to modern life, "and so they deal with the uncertainty and the anxieties of the modern world through their compulsions and their obsessions to gain a sense of control." Some of the same themes are echoed in the theories of sociologists. According to Giddens, "Modern institutions differ from all preceding forms of social order in respect of their dynamism, the degree to which they undercut traditional habits and customs, and their global impact."[26] As Gidden also pointed out:

> No one can show that it is not "rational" to worry constantly over the possibility of ecological catastrophe, nuclear war or the ravaging of humanity by as yet unanticipated scourges. Yet people who do spend every day worrying about such possibilities are not regarded as "normal." The crisis-prone nature of late modernity thus has unsettling consequences. . . . [It] fuels a general climate of uncertainty.[27]

To explain, in today's "modern" or "postmodern" society (scholars conceptualize and label these social changes somewhat differently),[28] Enlightenment hope in progress and reason has not brought us surety and complete safety. We have realized that our attempts to usher in an age of science and rationality, and better living through chemistry, have led to new problems, and not everything is within our control.[29] We are constantly revising our knowledge, which makes it hard for us in our daily lives to find solid ground on which to stand. Experts abound. For example, consider food. Today we are bombarded by experts telling us we need to eat this way or that, but who should we believe?[30] Are pasta and wheat bad or good for us? Should we choose margarine or butter? These macro or large-scale changes affect our individual lives. In the face of a multitude of choices, we constantly make and revise our decisions, reflexively building our selves.[31] We are living in what some people argue is an age of risk and others have called an age of anxiety.[32]

Life may not really be more risky than in the past, but the risks may be different, and a mindset of contemplating, calculating, and trying to minimize risk is what we use to operate in the world now.[33] Instead of surety, we are left with pervasive doubt. "Lay people are challenged by continual uncertainties," wrote the sociologist Deborah Lupton.[34] Some of our attention to risk is likely manufactured rather than real, for instance, our attention to risk heightened by the media's dire news stories. In any case, we monitor and control the minutiae of our lives as we seek to prevent illness.[35] You have surely seen and potentially participated in this yourself. Ask yourself if you do not already enact seemingly "compulsive" bodily routines to support health and well-being, such as counting calories. Rather than governments just maintaining a healthy water supply, sewer system, and so on, in twentieth-century Europe, North America, and some other regions, "the maintenance and promotion of personal, childhood, and familial health—regimen, personal hygiene, healthy child-reading, the identification and treatment of illness—became central to forms of self-management that authorities sought to inculcate into citizens and hence to their own hopes, fears, and anxieties."[36] This self-reflexivity and self-discipline have only been furthered by more recent biomedical and neuroscientific research, and the expansion of the pharmaceutical industry in concert with the way in which we study ever-smaller risks through clinical trials.[37] Instead of

healthy bodies that are beset by sickness at times, "a very different no-
tion of illness took center stage," where "health has come to be defined as
a reduction in risk."[38] The body we thought was healthy we now believe
may be harboring hidden symptoms or may be at risk for a future disease, so we treat the anticipated problem.

One response to these societal shifts has been for people to become
excessive about controlling risks to their health by becoming experts
themselves.[39] Even when we feel "healthy," we are expected to reduce
our risk and change our lifestyle or take medications. Another response
has been fear, leading to an "anxious duty to be healthy."[40] For Giddens,
our routines, and our vigilance and control of our bodies and discourse,
help minimize those anxieties I mentioned earlier.[41] Giddens argued
that these habits and routines provide a "bulwark" against threatening
anxieties. However, he warned that to hold too strictly to them can lead
to compulsive behaviors, melancholia, or schizophrenia; he stressed that
to live we have to have some trust and ability to live creatively. The sociologist Frank Furedi suggested that a culture of fear has developed
in our society, where our fear is free-floating, moving from fear of one
thing to another without any real rhyme or reason.[42] The more safety
precautions we put into place, the more we may actually feel insecure.
Like hamsters running on a wheel, people can become preoccupied with
reducing risk in the face of a growing specter of fear surrounding our
health, but the more attempts we make to stay "healthy" or be safe, the
more we may feel fear or insecurity.[43] The citizen today, wrote professor
of international politics Engin F. Isin, "arises from and responds to fears,
anxieties, and insecurities."[44]

Perhaps people with OCD are trying to cope with these societal
shifts, less willing or able to push aside the risks of today's world than
some other citizens, or are more concerned with controlling risks even
if such control is actually impossible. Some interviewees argued that
their OCD started when they found themselves in situations that were a
bit riskier than other contexts, and they began to institute precautions.
For instance, a couple of people described having jobs where they got
physically dirty, so they began enacting cleaning rituals. Aiten worked
in a motor vehicle garage as a teenager. He depicted these as "horrible
dirty places," so he started taking baths "and slowly the baths got longer
and longer." He wondered if his "habit" grew into OCD. Often people I

interviewed described what appeared to be worries about risks we all face today, and they commonly noted that their OCD seemed to get worse when they were under stress. For example, they described concerns about contracting illnesses or harm coming to loved ones, and as a result engaged in behaviors to try to minimize such. Nellie described her OCD as being akin to a "voice in your head telling you that something is or will be dangerous if you take a specific action." She said OCD "thrives" on the unknown. People with OCD's assessment of perceived risks sometimes became uncoupled from actual risks. The more people engaged in compulsions, sometimes the more they felt their anxiety, obsessions, and rituals increased. For people with OCD, behaviors could become excessive, or result in what an outsider would perceive as irrational or nonsensical. They sometimes stuck to their rituals, whereas others without OCD seem to be constantly managing and revising their behaviors to meet situational needs.[45] It was as if those with OCD sought safety in routine. I suggest it may be useful, at least in some cases, to see the mental and physical routines and behaviors of those with OCD as coping mechanisms, which was how a few people with the disorder described them. Zelda said that as such things go, OCD is "better than doing drugs." The routines/behaviors were extra insurance or an extra precaution against risk, even if irrational. For example, Giddens noted that the average person may ignore small risks.[46] In contrast, I found that some persons with OCD had trouble ignoring small risks or stopping what they clearly assessed as irrational actions, or actions linked to irrational thoughts. Jeff told me about an incident at a restaurant when he was a teenager. He saw a fry drop on the floor, "and I kind of felt like I ought to phone the restaurant owner and ask them, 'Did you pick up the fry to make sure no one falls and hurts themselves?' But I knew I shouldn't really do that, that it didn't really make sense." Jeff said that OCD at heart is not different from "ordinary" human life. It just seems different because it is "like zooming into something with a microscope . . . it's more of a hypersensitivity or hyperalertness to certain threatening or annoying experiences."

Taken far enough, people with OCD can be unsure or unable to trust their own actions. They may believe in their thoughts and behaviors; for instance, at times they really feel they are preventing harm by engaging in what an outsider would perceive as a clearly unrelated ritual. They can become afraid to live, to take risks. Phineas told me, "I constantly analyze every little thing in my life, to gain control, to see out the danger, and to get myself prepared for it. . . . Normal people live out in the bright lights of the world, I live in the dark alleys and shadows of the world." He explained compulsions as a way for people with OCD to "protect themselves from something bad happening; we feel that we always need to be in control." I want to clarify that I am not denying that OCD may have a neurobiological cause, nor am I claiming obsessions and compulsions only came into existence with modernity, but rather, that we should consider the disorder's current manifestation within the larger context in which we are now living.

In our risk society, a multitude of risks and fears abound, and contemporary society seems to provide fertile soil for obsessions and compulsions to grow. Regardless of how rational or irrational one might label the thoughts and behaviors of people with OCD, perhaps the motivation that undergirds it is the same one that drives people without the disorder: a desire to keep control over at least a portion of one's life in the face of a risky society, to set up barriers against the vagaries of society. Note that it is not my intention to paint modernity or postmodernity as all negative. We face a diversity of opportunities, perhaps more than ever before. Life is surely different from in the past. It is probably most accurate to say these changes have brought both good and bad, for example, new freedoms as well as new restrictions.

We Have All Got Problems and Flexible Institutions

Moreover, what some people with OCD told me, and what others with impairments or illnesses have reiterated in studies, is that many of us have problems. People with OCD are not alone. One woman told me, "I've found that once you open the door, and you let people know, you know, you're not perfect, that they walk through it with their own problems." Researcher Gill Green wrote, "Those who have traditionally been defined as 'not normal' or 'other' are challenging the definition of what is 'normal.'"[47] Therefore, how do we create a society that is communal but that also respects individual needs and impairments, as Bella envisioned in the previous chapter?

Institutions commonly assume a framework in which having an impairment is outside of the norm. For instance, I provide a variety of accommodations to students through my university's Office of Disability Accommodations, from athletes who have been injured to students with mental disorders. These can include having extended time to complete tests and seating near the door in class. Workplace-based return-to-work initiatives exist, applicable after someone has faced difficulties from a disorder or disability.[48] Some companies are more specifically addressing mental health in the work world with employee resource groups for mental health.[49] For instance, Johnson & Johnson has worked on improving access to care, as well as putting together employee resource groups, including one called the Alliance for Diverse Abilities.[50]

However, perhaps we need to reframe how we think about "normalcy" and illness. According to the National Institute of Mental Health, almost one in five people in the United States is living with a mental illness,[51] and many more may experience problems that do not reach the level of a diagnosis. In a study of the visually impaired, interviewees talked about how they are "just like everyone else and that the others are just like them. Everyone has some kind of disability and has some level of dependence on others."[52] Clyde said that "they're finding out that normal is not nearly as normal as they thought." Impairments can affect learning, and in some schools the majority of students with learning challenges might not disclose.[53] How do people manage who are too afraid to go to a healthcare professional, or who have "symptoms" below a threshold to be diagnosed, or who are too disheartened to directly ask for help? Sitting in my office, students have confessed their struggles to succeed in school. However, sometimes they languished for months without coming to me, or gave me all manner of explanations until they finally told me what was really happening in their lives—for example, that they were depressed.

Strategies can be employed in institutions that might benefit students or workers with a variety of stresses and problems across the mental health continuum without requiring them to necessarily label what they are experiencing or ask for special help. Pushes for "universal" and "inclusive" design in environments have been made, as well as cultures of care. We can imagine institutions that are made flexible enough to incorporate all types of participants. A little flexibility could make a huge difference in my students' lives as well as in the lives of my interviewees.

For instance, Melissa Mauldin, a sociologist who teaches in high schools, directed me to principles from the Universal Design of Learning (UDL) used by educators. These principles involve flexibility in the distribution of information and demonstration of accomplishments, as well as a reduction in barriers to instruction without lowering expectations.[54] UDL is based on universal design principles for the environment as well as research in neuroscience on how people learn. Options such as instruction in multiple formats, student output presented in diverse formats (i.e., not just written but possibly a podcast), and access to different learning environments can be beneficial. I have already observed institutions of higher education promoting some of these options. Some aspects of universal design could also be employed in the workplace, such as offering more flexible work hours.[55] Further, growth in telecommuting may provide people with disorders and disabilities more space to manage their symptoms. The downside is that there is some evidence that the extent to which one telecommutes can have some negative effects on careers (e.g., salary and promotions) in particular contexts,[56] but perhaps this may change as a result of the COVID-19 pandemic. A mental health report commissioned by the American Heart Association in 2019 depicted mental health on a continuum and provided more ideas for supporting workers.[57] The report outlined potential strategies for employee care at multiple points along the continuum. It argued that employers could reduce employee stress and prevent problems by investing in programs such as one for college loan repayment support. For those employees already facing difficulties such as anxiety and stress, employers could provide short-term counseling and referral to outside support. Importantly, employers could make mental health programs such as those involving cognitive behavior therapy available to all employees rather than just those with mental health concerns.

I concur with authors who believe we need to do more than foster personal development in institutions. Karp argued that "we need to rediscover community as the very best medicine for many of our ills, including the sadness of depression,"[58] and perhaps he is right. While I do value the everyday practices people with OCD put into place to reduce their stress and anxiety, we should question why people have so much stress and anxiety in the first place. An emphasis on individualism in society has been posed as a possible cause of increased anxiety in young people, and people's disconnection from each other has been linked to depression.[59] Therefore, telling people to become even more reliant upon themselves hardly seems the ultimate solution.

In a book about the influence of psychology on education, Jack Martin and Ann-Marie McLellan wrote, "What we believe mainstream educational psychology got fundamentally wrong was to conceptualize our selves (our psychological being) as isolated from and prior to our coordinated sociality within communities of others."[60] Educational psychologists work on promoting "self-esteem, self-concept, self-efficacy, and self-regulated learning" that "celebrate mostly individual ends."[61] Instead, Martin and McLellan drew from the ideas of the sociologist George Herbert Mead to promote the development of students in a community "that begins with the students' immediate situations and perspectives and moves gradually and progressively to enlarge and place them within the broader social context of human sociocultural perspectives, understandings, and accomplishments."[62] Education is both for personal and societal development in this way, and arguably other societal institutions should be so too.

Do Not Despair

What tips for others with OCD might we glean from my interviews? I began the book by mentioning jokes and memes that frustrate those with OCD. However, some people I interviewed told me how humor can be a great coping technique for life's stresses as well as the difficulties of experiencing obsessions and compulsions. It can be an interesting way to connect with people and share an inside joke. One study of people with various mental illnesses indicated that humor was linked to higher self-esteem.[63] I believe that Delia was offering some solid advice when she said that it is good to laugh at oneself or to share a joke with others. However, she advised that you should not allow others to insult you or make you feel like less of a person because you have OCD. Indeed, all of us can have bizarre thoughts pass through our minds. They do not have to mean something important, and therefore we do not necessarily need to judge them in ourselves or others.

Most important, if you have OCD, do not despair. You can find ways to treat and cope with your obsessions and compulsions. I believe the

Figure C.1. JangandFox's *Got You Covered* by Jang

most important message from interviewees for others with OCD would be to get trustworthy information and advocate for yourself. For anyone who wants to seek professional help, interviewees reiterated how it is wise to seek the counsel of someone experienced in contemporary treatments for OCD and who has treated a variety of OCD clients.

Despite fears of how the public would perceive them, those I interviewed did find many people in the world who took the time to listen and understand them. Therefore, I believe they would want me to conclude this book by saying thank you to the people who listen to, empathize with, show up for, and love those with OCD.

ACKNOWLEDGMENTS

This book would not exist without my editor, Ilene Kalish, who believed in this work and to whom I will forever be grateful. Her fast and insightful feedback was much appreciated and positively shaped the book before you. Thank you to everyone at New York University Press, as well as to the anonymous reviewers, for your time, help, and consideration. From the artwork to the copyediting, it has been a pleasure. This book is a joint effort between me and all the people I interviewed. I can never thank them enough for being willing to tell me their stories and for trusting that I would do them justice. To protect their identities, I cannot provide their names, but they know who they are. I hope this book lives up to your expectations. Thank you to the therapists and professionals whom I interviewed. I tried to bring your words to life. A special thank you to artists Jang (of JangandFox) and Hannah Hillam (of Verbal Vomit) for creating work that discusses mental well-being and letting me share their comics in this book.

I began studying OCD when I was a graduate student at the University of Florida, even though it was not the focus of my dissertation. I benefited from the mentorship of many people there, especially the late Hernán Vera, Barbara Zsembik, Stephen Perz, Robert Hatch, and Joe Feagin. I must thank the late Gordon Streib for his encouraging words when some of this work on OCD won an award named in his honor. I collaborated with Ana Liberato and Michael Boyd on aspects of my work on OCD, and I thank them for their patience and expertise. Other colleagues have supported this work and in the process encouraged me to continue this line of study, including David LoConto, Craig Forsyth of the journal *Deviant Behavior*, and Stephen E. Brown. At the University of Southern Mississippi, I am grateful for all my colleagues, especially for being part of this supportive group of sociologists: Amy Chasteen, Ann Marie Kinnell, Kari Kozlowski, Michelle McLeese, Julie Reid, and Matt Ward. I am extremely grateful for the sabbatical I was granted from the university to support my work on OCD. At Barry University, Karen Callaghan, Jung Min Choi, and Gary Grizzle first sparked my interest in sociology; Michael Melody encouraged me to go to graduate school, and that set me on the path that led to this book. Special thanks to David Karp for his feedback on an early draft of this work, and to Lavender Tan for providing me with feedback on psychological perspectives. Some of my students have asked me about this work and kept my creative juices flowing, so thank you to them, especially Anastasija Cobanovic.

Importantly, I have to thank my family for listening to my ideas, reading drafts, and putting up with me: Barbara Fennell (my mother and favorite editor from kindergarten to adulthood, whom I miss very much), Erin Fennell, and Roderick Fennell. Thank you to friends who sent positive vibes and discussed book ideas with me, notably Susan Astwood, Carmen Carracelas-Juncal, Guido Casorla, Ingmar Dechen, Elif Filiz, Bridget Hayden, Michael Helperin, Clay Hipke, Kriston Leagh, Nicholas Pagnucco, Sateesh Peddini and Keltoum Rowland. There are more of you who have supported me and this project than I can list. Your faith in this project has kept me moving forward, so thank you from the bottom of my heart.

NOTES

INTRODUCTION

1 Fennell, "If You're 'So OCD'"; Pavelko and Myrick, "Tweeting and Trivializing."
2 Pavelko and Myrick, "Tweeting and Trivializing," 42.
3 Schuster, "16 Hilarious OCD Memes."
4 American Psychiatric Association, *DSM-5*; World Health Organization, "ICD-11."
5 American Psychiatric Association, *DSM-5*, 23.
6 Penzel, "'But I Love My Kids . . .'"
7 Shapiro, *Understanding OCD*, chap. 1. According to Nikodijevic et al., "Unwanted intrusive thoughts that are contrary to the person's self-view are more likely to be interpreted as significant and threatening, and may lead to the individual questioning their self-concept" ("Fear of Self," 165).
8 American Psychiatric Association, *DSM-5*; Rachman and De Silva, *Obsessive-Compulsive Disorder*.
9 Adam et al., "Obsessive-Compulsive Disorder"; Albert et al., "Suicide"; American Psychiatric Association, *DSM-5*; de la Cruz et al., "Suicide"; Huppert et al., "Quality of Life"; Rachman and De Silva, *Obsessive-Compulsive Disorder*; Stengler-Wenzke et al., "Subjective Quality"; Subramaniam et al., "Quality of Life"; Welkowitz et al., "Obsessive-Compulsive."
10 Subramaniam et al., "Quality of Life," 375.
11 Boschen, "Publication Trends"; Rapoport, *Boy Who Couldn't Stop Washing*; Rasmussen and Eisen, "Epidemiology"; Wahl, "Obsessive-Compulsive." It is unclear why prevalence rates increased. Rapoport suggested that people with OCD who had previously been hiding their problem became more open as a result of increased scientific interest and treatment accessibility. However, perhaps the definition of OCD, or at least obsessionality and compulsiveness, has expanded or will expand in the future (see Kramer, *Listening to Prozac*). Also, there appears to be a period in the 1990s when the prevalence of the disorder was overestimated (e.g., see Crino, Slade, and Andrews, "Changing Prevalence").
12 Coles et al., "Obsessive Compulsive Disorder Prevalence"; Fawcett, Power, and Fawcett, "Women"; Fontenelle, Mendlowicz, and Versiani, "Descriptive Epidemiology"; Subramaniam et al., "Prevalence, Correlates, Help-Seeking." The actual prevalence of OCD worldwide is a bit uncertain. Widely varying prevalence rates are due to in part to differences in study methodology. Other social and environmental factors are also relevant.
13 Schneider and Conrad, *Having Epilepsy*, 3.

14 For instance, see Durkheim, *Suicide*.

15 For instance, see Barker, *Fibromyalgia Story*; Beard, *Living with Alzheimer's*; Charmaz, *Good Days*; Karp, *Speaking of Sadness*; Schneider and Conrad, *Having Epilepsy*; Weitz, *Life with AIDS*.

16 Frank, *Wounded Storyteller*, xiii.

17 Holstein and Gubrium, *Self We Live By*.

18 Frank, *Wounded Storyteller*, xii.

19 Bury, "Illness Narratives."

20 Frank, *Wounded Storyteller*, 5.

21 Frank, 6.

22 Albert et al., "Duration of Untreated Illness"; Gershkovich et al., "Exposure and Response"; Schwartz et al., "Treatment-Seeking"; Subramaniam et al., "Prevalence, Correlates, Help-Seeking."

23 I interviewed the first group of people in 2003. Years later I expanded the project and more than doubled the number of interviews, plus I was able to recontact some of my first interviewees. There were a few people who stayed in touch over a number of years.

24 Online interviewing has been a growing methodological approach for researchers, one that is especially useful for communicating with vulnerable populations. I created a semi-structured list of questions covering core topics, including treatment, interactions with others, and stigma.

25 One person's age is an estimate based on work history.

26 Interviewees were asked to identify their own race/ethnicity. Of the group of fifty-five respondents, five did not answer. Of those who did, there was one Native American man, one Haitian woman, one Cuban woman, one Indian woman, and one Jewish woman. The rest identified themselves as White or Caucasian.

27 Of the fifty-five core interviewees, thirteen said they had not been, or were not sure if they had been, professionally diagnosed as having OCD (although Alvira received treatment from a healthcare professional and was told she had or could someday develop OCD; Janet felt her therapist seemed to think she probably had OCD, and Janet considered herself diagnosed; Monica said a psychologist went along with her self-diagnosis; Percy said a telephone counselor for an OCD organization thought it sounded like he had OCD; and Mable was being given medication for her symptoms by an MD). I asked respondents to answer questions from the Obsessive-Compulsive Inventory-Revised (OCI-R). It is condensed, compared with other instruments, consisting of eighteen questions (six subscales). People report on a scale of 0 to 4 the degree to which they are bothered by experiences such as seeing objects out of place (see Foa et al., "Obsessive-Compulsive Inventory"). In different samples Foa identified a cutscore between 18 and 21 for the total OCI-R, and between 4 and 5 for the obsessing subscale. Other researchers determined an optimal cutscore of 7 for the obsessing subscale, 7 for symmetry and ordering, 7 for checking, 5 for hoarding, 3 and 4 for neutralizing/superstition, and 3 and 4 for contamination and washing (see Gönner, Ecker, and Leonhart, "Diagnostic Discrimination").

Of the thirteen interviewees who had not been diagnosed, nine had scores of 23 or greater. Of the other four, Monica had a score of 17 total (but 9 on the obsessing subscale); Percy had a score of 15 total (but 12 on the obsessing subscale); Katie had a score 17 total (but 11 on the hoarding subscale); and Lily had a score of 6 total (but 5 on the hoarding subscale). A note of caution in interpreting these numbers—the OCI-R asks people to say how much particular things distress them over the "past month." However, respondents said their symptoms waxed and waned and were affected by treatment. At the time of the interview, some respondents felt they were in remission or had few symptoms to report. Interviewees' answers to the OCI-R did not all reflect their symptoms as of the past month but were based on various time periods. Some persons, for example, answered these questions based on how they felt before treatment or when symptoms were at their worst.

Most of these people diagnosed themselves as having OCD. However, despite having a healthcare practitioner tell her that she had or could develop OCD, Alvira hesitated to define herself as having a problem. Mable learned about OCD in college and felt she might have had OCD when she was a child; she was "obsessive about thoughts" as an adult but seemed to not consider this OCD because she did not engage in overt compulsions. Adrian felt he had OCD or at least was on his way to developing it, before he got his thoughts/behaviors under control. Two more participants were unsure if they had OCD but explained that they hoarded.

28 American Psychiatric Association, *DSM-IV-TR*.
29 Jutel, *Putting a Name to It*, introduction.
30 Jutel. According to Lakoff, "Two centuries after its invention, psychiatry's illnesses have neither known causes nor definitive treatments. The field's difficulty in stabilizing its forms of knowledge and intervention has contributed to its problematic position within contemporary biomedicine" (*Pharmaceutical Reason*, introduction).
31 Hollander, Braun, and Simeon, "Should OCD Leave."
32 American Psychiatric Association, *DSM-5*, 235.
33 Mataix-Cols et al., "Hoarding Disorder."
34 For instance, in one study in the United States, 90 percent of participants who met the criteria for lifetime OCD also met the threshold for another lifetime disorder (see Ruscio et al., "Epidemiology").
35 For instance, one person I interviewed said that at first she hid information about what she was going through, which she felt led to a misdiagnosis. For one person, I have missing data on this issue.
36 Karp, *Speaking of Sadness*; UNM Center for Social Policy, "Medicalization."
37 Blumer, *Symbolic Interactionism*; Mead, *Mind, Self and Society*.
38 Holstein and Gubrium, *Self We Live By*.
39 To analyze the interviews and online materials, I alternated between inductive (looking for themes in people's words) and deductive (comparing their words to

existing research and theoretical concepts) approaches. I highlighted interviewees' words that reflected themes and concepts, as well as utilized techniques of display to identify patterns and connections among them (see Miles and Huberman, *Qualitative Data Analysis*).

40 Aneshensel, "Mental Illness as a Career"; Becker, "Becoming a Marihuana User"; Biddle et al., "Explaining Non-Help-Seeking"; Crossley, *In the Gym*; Goffman, "Moral Career"; Karp, *Speaking of Sadness*; Suchman, "Stages of Illness."

41 Since people could move through the stages in different ways, they technically could be said to follow multiple trajectories (see Aneshensel, "Mental Illness as a Career").

42 Karp, *Speaking of Sadness*, 57.

43 Karp, 56.

44 For instance, see Beard, *Living with Alzheimer's*.

45 Conrad, Bandini, and Vasquez "Illness and the Internet"; Frank, *Wounded Storyteller*; Harrison, "Regressing or Progressing"; Hult et al., "Flipped Healthcare"; Lewis, "DIY Selves"; Petersen, "Risk."

46 Glazier et al., "High Rates"; Wilson and Thayer, "Cross-Cultural Differences."

47 Fennell and Liberato, "Learning to Live."

48 Fennell, "If You're 'So OCD' "; Schmelkin, "Hierarchy"; Tringo, "Hierarchy."

49 Levy, "Am I a Monster?"

50 Goffman, *Stigma*; Link and Phelan, "Labeling and Stigma."

51 Corrigan and Rao, "Self-Stigma."

52 Cummings, Lucas, and Druss, "Addressing Public Stigma," e1.

53 Fennell, "If You're 'So OCD' "; Warman, Phalen, and Martin, "Impact."

54 Fennell and Boyd, "Obsessive-Compulsive Disorder."

55 Julien, O'Connor, and Aardema, "Intrusions Related to Obsessive-Compulsive Disorder"; Radomsky et al., "You Can't Hide."

56 Beck, *Risk Society*; Giddens, *Modernity and Self-Identity*. Whether the prevalence of mental disorders increased over time prior to the COVID-19 pandemic is controversial. For instance, see Baxter et al., "Challenging"; Booth, Sharma, and Leader, "Age of Anxiety"; Richter, Bruen, and Whittington, "Global Prevalence"; and Twenge, "Age of Anxiety."

57 McLean Hospital, "Living with OCD."

58 Khosravani et al., "Impact of the Coronavirus Pandemic"; Nissen, Højgaard, and Thomsen, "Immediate Effect."

59 McLean Hospital, "Living with OCD."

60 American Heart Association, *Mental Health*; Cole and Warman, "Examination of Continuum"; Peter et al., "Continuum Beliefs"; Schomerus, Matschinger, and Angermeyer, "Continuum Beliefs."

61 I reproduce interviewees' words as faithfully as possible, with a few minor corrections for obvious grammatical, wording, and spelling errors or repetitions.

62 At times I reference material from online forums. Using this as part of research can be controversial, because even though the material may be publicly available,

authors/creators may not realize. For their protection, I do not identify the sites I visited and only paraphrase their words—never quoting them directly. I systematically analyze posts from one site in chapter 7; I identified myself as a researcher and gained permission to study the posts.

1. WHAT IS OCD?

1 Pavelko and Myrick, "Tweeting and Trivializing"; Rapoport, *Boy Who Couldn't Stop Washing*; Wahl, "Obsessive-Compulsive."

2 Pavelko and Myrick, "Tweeting and Trivializing."

3 Beveridge, "Images of Madness"; Carmichael et al., "Media Coverage"; Diefenbach and West, "Television and Attitudes"; Johnson and Riles, "'He Acted'"; Philo and Glasgow University Media Group, *Media and Mental Distress*; Pirkis et al., "On-Screen"; Stout, Villegas, and Jennings, "Images of Mental Illness"; Wahl, *Media Madness*.

4 Diefenbach and West, "Television and Attitudes."

5 Philo and Glasgow University Media Group, *Media and Mental Distress*; Stout, Villegas, and Jennings, "Images of Mental Illness"; Wahl, *Media Madness*.

6 Robinson et al., "Measuring Attitudes."

7 For instance, see Maier et al., "Media Influences"; Maiorano et al., "Reducing Stigma"; Ross et al., "Systematic Review."

8 Cefalu, "What's So Funny"; Davis, *Obsession*; Fennell and Boyd, "Obsessive-Compulsive Disorder"; Wahl, "Obsessive-Compulsive."

9 American Psychiatric Association, *DSM-5*.

10 Pavelko and Myrick, "Tweeting and Trivializing"; Wahl, "Obsessive-Compulsive."

11 Coles, Heimberg, and Weiss, "Public's Knowledge."

12 García-Soriano and Roncero, "What Do Spanish Adolescents Think."

13 Fennell and Boyd, "Obsessive-Compulsive Disorder."

14 Siegel, "Portrayal."

15 Clark and Rhyno, "Unwanted Intrusive Thoughts."

16 American Psychiatric Association, *DSM-5*; World Health Organization, "ICD-11."

17 American Psychiatric Association, *DSM-5*, 237.

18 Steketee, Pigott, and Schemmel, *Latest Assessment*, 1.

19 Rachman and De Silva, *Obsessive-Compulsive Disorder*, 7.

20 American Psychiatric Association, *DSM-5*; World Health Organization, "ICD-11."

21 Kramer, *Listening to Prozac*, 26.

22 Adam et al., "Obsessive-Compulsive Disorder"; Fullana et al., "Obsessions and Compulsions."

23 Conrad and Potter, "Expansion of Medical Categories."

24 Maggini et al., "Epidemiological Survey."

25 Cameron et al., "Comparison"; Eisen et al., "Five-Year Course"; Li et al., "Symptom Dimensions." In one study, "negative appraisals of intrusive thoughts were the most central symptoms in the OCD network, and they uniquely predict co-occurring symptoms of anxiety and depression" (Olatunji et al., "Core of OCD," 45).

26 For instance, see Grant and Chamberlain, "Exploring the Neurobiology."
27 D'Amico, Estivill, and Terriente, "Switching," 144.
28 Grant and Chamberlain, "Exploring the Neurobiology," n.p.
29 Buchman et al., "Neurobiological Narratives"; Hauschildt and Dar, "On the Relevance"; Hinshaw and Cicchetti, "Stigma"; Stoppard and McMullen, *Situating Sadness*.
30 Buchman et al., "Neurobiological Narratives," 67.
31 Linden, "Biological Psychiatry"; Priebe, Burns, and Craig, "Future"; Rose, *Our Psychiatric Future*.
32 Bracken et al., "Psychiatry beyond the Current Paradigm"; Zion and Crum, "Mindsets Matter."
33 Zion and Crum, "Mindsets Matter."
34 Bracken et al., "Psychiatry Beyond the Current Paradigm," 432.
35 Hinshaw and Cicchetti, "Stigma."
36 Bhui, "Cultural Neuroscience"; Bracken et al., "Psychiatry Beyond the Current Paradigm"; Fingelkurts and Fingelkurts, "Brain Space"; Linden, "Biological Psychiatry."
37 Bhui, "Cultural Neuroscience," 89.
38 Rose, *Our Psychiatric Future*.
39 Rosso et al., "Stressful Life Events."
40 Coles et al., "Obsessive Compulsive Disorder Prevalence"; Nicolini et al., "Influence of Culture"; Taylor, "Etiology."
41 Julien, O'Connor, and Aardema, "Intrusions Related to Obsessive-Compulsive Disorder"; Rachman, "Cognitive Theory of Obsessions," Radomsky et al., "You Can't Hide."
42 Belayachi and Van der Linden, "Looking for Outcomes," 158.
43 Julien, O'Connor, and Aardema, "Intrusions Related to Obsessive-Compulsive Disorder," 710.
44 Llorens-Aguilar et al., "Context"; Rachman, "Cognitive Theory of Obsessions."
45 Fisher and Wells, "Metacognitive Therapy," 118–19.
46 Fisher and Wells, 118.
47 Audet et al., "Not All Intrusions"; Nikodijevic et al., "Fear of Self."
48 Julien, O'Connor, and Aardema, "Inference-Based Approach," 189.
49 Julien, O'Connor, and Aardema, 189.
50 Aardema, "COVID-19"; Nikodijevic et al., "Fear of Self."
51 Fradkin et al., "Searching," 673.
52 American Psychiatric Association, *DSM-5*.
53 Rapoport, *Boy Who Couldn't Stop Washing*.
54 Rapoport, 177.
55 Davis, *Obsession*, 18.
56 For instance, see Coles et al., "Obsessive Compulsive Disorder Prevalence"; Fontenelle, Mendlowicz, and Versiani, "Descriptive Epidemiology"; Olson et al., "Culturally Sensitive OCD Research"; Subramaniam et al., "Prevalence, Correlates, Help-Seeking."

57 Guzick et al., "Diagnostic Description and Prevalence," 25.
58 Williams et al., "Cross-Cultural Phenomenology," 68.
59 Li et al., "Symptom Dimensions."
60 Li et al.; Wilson and Thayer, "Cross-Cultural Differences"; Yorulmaz, Gençöz, and Woody, "Vulnerability Factors."
61 Yorulmaz, Gençöz, and Woody, "Vulnerability Factors."
62 Ozcanli et al., "Obsessions across Two Cultures"; Williams and Jahn, "Obsessive-Compulsive Disorder"; Wilson and Thayer, "Cross-Cultural Differences."
63 Rapoport, *Boy Who Couldn't Stop Washing*.
64 Jutel, *Putting a Name to It*, introduction.
65 Davis, *Obsession*.
66 Davis, 212.
67 Berrios, *History of Mental Symptoms*; Davis, *Obsession*; Rachman and Hodgson, *Obsessions and Compulsions*.
68 Climacus, *Ladder*, 143.
69 Berrios, *History of Mental Symptoms*, 140.
70 Osborn, *Can Christianity Cure*, 30.
71 Friedrich, *Literary and Linguistic Construction*, 31.
72 Rachman and Hodgson, *Obsessions and Compulsions*.
73 Aardema, "COVID-19," 2.
74 Berrios, *History of Mental Symptoms*, 140.
75 Davis, *Obsession*, 13.
76 Rachman and Hodgson, *Obsessions and Compulsions*.
77 Rapoport, *Boy Who Couldn't Stop Washing*; Steketee, Pigott, and Schemmel, *Latest Assessment*.
78 Rachman and Hodgson, *Obsessions and Compulsions*, 28.
79 Rachman and Hodgson, 22.
80 Porter, *Madness*, chap. 2.
81 Porter, chap. 1.
82 Porter, chap. 2.
83 Adler and Adler, *Tender Cut*, chap. 12.
84 Conrad and Schneider, *Deviance and Medicalization*, chap. 3.
85 Conrad and Schneider, chap. 3.
86 For instance, see Priebe, Burns, and Craig, "Future."
87 Porter, *Madness*.
88 Boschen, "Publication Trends"; Davis, *Obsession*; Rapoport, *Boy Who Couldn't Stop Washing*; Rasmussen and Eisen, "Epidemiology"; Wahl, "Obsessive-Compulsive."
89 Jenike, "Hidden Epidemic," 539.

2. BUT WHAT IS IT REALLY LIKE?

1 Grayson, *Freedom*, introduction.
2 Someone asked me if people with OCD have a type of "double-consciousness." The sociologist W. E. B. DuBois wrote about having a double consciousness in *The*

Souls of Black Folk from 1903, where he pointed out that Black people have "this sense of always looking at one's self through the eyes of others, of measuring one's soul by the tape of a world that looks on in amused contempt and pity. One ever feels his two-ness,—an American, a Negro; two souls, two thoughts, two unreconciled strivings; two warring ideals" (8). People with OCD experience a different kind of double perspective, but it is there nonetheless.

3   Davis et al., "Impact," 751.

4   Agency stands in contrast to determinism (see Franks, *Neurosociology*). "A tentative list of the features distinguishing the concept of agency includes awareness of a goal, of an intention to act, and of initiation of action; awareness of movements; a sense of activity, of mental effort, and of control; and the concept of authorship" (Balconi, "Preface," v).

5   Balconi, "Sense of Agency," 3.

6   Holstein and Gubrium, *Self We Live By*.

7   Charmaz, *Good Days*; Goffman, *Presentation of Self*.

8   Control has long been a component in theoretical understandings of OCD, but in different ways. For instance, when speaking of obsessions, Aardema and O'Connor noted the "tendency" of people with some forms of OCD to engage in "metacognitive thought and control" and wrote that "other researchers before us have noted the excessive control exercised by OCD patients in regulating their mental states" ("Menace Within," 188). However, for Aardema and O'Connor it is not that people with OCD are inherently overly concerned with control, but "the belief that the person is really experiencing a motivated impulse while in fact this is not the case leads to obvious problems with a sense of control since the person attempts to remove motivated thoughts that are not there" (189). Other researchers found that "the fear of cognitive dyscontrol resulting from anxious arousal was uniquely predictive of difficulties with unacceptable thoughts" (Wheaton et al., "Relationship," 895). Meanwhile, an article published in *Brain and Cognition* suggested "the main problem in OCD might be difficulty activating the right frontoparietal networks during tasks that require cognitive control, which might result in the intrusiveness of obsessive thoughts" (Koçak et al., "Cognitive Control," 390). Grayson wrote, "Almost all rituals [compulsions] involve the attempt to control or stop feelings, with anxiety being the most common feeling" (*Freedom*, chap. 3).

Part of having agency is engaging in acts; researchers found that "OCD patients fail to predict and suppress the sensory consequences of their own actions. The increased mismatch between expected and actual outcomes caused by this forward model dysfunction may explain persistent feelings of incompleteness even after properly executed actions and the augmented search for control in these patients" (Gentsch et al., "Dysfunctional," 652). Timpano and Schmidt, when looking at self-control and hoarding, found that "depleting self-control resources was associated with an increase in subsequent saving behaviors" ("Relationship," 13). As part of a treatment method, Schwartz and

Beyette advocated that people with OCD change their own brain chemistry (*Brain Lock*). For examples of how OCD can be understood as a "disturbance of agency," see Belayachi and Van der Linden, "Looking for Outcomes," 167.

9 Gagné and Radomsky, "Manipulating Beliefs."
10 OCD Center of Los Angeles, "Harm OCD."
11 Grayson, *Freedom*.
12 Hershfield, "Mistaken Beliefs."
13 Fennell and Liberato, "Learning to Live."
14 Seay, "Suicide Obsessions."
15 Barker, *Fibromyalgia Story*.
16 Kelly and Field, "Medical Sociology," 248.
17 Bowen, Brenton, and Elliott, *Pressure Cooker*, chap. 7.
18 Belayachi and Van der Linden, "Looking for Outcomes."
19 Boschen and Vuksanovic, "Deteriorating Memory Confidence"; March and Benton, *Talking Back*; Ouellet-Courtois, Wilson, and O'Connor, "Cognitive Confidence"; Radomsky and Alcolado, "Don't Even."
20 McGuire et al., "Role of Avoidance."
21 Coles and Ravid, "Clinical Presentation."
22 Burchi and Pallanti, "Diagnostic Issues."
23 Rachman and De Silva, *Obsessive-Compulsive Disorder*.
24 Capawana, "Developmental Psychopathology," 106.
25 Steketee and van Noppen, "Family Approaches," 44.
26 Fennell and Liberato, "Learning to Live."
27 Rigney, *Metaphorical Society*; Sontag, *Illness as Metaphor*.
28 March and Benton, *Talking Back*, chap. 6.
29 Other common metaphors interviewees used treated OCD as chaotic or overmuch in some way, e.g., as a blockage or limiting force, as something repeating or stuck (sometimes leading them to feel stuck), or as a facade or other reality.
30 Fennell and Liberato, "Learning to Live."
31 Purdon et al., "Development," 200.
32 Foucault, "About the Beginning," 201.
33 American Psychiatric Association, *DSM-5*.
34 American Psychiatric Association, 238.

3. TREATMENTS, OLD AND NEW

1 For instance, see Hershfield, "Mistaken Beliefs"; Grayson, *Freedom*; Salkovskis and Kobori, "Reassuringly Calm."
2 Penzel, "To Be or Not to Be."
3 Wegner et al., "Paradoxical."
4 Hershfield and Corboy, *Mindfulness Workbook*; Penzel, "'But I Love My Kids . . .'"
5 Esman, "Obsessive-Compulsive."
6 McKay, Abramowitz, and Storch, "Ineffective."
7 Rapoport, *Boy Who Couldn't Stop Washing*, 101.

8 Siev, Huppert, and Zuckerman, "Understanding," 535.

9 McKay, Abramowitz, and Storch, "Ineffective."

10 Steketee, Pigott, and Schemmel, *Latest Assessment*, 39.

11 Keyes, Nolte, and Williams, "Battle."

12 Dumit, *Drugs for Life*, introduction.

13 Kramer, *Listening to Prozac*.

14 Kramer, 33.

15 Pittenger and Bloch, "Pharmacological Treatment."

16 Greist, "Comparative Effectiveness."

17 Goddard et al., "Serotoninergic Mechanisms."

18 Stokes and Holtz, "Fluoxetine."

19 Catapano et al., "Obsessive-Compulsive Disorder"; Skapinakis et al., "Systematic Review"; Stein et al., "Obsessive-Compulsive Disorder"; Steketee, Pigott, and Schemmel, *Latest Assessment*.

20 Kotapati et al., "Effectiveness," 12.

21 Rose, *Our Psychiatric Future*.

22 It is expensive to carry out studies involving medications, so research has often been conducted by pharmaceutical companies, which arguably is a conflict of interest (Dumit, *Drugs for Life*). Negative studies have been published less often than those showing positive results. Research and development have been conducted in such a way to promote the most use of medications and earn the most money, not necessarily what is best for health or the most efficient use of medications. Many issues have not been prioritized in research, such as the best methods to get off medications and their long-term side effects (Dumit, *Drugs for Life*; Rose, *Our Psychiatric Future*).

23 Roberts, Sahakian, and Robbins, "Psychological Mechanisms"; Rose, *Our Psychiatric Future*.

24 Bloch et al., "Long-Term Outcome"; Eisen et al., "Five-Year Course"; Hirschtritt, Bloch, and Mathews, "Obsessive-Compulsive Disorder"; Skapinakis et al., "Systematic Review"; Skoog and Skoog, "40-Year Follow-Up"; Springer, Levy, and Tolin, "Remission"; Stein et al., "Obsessive-Compulsive Disorder." Authors of one metanalysis wrote, "Remission rates in the modern era have not improved compared with those reported in earlier studies . . . despite the wide availability of effective treatments," but more data are needed (Skapinakis et al., "Systematic Review," 9).

25 Abramowitz, Taylor, and McKay, "Potentials and Limitations"; Skapinakis et al., "Systematic Review"; Uhre et al., "Systematic Review."

26 Hauschildt and Dar, "On the Relevance," 1.

27 International OCD Foundation, "Ineffective."

28 Schwartz and Beyette, *Brain Lock*.

29 Rachman, "Evolution."

30 Salkovskis and Kirk, "Obsessive-Compulsive Disorder," 181–82.

31 Salkovskis and Kirk, "Obsessive-Compulsive Disorder"; Stein et al., "Obsessive-Compulsive Disorder."

32 Keleher, Jassi, and Krebs, "Clinician-Reported Barriers."
33 Clark, "Focus"; Rachman, "Evolution"; Wilhelm et al., "Mechanisms of Change."
34 Abramowitz, Taylor, and McKay, "Potentials and Limitations," 141.
35 Abramowitz, Taylor, and McKay, 142.
36 One issue of debate is whether people with OCD have cognitive deficits (like dysfunctions in how they process certain types of information) or cognitive biases (like having distorted beliefs about how dangerous certain things are) (Ouimet, Ashbaugh, and Radomsky, "Hoping for More").
37 Inference Based Approach, "What Is IBA?," n.p.
38 O'Connor and Audet, "OCD Is Not a Phobia," 45.
39 Clark, "Focus"; O'Connor and Audet, "OCD Is Not a Phobia"; Ong, "Dropout"; Schneider et al., "Serious."
40 Abramowitz et al., "New Directions"; Manjula and Sudhir, "New-Wave Behavioral Therapies."
41 Manjula and Sudhir, "New-Wave Behavioral Therapies," S105.
42 Hayes, Strosahl, and Wilson, *Acceptance and Commitment Therapy*.
43 Kelly, "Buddhist Psychology"; Olson, "Buddhism."
44 Schwartz and Beyette, *Brain Lock*, xxxv.
45 Fennell, "Explorations."
46 Ñāṇamoli and Bodhi, *Middle Length Discourses*, pt. 1.
47 Schwartz and Beyette, *Brain Lock*, 7.
48 Schwartz and Beyette, 7.
49 Franks, *Neurosociology*.
50 Hershfield and Corboy, *Mindfulness Workbook*.
51 Karcı and Celik, "Nutritional and Herbal"; Sarris, Camfield, and Berk, "Complementary Medicine."
52 Balachander, Arumughan, and Srinivas, "Ablative Neurosurgery"; Kumar et al., "Comparative Effectiveness"; Mian et al., "Deep Brain Stimulation."
53 Nuñez, Zinbarg, and Mittal, "Efficacy and Mechanisms"

4. IS IT ME OR IS THERE A PROBLEM?

1 One doctor said that Zelda had schizophrenia-like symptoms, but she thought he misunderstood her symptoms.
2 Schur, *Labeling Deviant Behavior*.
3 Foa and Wilson, *Stop Obsessing*; personal communication with an OCD specialist.
4 Bury, "Sociology of Chronic Illness."
5 Goffman, "Moral Career."
6 Goffman, 126.
7 Beard, *Living with Alzheimer's*.
8 Parsons, *Social System*.
9 Belloch et al., "To Seek Advice."
10 Albert et al., "Duration of Untreated Illness"; Belloch et al., "To Seek Advice"; Jorm et al., "Increased Provision"; Levy et al., "Characteristics"; Marques et al.,

"Barriers"; Rapoport, *Boy Who Couldn't Stop Washing*; Schwartz et al., "Treatment-Seeking"; Subramaniam et al., "Prevalence, Correlates, Help-Seeking"; Torres et al., "Treatment Seeking"; Wang et al., "Use of Mental Health Services."

11 Belloch et al., "To Seek Advice"; Beşiroğlu, Çilli, and Aşkın, "Predictors"; García-Soriano et al., "Factors"; Goodwin et al., "Helpseeking"; Mayerovitch et al., "Treatment Seeking"; Stengler et al., "Mental Health Treatment"; Williams and Jahn, "Obsessive-Compulsive Disorder."

12 Goffman defined stigma as an undesirable gap between "virtual social identity" and "actual social identity" (*Stigma*, 2). Building from these ideas, I am describing a type of self-stigma linked to people's perceptions of their thoughts/behaviors (see Fennell and Liberato, "Learning to Live").

13 American Psychiatric Association, *DSM-5*, 21.

14 Blumer, *Symbolic Interactionism*.

15 Watson, *Golden Arches East*.

16 Watson.

17 Williams, "Chronic Illness."

18 Williams, 57.

19 Holstein and Gubrium, *Self We Live By*.

20 Fennell and Liberato, "Learning to Live."

21 Mead, *Mind, Self and Society*.

22 Holstein and Gubrium, *Self We Live By*, 29.

23 Karp, *Speaking of Sadness*.

24 Karp, 58.

25 Belloch et al., "To Seek Advice"; Thompson, Issakidis, and Hunt, "Delay."

26 For instance, see Suchman, "Stages of Illness."

27 Berkman et al., "Family-Based Treatment."

28 Farrell and Barrett, "Function of the Family," 313.

29 Farrell and Barrett.

30 At various points in the illness experience, we can find people trying to "normalize" what is happening. For instance, researchers have used the term "normalization" to refer to aspects of living with an illness or disability, such as attempts to maintain or regain a sense of the typical (e.g., Strauss *Chronic Illness*). The concept of "normalization" was perhaps first used in the Danish human services context to ensure the "mentally retarded" were granted the resources to achieve the same life conditions as everyone else (Wolfensberger, *Principle of Normalization*). My interviewees were describing something a bit different (i.e., perceiving what they were thinking/doing as nonproblematic). Researchers have noticed this, and at times referred to this as normalization, but I find it a bit confusing to use the same terminology.

31 Cicourel, *Cognitive Sociology*; Garfinkel, "Studies of the Routine"; Heritage, *Garfinkel and Ethnomethodology*.

32 Boydell et al., "Youth."

33 Frances, "*DSM5* in Distress."

34 Fontenelle and Yücel, "Clinical Staging."

35 Albert et al., "Duration of Untreated Illness"; Fontenelle and Yücel, "Clinical Staging."

36 García-Soriano et al., "Factors"; Suchman, "Stages of Illness."

37 Rapoport, *Boy Who Couldn't Stop Washing*, 13.

38 We can understand this through Goffman's theories on the presentation of the self. In chapter 8, I explain this theory and provide a move comprehensive depiction of the different ways people with OCD hid and revealed their thoughts/behaviors.

39 American Psychiatric Association, *DSM-5*; Purdon et al., "Development"; Storch, Geffken, and Murphy, *Handbook of Child*.

40 Nikodijevic et al., "Fear of Self."

41 Karp, in *Speaking of Sadness*, found that people with depression commonly blamed external circumstances at first for ill feelings, while the people I interviewed seemed to draw from more explanations, especially internal and psychological ones.

42 Jorm, "Mental Health Literacy."

43 For instance, see Picco et al., "Association."

44 Simonds and Elliott, "OCD Patients," 439.

45 Holstein and Gubrium, *Self We Live By*, 96.

5. STIGMA AND TRIVIALIZATION

1 Jutel, *Putting a Name to It*.

2 Fennell and Boyd, "Obsessive-Compulsive Disorder."

3 In about 5.5 percent of cases, other people (such as friends) helped interviewees perceive their thoughts/behaviors as OCD. One person told me they just knew it was OCD. In 9.1 percent of cases, how they came to see themselves as having OCD was unclear.

4 Wahl, "Obsessive-Compulsive."

5 Rapoport, *Boy Who Couldn't Stop Washing*.

6 For instance, see Coles, Heimberg, and Weiss, "Public's Knowledge"; García-Soriano and Roncero, "What Do Spanish Adolescents Think."

7 Coles, Heimberg, and Weiss, "Public's Knowledge."

8 Glazier et al., "High Rates."

9 Jenike, "Obsessive-Compulsive Disorder," 259.

10 Penzel, "'But I Love My Kids . . .'"; Rachman, "Cognitive Theory of Obsessions."

11 Glazier et al., "High Rates."

12 Glazier et al., 208.

13 Booth et al., "Obsessions."

14 Challacombe and Wroe, "A Hidden Problem."

15 Conrad, "Medicalization and Social Control"; Jutel, *Putting a Name to It*.

16 Liegghio, "Too Young to Be Mad."

17 Pattyn et al., "Medicalizing versus Psychologizing."
18 Barker, *Fibromyalgia Story*, 11.
19 Barker, "Social Construction."
20 Dumit, Drugs for Life, chap. 2.
21 Conrad and Potter, "Expansion of Medical Categories."
22 Barker, "Social Construction," 152.
23 Beard, *Living with Alzheimer's*; Jutel, *Putting a Name to It*.
24 Guthman, *Obesity*, 25–26.
25 Parsons, *Social System*.
26 Barker, *Fibromyalgia Story*; Hilbert, "Acultural Dimensions"; Kroll-Smith and Floyd, *Bodies in Protest*.
27 Jutel, *Putting a Name to It*, introduction.
28 Barker, *Fibromyalgia Story*, 65.
29 Jutel, *Putting a Name to It*.
30 Harrington, *Cure Within*.
31 Beard, *Living with Alzheimer's*.
32 Karp, *Speaking of Sadness*, 65.
33 Goffman, *Stigma*; Link and Phelan, "Labeling and Stigma."
34 Goffman, *Stigma*, 2.
35 Link and Phelan, "Labeling and Stigma."
36 Link, Phelan, and Sullivan, "Mental and Physical."
37 Hinshaw and Cicchetti, "Stigma."
38 Baldwin and Marcus, "Labor Market"; Corker et al., "Viewpoint Survey"; Elraz, "Identity"; Hipes et al., "Stigma"; Pescosolido, "Public Stigma"; Thornicroft, *Shunned*.
39 Thoits, "Disentangling."
40 Corrigan and Rao, "Self-Stigma"; Marcussen, Gallagher, and Ritter, "Mental Illness."
41 For instance, see Schmelkin, "Hierarchy"; Tringo, "Hierarchy."
42 Fennell and Boyd, "Obsessive-Compulsive Disorder."
43 I performed this search in 2017. I engaged in a type of research called a content analysis, where I filled out a "coding protocol" that had a list of elements I wanted to document about each piece, including how they represented stigma and trivialization.
44 Raiola, "Why You Need to Stop."
45 Singh, "Disorder of Anger and Aggression."
46 Grayson, *Freedom*, chap. 1.
47 Rüsch, Angermeyer, and Corrigan, "Mental Illness Stigma."
48 Gergel, "Too Similar, Too Different," 148.
49 Warman, Phalen, and Martin, "Impact."
50 The study was approved by the institution's institutional review board, and participants provided informed consent. Students completed the survey online, and any participants who started but did not complete the majority of the survey were

omitted. Where possible, vignettes were drawn from other studies to facilitate comparisons. The vignette about *inadvertent harm* depicted someone with worries about something bad or harmful happening and who engaged in checking behaviors (modified from Koutoufa and Furnham, "Mental Health Literacy"), e.g., worries about the stove being turned off. *Sexual orientation* depicted someone in a heterosexual relationship who wondered if they were gay, and who tried to assess their sexual arousal when in the presence of the same sex (taken from Glazier et al., "High Rates"). *Blasphemy* depicted someone who was concerned about people saying negative comments about God or other spiritual entities; therefore, they prayed repeatedly to feel safe from harm (modified from Glazier et al., "High Rates" to be open to multiple faiths). *Contamination* depicted someone concerned about dirt and germs to the point that they avoided touching contaminated objects and washed their hands (modified from Glazier et al. "High Rates" to include how someone with OCD can feel that people who touch contaminated objects become contaminated). This was done to make the scenario more equivalent to the other vignettes which depicted symptoms that had impacts on the lives of those around people with OCD. *Order/symmetry* depicted someone concerned with symmetry and exactness and magical thinking, to the point where they felt uneasy if their family moved things in the house and therefore later adjusted them; this vignette was created based on the Yale-Brown Obsessive-Compulsive Scale-Symptom Checklist (Goodman et al., "Yale-Brown") and examples from Grayson's *Freedom from Obsessive-Compulsive Disorder*. The vignette about *harm* OCD depicted taboo thoughts about physical aggression/harm, i.e., someone who feared harming a woman at the subway station and visualized the situation to make sure they did not cause harm (taken from Glazier et al., "High Rates"). *Child sexual* depicted someone with "pedophilia OCD" or someone who had thoughts about touching their nieces/nephews in a sexually inappropriate manner and began to avoid contact with them (taken from Glazier et al., "High Rates"). *Relationship* depicted "relationship OCD," where someone noticed an attractive person at the store and began to worry if that meant they did not love their partner; they began to assess their attraction to their significant other and confess their doubts to their partner. This was created based on examples from the OCD Center of Los Angeles ("ROCD"). Vignettes depicted someone who was twenty-one years old (to be college-age, akin to the respondents), and who was generically referred to as Person A (Person B, and so on), to avoid gender bias. The vignettes and questions about social distance and accommodation were the same in every survey, but some students were asked additional questions (e.g., for more in-depth information).

51 Note that many participants expressed some uncertainty. I grouped their free-form answers into categories. If they mentioned general terms such as "anxiety" or "anxiety disorder" (even if they were not completely sure of their answers), I called that *anxiety*. If they mentioned the name of another mental disorder or illness (including a specific anxiety disorder like GAD), generally spoke of the

person having an illness/disorder/disability of some kind, or wrote down a term/symptom commonly associated with an illness/disorder/disability (even if they expressed uncertainty)—I categorized this as *other type of illness/disorder/disability*. If they indicated that the person did not have an illness/disorder/disability, I marked *none*; some people seemed to be using the term "stress" to downplay the content of the vignette, or they used other terminology that did not appear to signify an illness/disorder disability (e.g. "homosexuality," "highly religious"), so I also marked this as *none*. If the only thing they said was that they were unsure, or they wrote down terms that I was not sure how to categorize (e.g., "bad person," "suicide," "identity crisis"), I labeled this *don't know/unclear response*. If people marked down two illnesses/disorders/disabilities and one was OCD, I counted this in the *OCD* category; I did the same for anxiety. If they said "none" or similar wording, while also mentioning the possibility of an illness/disorder/disability, I categorized this as *don't know/unclear response*. I reported some of my initial results previously in Fennell, "If You're 'So OCD.'"

52 For that vignette, the table shows 45.8 percent of respondents marked no illness/disorder/disability. More specifically, 35.7 percent indicated none. A few respondents indicated the person was not heterosexual (e.g., gay); a number of others mentioned that the person could be confused or disoriented regarding their sexuality, but it was not always clear if respondents were arguing this confusion reached the level of an illness/disorder/disability.

53 OCD Center of Los Angeles, "Harm OCD."

54 To assess significance, I used the nonparametric Friedman test (see the last column of table 5.4). Results showed that people's willingness to interact with people with OCD did vary by vignette (or form of OCD); people's support for accommodations also varied by vignette. To assess which forms affected people's responses specifically, I used SPSS to calculate pairwise multiple comparisons using the Dunn-Bonferroni test. Listwise deletion for missing data was used. More specifically, there were significant differences in support for accommodations when I compared answers about obsessions dealing with inadvertent harm to all other types of OCD. This was also true between obsessions about causing harm and all other types of OCD. Additional significant differences were detected; please contact the author for more information.

55 Results from post hoc analyses showed that the most salient differences were related to thoughts of harm and pedophilia. Students wanted increased distance from people with these forms of OCD compared with other types of OCD. Meanwhile, differences in willingness to interact with people with the other concerns were sometimes, but not always, significantly different.

56 Pachankis et al., "Burden."

6. COPING AND TREATMENT

1 It is tricky to assess the rates at which people with OCD improve over the long term and achieve remission. Studies measure remission in various ways; research-

ers monitor groups of people with OCD over different time periods (from a couple years to forty years), and samples can include people who participated in various forms of treatment.

2 Balachander, Arumughan, and Srinivas, "Ablative Neurosurgery,"; Bloch et al., "Long-Term Outcome"; Eisen et al., "Five-Year Course"; Hirschtritt, Bloch, and Mathews, "Obsessive-Compulsive Disorder"; Kotapati et al., "Effectiveness"; Skapinakis et al., "Systematic Review"; Skoog and Skoog, "40-Year Follow-Up"; Springer, Levy, and Tolin, "Remission." For instance, in one long-term study of a sample of people with OCD in the United States who took SRI medications, 49 percent still faced clinically significant symptoms (Bloch et al., "Long-Term Outcome").

3 Balachander, Arumughan, and Srinivas, "Ablative Neurosurgery," S77.

4 Barker, *Fibromyalgia Story*; Karp, *Speaking of Sadness*.

5 Karp, *Is It Me*, 62.

6 Albert et al., "Duration of Untreated Illness"; Torres et al., "Treatment Seeking."

7 Jorm et al., "Increased Provision."

8 Shapiro, *Understanding OCD*, chap. 9.

9 Parsons, *Social System*.

10 Mick's OCD started when he was a child, and even then, he wanted to protect his compulsions. Mick's mother took him to a psychiatrist and psychologist, but he confessed that "my mom and I had different ideas about the purpose of these visits. She wanted my compulsions brought to heel, reduced, so I'd seem less weird to casual observers and, more importantly, be less burdened, more functional. I was fiercely and stubbornly defensive about my compulsions, but wanted the psychiatry to reduce my anxiety and obsessions, to help me better understand and manage my psyche, and learn to control my thoughts. Consequently, the only treatment I received in those years was psychotherapy. It is not generally effective for OCD, but I would've refused treatment against compulsions." As an adult, Mick maintained the same view on compulsions.

11 Polimeni, Reiss, and Sareen, "Could Obsessive-Compulsive Disorder Have Originated," 658.

12 Carey, "Marijuana and OCD."

13 Coping strategies can be defined as "constantly changing cognitive and behavioral efforts to manage specific external and/or internal demands that are appraised as taxing or exceeding the resources of the person" (Lazarus and Folkman, *Stress, Appraisal, and Coping*, 141). In the chronic illness literature, Bury argued that we should distinguish cognitive attempts that people make to deal with illness and maintain a sense of who they are (which he labeled "coping") from actions people take in response to their illness (which he labeled "strategies") (Bury, "Sociology of Chronic Illness"). In the case of OCD, I did not find that these were clearly separable.

14 Rachman and De Silva, *Obsessive-Compulsive Disorder*; Steketee, Pigott, and Schemmel, *Latest Assessment*.

15 Purdon and Clark, *Overcoming Obsessive Thoughts*, 71.

16 Purdon, "Empirical"; Wegner et al., "Paradoxical."

17 Williams and Jahn, "Obsessive-Compulsive Disorder."

18 Karp, *Is It Me*; Karp, *Speaking of Sadness*.

19 Fennell, "If You're 'So OCD'"; Karp, *Is It Me*; Karp, *Speaking of Sadness*.

20 Hirschtritt, Bloch, and Mathews, "Obsessive-Compulsive Disorder."

21 Bury, "Sociology of Chronic Illness," 460.

22 For Grayson, OCD is "both a learned and a biological disorder," although he said the biological aspect "is not always active" (*Freedom*, chap. 2). He advised readers that medication is useful when the latter is active or else it can feel like you are "trying to stop drinking while you are in a bar with all your drinking buddies" (*Freedom*, chap. 4).

23 Karp, *Is It Me*; Karp, *Speaking of Sadness*.

24 Schwartz and Beyette, *Brain Lock*, 8.

25 Schwartz and Gladding, *You Are Not*, 73.

26 Their approach focuses on CBT and ACT but also includes expressive therapies such as yoga, mindfulness, and art (see https://www.mcleanhospital.org/).

27 For instance, see Bucarelli and Purdon, "Diary Study"; Salkovskis and Kobori, "Reassuringly Calm"; Veale, "Psychopathology."

28 March and Benton, *Talking Back*, introduction.

29 For instance, see Bucarelli and Purdon, "Diary Study"; Rachman et al., "Remain Neutral"; Salkovskis and Kobori, "Reassuringly Calm."

30 Rachman et al., "Remain Neutral," 889.

31 Bucarelli and Purdon, "Diary Study"; Haciomeroglu, "Role of Reassurance"; Rachman, "Cognitive Theory of Obsessions"; Rachman, "Cognitive Theory of Compulsive Checking"; Rachman et al., "Remain Neutral."

32 Rachman, "Cognitive Theory of Compulsive Checking," 629.

33 Rachman.

34 Boschen and Vuksanovic, "Deteriorating Memory Confidence"; Bucarelli and Purdon, "Diary Study"; Ouellet-Courtois, Wilson, and O'Connor, "Cognitive Confidence"; Radomsky and Alcolado, "Don't Even."

35 Van Dis and van den Hout, "Not Just Right Experiences," 100.

36 OCD Center of Los Angeles, "HOCD/Gay OCD."

37 Veale, "Psychopathology," 67.

38 Penzel, "'But I Love My Kids . . .'"

39 OCD Center of Los Angeles, "Imaginal Exposure."

40 Cobb, "Understanding Scrupulosity," 26.

41 Grayson, *Freedom*, chap. 6.

42 Grayson.

43 O'Connor and Audet, "OCD Is Not a Phobia."

44 Rachman, Radomsky, and Shafran, "Safety Behaviour."

45 Bucarelli and Purdon, "Diary Study," 214.

46 "This occurs when the OCD sufferer starts to experience less anxiety in response to their unwanted thoughts, and then begins to obsess that they are *not anxious enough* about these thoughts" (OCD Center of Los Angeles, "Doubt").

47 Charmaz, *Good Days*.

48 Remmerswaal, Batelaan, and van Balkom, "Relieving."

49 Stengler-Wenzke et al., "Coping Strategies"; Walseth et al., "Obsessive-Compulsive Disorder's Impact."

50 Shapiro, *Understanding OCD*, chap. 10.

51 Boeding et al., "Let Me Check"; Lebowitz, Panza, and Bloch, "Family Accommodation"; Steketee and van Noppen, "Family Approaches."

52 Francazio et al., "Parental Accommodation."

53 Salkovskis and Kobori, "Reassuringly Calm."

54 Elements of expressed emotion can negatively affect those with OCD. Research has shown that expressed emotion "assessed mainly via a combination of criticism and emotional over-involvement" (Steketee and van Noppen, "Family Approaches," 45) can negatively affect the treatment response of those with mental disorders. For examples, see Peris et al., "Pediatric Obsessive"; Steketee and van Noppen, "Family Approaches."

55 Angermeyer, Schulze, and Dietrich, "Courtesy Stigma"; Goffman, *Stigma*.

56 Wu et al., "Quality of Life."

7. THE POWER OF KNOWLEDGE

1 Barker, *Fibromyalgia Story*; Karp, *Speaking of Sadness*; Schneider and Conrad, *Having Epilepsy*.

2 Bourdieu, "Forms of Capital"; Lamont and Lareau, "Cultural Capital."

3 Adler and Adler, *Tender Cut*.

4 Lewis, "DIY Selves," 462.

5 Samerski, "Health Literacy," 5.

6 Bury, "Researching Patient-Professional Interactions"; Weiss and Fitzpatrick, "Challenges to Medicine."

7 Conrad, "Medicalization and Social Control."

8 Bury, "Researching Patient-Professional Interactions"; Pescosolido and Boyer, "American Health Care"; Traynor, Boland, and Buus, "Professional Autonomy"; Weiss and Fitzpatrick, "Challenges to Medicine"; Willis, "Introduction"; Winnick, "From Quackery"; Ziebland, "Importance of Being Expert."

9 Bellack and Drapalski, "Issues and Developments," 156.

10 Williams and Jahn, "Obsessive-Compulsive Disorder."

11 Adler and Adler, *Tender Cut*.

12 Dumit, *Drugs for Life*.

13 Linardon et al., "Efficacy of App-Supported," 325.

14 Linardon et al., 325.

15 How do these other forms of capital relate to economics? To quote Bourdieu, "It has to be posited simultaneously that economic capital is at the root of all the

other types of capital and that these transformed, disguised forms of economic capital, never entirely reducible to that definition, produce their most specific effects only to the extent that they conceal (not least from their possessors) the fact that economic capital is at their root, in other words—but only in the last analysis—at the root of their effects" (Bourdieu, "Forms of Capital," 252).

16 Cockerham, *Sociology of Mental Disorder*, 149.
17 Verlinde et al., "Social Gradient."
18 Verlinde et al.
19 Ong et al., "Doctor-Patient Communication"; Schneider and Conrad, *Having Epilepsy*.
20 Bourdieu, "Forms of Capital"; Bourdieu and Wacquant, *Invitation*.
21 Bourdieu used the term "fields" (see Bourdieu and Wacquant, *Invitation*).
22 Lamont and Lareau explaining Bourdieu, "Cultural Capital," 154.
23 Abel, "Cultural Capital," n.p.
24 Grineski, "Parental Accounts"; Shim, "Cultural Health Capital." Cultural capital (a concept developed by Bourdieu and Passeron) has been defined in different ways (see Lamont and Lareau, "Cultural Capital"). It includes educational qualifications or credentials that are institutionalized in society. People can have cultural capital in themselves as well, e.g., an ability to speak a particular language. Cultural capital can also exist in the form of objects like books and instruments, but of course for these to be used successfully one must have personal knowledge of how to use/read them or have access to others with this ability (see Bourdieu, "Forms of Capital").
25 Grineski, "Parental Accounts."
26 Parsons, *Social System*; Siu, "Seeing."
27 Timothy's Law improved coverage for mental illness in New York State.
28 Kirsch, Wampold, and Kelley, "Controlling," 127.
29 Beard, *Living with Alzheimer's*; Kirsch, Wampold, and Kelley, "Controlling"; Moerman and Jonas, "Deconstructing"; Ong et al., "Doctor-Patient Communication"; Zion and Crum, "Mindsets Matter."
30 Moerman and Jonas, "Deconstructing," 473.
31 Karp, *Is It Me*.
32 Parsons, *Social System*.
33 MacDonald, Sohn, and Ellis, "Privacy."
34 Kusalaruk, Saipanish, and Hiranyatheb, "Attitudes."
35 Steinberg and Wetterneck, "OCD Taboo."
36 Olbrich, Stengler, and Olbrich, "Smartphone."
37 Luu et al., "Internet-Based"; Mataix-Cols and Marks, "Self-Help."
38 Whittal and McLean, "CBT for OCD."
39 Grayson, "Series Response," 416–17.
40 Rosmarin, Pirutinsky, and Siev, "Recognition of Scrupulosity."
41 Conrad, Bandini, and Vasquez, "Illness and the Internet."
42 Adler and Adler, *Tender Cut*.
43 Bourdieu and Wacquant, *Invitation*, 119.

44 Ferlander, "Importance."

45 Meier and Schäfer, "Positive Side."

46 Adler and Adler, *Tender Cut*; Beard, *Living with Alzheimer's*.

8. LIFE GOES ON

1 Brown, Huszar, and Chapman, "'Betwixt and Between.'"

2 Fennell and Liberato, "Learning to Live."

3 Dumit, *Drugs for Life*.

4 Steketee and van Noppen, "Family Approaches."

5 Steketee and van Noppen, 44.

6 Steketee and van Noppen.

7 Steketee and van Noppen.

8 Nikodijevic et al., "Fear of Self"; Shapiro, *Understanding OCD*.

9 In *Stigma*, Goffman talked about hidden failings or flaws.

10 Hochschild, *Managed Heart*.

11 Goffman, *Stigma*.

12 Goffman; Hochschild, *Managed Heart*.

13 Brohan et al., "Development."

14 Brooks, "Social Performance," 258.

15 Goffman, *Stigma*, chap. 2.

16 Interviewees generally did not frame their interactions as hiding their "true" selves while presenting a fake self. However, in a different study, some people portrayed a mental distance between themselves and romantic partners because they "did not reveal a genuine version of themselves" (Walseth et al., "Obsessive-Compulsive Disorder's Impact," 205).

17 Fennell and Liberato, "Learning to Live."

18 There is some evidence that being secretive, overcompensating, and trying to disprove stereotypes can have negative effects on self-esteem (Ilic et al., "Protecting Self-Esteem").

19 Heritage, *Garfinkel and Ethnomethodology*.

20 In another study, some people with OCD found this humiliating (Walseth et al., "Obsessive-Compulsive Disorder's Impact").

21 Charmaz, *Good Days*.

22 Fennell, "If You're 'So OCD.'"

23 Fennell.

24 Goffman, *Presentation of Self*.

25 For instance, see Chaudoir, Earnshaw, and Andel, "'Discredited.'"

26 Ramos-Cerqueira et al., "Emotional Burden."

27 This has been mentioned in other research; for example, see Steketee and van Noppen, "Family Approaches."

28 Keyes, Nolte, and Williams, "Battle."

29 Thornicroft, *Shunned*.

30 Shapiro, *Understanding OCD*, chap. 1.

31 Fleischer and Zames, *Disability Rights*, xix.
32 Barnes, "Understanding"; Fleischer and Zames, *Disability Rights*.
33 Union of the Physically Impaired Against Segregation and Disability Alliance, *Fundamental Principles*, 3–4.
34 Barnes, "Understanding"; Thomas, "Medical Sociology"; Union of the Physically Impaired Against Segregation and Disability Alliance, *Fundamental Principles*.
35 People can have impairments that are mental, physical, or intellectual, and these can overlap. Those with disabilities are not a small and isolated group. In the United States alone, millions of people are disabled; more than 25 percent of people had a disability in 2014 (Taylor, *Americans with Disabilities*).
36 Beresford, "Psychiatric"; Campbell and Rose, "Action for Change"; Mulvany, "Disability." For instance, the United States has been divided at times by those who want to modify the current system versus those who seek alternatives. The disability movement has also been in tension with medical sociology, the latter being more reductionistic and medico-centric. Disability studies has placed more emphasis on social oppression, social structure, interpersonal consequences, and the agency of those who are disabled (Ostrow and Adams, "Recovery"; Thomas, "Medical Sociology").
37 Beresford, "Psychiatric," 152.
38 Myrick, Major, and Jankowski, "Sources."
39 Gordon and Rosenblum, "Bringing Disability," 16.
40 Graby, "Neurodiversity," 234.
41 Rose, "Mainstreaming."

CONCLUSION

1 Beard, *Living with Alzheimer's*.
2 Green, *End of Stigma*.
3 Link and Phelan, "Labeling and Stigma."
4 Pavelko and Myrick, "Measuring Trivialization."
5 Myrick and Pavelko, "Examining Differences," 876.
6 Corrigan and Fong, "Competing"; Schomerus, Matschinger, and Angermeyer, "Continuum Beliefs"; Wong et al., "Effects."
7 Time to Change.
8 For instance, see Schomerus, Matschinger, and Angermeyer, "Continuum Beliefs."
9 Buchman et al., "Neurobiological Narratives."
10 Karp, *Is It Me*, 211–12.
11 Pescosolido et al., "'Backbone,'" 857.
12 Pescosolido et al.; Buchman et al., "Neurobiological Narratives"; Kvaale, Gottdiener, and Haslam, "Biogenetic Explanations"; Loughman and Haslam, "Neuroscientific Explanations."
13 Makowski et al., "Continuum Beliefs"; Peter et al., "Continuum Beliefs"; Schomerus, Matschinger, and Angermeyer, "Continuum Beliefs"; Subramaniam et al., "Continuum"; Thibodeau, Shanks, and Smith, "Continuum."

14 Schomerus, Matschinger, and Angermeyer, "Continuum Beliefs," 665.
15 Thibodeau, Shanks, and Smith, "Continuum."
16 Corrigan and Fong, "Competing," 115.
17 Cole and Warman, "Examination of Continuum"; Fontenelle and Yücel, "Clinical Staging."
18 Cole and Warman, "Examination of Continuum," n.p.
19 Carter et al., "Downsides."
20 Adam et al., "Obsessive-Compulsive Disorder."
21 Fontenelle and Yücel, "Clinical Staging."
22 Beck, *Risk Society*; Furedi, *Culture of Fear*; Giddens, *Modernity and Self-Identity*; Lupton, "Sociology and Risk"; Mythen and Walklate, "Introduction."
23 Beck, *Risk Society*.
24 Giddens, *Modernity and Self-Identity*, chap. 2.
25 Wilkinson, *Anxiety*, 3.
26 Giddens, *Modernity and Self-Identity*, introduction.
27 Giddens, chap. 6.
28 Some authors like Giddens have theorized that there are partitions within modernity, such as his discussion of "high modernity" (*Modernity and Self-Identity*). Others "claim that in the contemporary high tech media society, emergent processes of change and transformation are producing a new postmodern society" (Best and Kellner, *Postmodern Theory*, 3).
29 Beck, *Risk Society*.
30 Pollan, *Omnivore's Dilemma*.
31 Giddens, *Modernity and Self-Identity*.
32 Baxter et al., "Challenging"; Booth, Sharma, and Leader, "Age of Anxiety"; Schürmann and Margraf, "Age of Anxiety."
33 Furedi, *Culture of Fear*; Giddens, *Modernity and Self-Identity*.
34 Lupton, "Sociology and Risk," 12.
35 Dumit, *Drugs for Life*; Foucault, "About the Beginning"; Lupton, "Digitized"; Johnson, "Managing"; Petersen, "Risk."
36 Rose, *Politics*, chap. 1.
37 Dumit, *Drugs for Life*; Rose, *Politics*.
38 Dumit, *Drugs for Life*, introduction.
39 Dumit.
40 Dumit, chap. 6.
41 Giddens, *Modernity and Self-Identity*.
42 Furedi, *Culture of Fear*.
43 Furedi; Isin, "Neurotic Citizen"; Zedner, "Too Much Security."
44 Isin, "Neurotic Citizen," 217.
45 Garfinkel, "Studies of the Routine"; Heritage, *Garfinkel and Ethnomethodology*.
46 Giddens, *Modernity and Self-Identity*.
47 Green, *End of Stigma*, 4.
48 Cullen et al., "Effectiveness."

49 Wong, "What Companies."

50 Johnson and Johnson, "Employee Resource Groups."

51 National Institute of Mental Health, "Statistics."

52 Almog, " 'Everyone Is Normal,' " 222. This is different from privileging those without impairments (i.e., ableism).

53 Grimes et al., "Non-disclosing Students."

54 Burgstahler, *Universal Design*; McGuire and Scott, "Universal"; Meyer, Rose, and Gordon, *Universal Design for Learning*.

55 Rathbun-Grubb, "Lived Experience."

56 Golden and Eddleston, "Price Telecommuters."

57 American Heart Association, *Mental Health*.

58 Karp, *Speaking of Sadness*, 187.

59 Karp.

60 Martin and McLellan, *Education of Selves*, 177.

61 Martin and McLellan, 178.

62 Martin and McLellan, 190.

63 Ilic et al., "Protecting Self-Esteem."

BIBLIOGRAPHY

Aardema, Frederick. "COVID-19, Obsessive Compulsive Disorder and Invisible Life Forms That Threaten the Self." *Journal of Obsessive-Compulsive and Related Disorders* 26 (2020): n.p.

Aardema, Frederick, and Kieron O' Connor. "The Menace Within: Obsessions and the Self." *Journal of Cognitive Psychotherapy: An International Quarterly* 21 (2007): 182–97.

Abel, T. "Cultural Capital and Social Inequality in Health." *Journal of Epidemiology and Community Health* 62 (2008): e13.

Abramowitz, Jonathan S., Shannon M. Blakey, Lillian Reuman, and Jennifer L. Buchholz. "New Directions in the Cognitive-Behavioral Treatment of OCD: Theory, Research, and Practice." *Behavior Therapy* 49 (2018): 311–22.

Abramowitz, Jonathan S., Steven Taylor, and Dean McKay. "Potentials and Limitations of Cognitive Treatments for Obsessive-Compulsive Disorder." *Cognitive Behaviour Therapy* 34 (2005): 140–47.

Adam, Yuki, Gunther Meinlschmidt, Andrew T. Gloster, and Roselind Lieb. "Obsessive-Compulsive Disorder in the Community: 12-Month Prevalence, Comorbidity and Impairment." *Social Psychiatry and Psychiatric Epidemiology* 47 (2012): 339–49.

Adler, Patricia A., and Peter Adler. *The Tender Cut: Inside the Hidden World of Self-Injury*. New York: New York University Press, 2011. Kindle.

Albert, Umberto, Francesca Barbaro, Stefano Bramante, Gianluca Rosso, Diana De Ronchi, and Giuseppe Maina. "Duration of Untreated Illness as a Response to SRI Treatment in Obsessive-Compulsive Disorder." *European Psychiatry* 58 (2019): 19–26.

Albert, Umberto, Diana De Ronchi, Giuseppe Maina, and Maurizio Pompili. "Suicide Risk in Obsessive-Compulsive Disorder and Exploration of Risk Factors: A Systematic Review." *Current Neuropharmacology* 17 (2019): 681–96.

Almog, Nitsan. "'Everyone Is Normal, and Everyone Has a Disability': Narratives of University Students with Visual Impairment." *Social Inclusion* 6 (2018): 218–29.

American Heart Association. *Mental Health: A Workforce Crisis*. 2019. https://ceoroundtable.heart.org.

American Psychiatric Association. *Diagnostic and Statistical Manual of Mental Disorders: DSM-IV-TR*. Washington, DC: American Psychiatric Association, 2000.

———. *Diagnostic and Statistical Manual of Mental Disorders: DSM-5*. Washington, DC: American Psychiatric Association, 2013.

Aneshensel, Carol S. "Mental Illness as a Career: Sociological Perspectives." In *Handbook of the Sociology of Mental Health*, edited by Carol. S. Aneshensel and Jo. C. Phelan, 585–603. New York: Springer, 1999.

Angermeyer, Matthias C., Beate Schulze, and Sandra Dietrich. "Courtesy Stigma." *Social Psychiatry and Psychiatric Epidemiology* 38 (2003): 593–602.

Audet, Jean-Sébastien, Shiu F. Wong, Adam S. Radomsky, and Frederick Aardema. "Not All Intrusions Are Created Equal: The Role of Context, Feared-Self Perceptions and Inferential Confusion in the Occurrence of Abnormal Intrusions." *Journal of Obsessive-Compulsive and Related Disorders* 26 (2020): n.p.

Balachander, Srinivas, Shyam Sundar Arumughan, and Dwarakanath Srinivas. "Ablative Neurosurgery and Deep Brain Stimulation for Obsessive-Compulsive Disorder." *Indian Journal of Psychiatry* 61 (2019): S77–S84.

Balconi, Michela. "Preface." In *Neuropsychology of the Sense of Agency*, edited by Michela Balconi, v–vii. Milan: Springer, 2010.

———. "The Sense of Agency in Psychology and Neuropsychology." In *Neuropsychology of the Sense of Agency*, edited by Michela Balconi, 3–22. Milan: Springer, 2010.

Baldwin, Marjorie L., and Steven C. Marcus. "Labor Market Outcomes of Persons with Mental Disorders." *Industrial Relations: A Journal of Economy and Society* 46 (2007): 481–510.

Barker, Kristin K. *The Fibromyalgia Story: Medical Authority and Women's Worlds of Pain*. Philadelphia: Temple University Press, 2005.

———. "The Social Construction of Illness: Medicalization and Contested Illness." In *Handbook of Medical Sociology*, 6th ed., edited by Chloe E. Bird, Peter Conrad, Allen M. Fremont, and Stefan Timmermans, 147–62. Nashville, TN: Vanderbilt University Press, 2010.

Barnes, Colin. "Understanding the Social Model of Disability." In *Routledge Handbook of Disability Studies*, 2nd ed., edited by Nick Watson and Simo Vehmas, 14–34. New York: Routledge, 2020.

Baxter, Amanda J., Kate M. Scott, Alize J. Ferrari, Rosana E. Norman, Theo Vos, and Harvey Whiteford. "Challenging the Myth of an 'Epidemic' of Common Mental Disorders: Trends in the Global Prevalence of Anxiety and Depression between 1990 and 2010." *Depression and Anxiety* 31 (2014): 506–16.

Beard, Renée L. *Living with Alzheimer's: Managing Memory Loss, Identity, and Illness*. New York: New York University Press, 2016. Kindle.

Beck, Ulrich. *Risk Society: Towards a New Modernity*. Los Angeles: Sage, 2007.

Becker, Howard S. "Becoming a Marihuana User." *American Journal of Sociology* 59 (1953): 235–42.

Belayachi, Sanaâ, and Martial Van der Linden. "Looking for Outcomes: The Experience of Control and Sense of Agency in Obsessive-Compulsive Behaviors." In *Neuropsychology of the Sense of Agency*, edited by Michela Balconi, 157–71. Milan: Springer, 2010.

Bellack, Alan S., and Amy Drapalski. "Issues and Developments on the Consumer Recovery Construct." *World Psychiatry* 11 (2012): 156–60.

Belloch, Amparo, Gema del Valle, Carmen Morillo, Carmen Carrió, and Elena Cabedo. "To Seek Advice or Not to Seek Advice about the Problem: The Help-Seeking Dilemma for Obsessive-Compulsive Disorder." *Social Psychiatry and Psychiatric Epidemiology* 44 (2009): 257–64.

Beresford, Peter. "Psychiatric System Survivors: An Emerging Movement." In *Routledge Handbook of Disability Studies*, edited by Nick Watson, Alan Roulstone, and Carol Thomas, 151–64. London: Routledge, 2012.

Berkman, Julia M., Jennifer B. Freeman, Abbe M. Garcia, and Henrietta L. Leonard. "Family-Based Treatment of Early Onset Obsessive-Compulsive Disorder." In *Handbook of Child and Adolescent Obsessive-Compulsive Disorder*, edited by Eric A. Storch, Gary R. Geffken, and Tanya K. Murphy, 295–312. Mahwah, NJ: Lawrence Erlbaum, 2007.

Berrios, German E. *The History of Mental Symptoms: Descriptive Psychopathology since the Nineteenth Century*. Cambridge: Cambridge University Press, 1996.

Beşiroğlu, Lütfullah, Ali Savaş Çilli, and Rüstem Aşkın. "The Predictors of Health Care Seeking Behavior in Obsessive Compulsive Disorder." *Comprehensive Psychiatry* 45 (2004): 99–108.

Best, Steven, and Douglas Kellner. *Postmodern Theory*. New York: Guilford Press, 1991.

Beveridge, Allan. "Images of Madness in the Films of Walt Disney." *Psychiatry Bulletin* 20 (1996): 618–20.

Bhui, Kamaldeep. "Cultural Neuroscience: A Meta-paradigm for Psychiatry." *British Journal of Psychiatry* 210 (2017): 89–90.

Biddle, Lucy, Jenny Donovan, Debbie Sharp, and David Gunnell. "Explaining Non-Help-Seeking amongst Young Adults with Mental Distress: A Dynamic Interpretive Model of Illness Behaviour." *Sociology of Health and Illness* 29 (2007): 983–1002.

Bloch, Michael H., Christy Green, Stephen A. Kichuk, Philip A. Dombrowski, Suzanne Wasylink, Eileen Billingslea, Angeli Landeros-Weisenberger, Benjamin Kelmendi, Wayne K. Goodman, James F. Leckman, Vladimir Coric, and Christopher Pittenger. "Long-Term Outcome in Adults with Obsessive-Compulsive Disorder." *Depression and Anxiety* 30 (2013): 716–22.

Blumer, Herbert. *Symbolic Interactionism*. Berkeley: University of California Press, 1969.

Boeding, Sara E., Christine M. Paprocki, Donald H. Baucom, Jonathan S. Abramowitz, Michael G. Wheaton, Laura E. Fabricant, and Melanie S. Fischer. "Let Me Check That for You: Symptom Accommodation in Romantic Partners of Adults with Obsessive-Compulsive Disorder." *Behaviour Research and Therapy* 51 (2013): 316–22.

Booth, Bradley D., Susan Hatters Friedman, Susan Curry, Helen Ward, and S. Evelyn Stewart. "Obsessions of Child Murder: Underrecognized Manifestations of Obsessive-Compulsive Disorder." *Journal of the American Academy of Psychiatry and the Law* 42 (2014): 66–74.

Booth, Rob, Dinkar Sharma, and Tirza Leader. "The Age of Anxiety? It Depends Where You Look: Changes in STAI Trait Anxiety, 1970–2010." *Social Psychiatry and Psychiatric Epidemiology* 51 (2015): 193–202.

Boschen, Mark J. "Publication Trends in Individual Anxiety Disorders: 1980–2015." *Journal of Anxiety Disorders* 22 (2008): 570–75.

Boschen, Mark J., and Dean Vuksanovic. "Deteriorating Memory Confidence, Responsibility Perceptions and Repeated Checking: Comparisons in OCD and Control Samples." *Behaviour Research and Therapy* 45 (2007): 2098–109.

Bourdieu, Pierre. "Forms of Capital." In *Handbook of a Theory of Research for the Sociology of Education*, edited by J. E. Richardson, translated by Richard Nice, 241–58. New York: Greenwood Press, 1986.

Bourdieu, Pierre, and L. J. D. Wacquant. *An Invitation to Reflexive Sociology.* Chicago: University of Chicago Press, 1992.

Bowen, Sarah, Joslyn Brenton, and Sinikka Elliott. *Pressure Cooker: Why Home Cooking Won't Solve Our Problems and What We Can Do about It.* New York: Oxford University Press, 2019. Kindle.

Boydell, Katherine M., Tiziana Volpe, Brenda M. Gladstone, Elaine Stasiulis, and Jean Addington. "Youth at Ultra High Risk for Psychosis: Using the Revised Network Episode Model to Examine Pathways to Mental Health Care." *Early Intervention in Psychiatry* 7 (2013): 170–86.

Bracken, Pat, Philip Thomas, Sami Timimi, Eia Asen, Graham Behr, Carl Beuster, Seth Bhunnoo, et al. "Psychiatry beyond the Current Paradigm." *British Journal of Psychiatry* 201 (2012): 430–34.

Brohan, Elaine, Claire Henderson, Mike Slade, and Graham Thornicroft. "Development and Preliminary Evaluation of a Decision Aid for Disclosure of Mental Illness to Employers." *Patient Education and Counseling* 94 (2014): 238–42.

Brooks, Catherine Francis. "Social Performance and Secret Ritual: Battling against Obsessive-Compulsive Disorder." *Qualitative Health Research* 21 (2011): 249–61.

Brown, Brian, Kate Huszar, and Rosemary Chapman. "'Betwixt and Between'; Liminality in Recovery Stories from People with Myalgic Encephalomyelitis (ME) or Chronic Fatigue Syndrome (CFS)." *Sociology of Health and Illness* 39 (2017): 696–710.

Bucarelli, Bianca, and Christine Purdon. "A Diary Study of the Phenomenology and Persistence of Compulsions." *Journal of Behavior Therapy and Experimental Psychiatry* 49 (2015): 209–15.

Buchman, Daniel Z., Emily L. Borgelt, Louise Whiteley, and Judy Illes. "Neurobiological Narratives: Experiences of Mood Disorder through the Lens of Neuroimaging." *Sociology of Health and Illness* 35 (2013): 66–81.

Burchi, Elisabetta, and Stefano Pallanti. "Diagnostic Issues in Early-Onset Obsessive-Compulsive Disorder and Their Treatment Implications." *Current Neuropharmacology* 17 (2019): 672–80.

Burgstahler, Sheryl E., ed. *Universal Design in Higher Education: From Principles to Practice.* 2nd ed. Cambridge, MA: Harvard Education Press, 2015.

Bury, Mike. "Illness Narratives: Fact or Fiction?" *Sociology of Health and Illness* 23 (2001): 263–85.

———. "Researching Patient-Professional Interactions." *Journal of Health Services Research and Policy* 9 (2004): S48–S54.

———. "The Sociology of Chronic Illness: A Review of Research and Prospects." *Sociology of Health and Illness* 13 (1991): 451–68.

Cameron, Duncan H., David L. Streiner, Laura J. Summerfeldt, Karen Rowa, Margaret C. McKinnon, and Randi E. McCabe. "A Comparison of Cluster and Factor Analytic Techniques for Identifying Symptom-Based Dimensions of Obsessive-Compulsive Disorder." *Psychiatry Research* 278 (2019): 86–96.

Campbell, Peter, and Diana Rose. "Action for Change in the UK: Thirty Years of the User/Survivor Movement." In *The Sage Handbook of Mental Health and Illness*, edited by David Pilgrim, Anne Rogers, and Bernice Pescosolido, 452–70. Los Angeles: Sage, 2011.

Capawana, Michael R. "A Developmental Psychopathology Perspective of Obsessive-Compulsive Disorder." *Current Psychiatry Research and Reviews* 15 (2019): 105–15.

Carey, Patrick. "Marijuana and OCD: Will It Help or Hurt? Ask Dr. Reilly Kayser." NOCD. Accessed January 28, 2019. https://www.treatmyocd.com.

Carmichael, Victoria, Gavin Adamson, Kathleen C. Sitter, and Rob Whitley. "Media Coverage of Mental Illness: A Comparison of Citizen Journalism vs. Professional Journalism Portrayals." *Journal of Mental Health* 28 (2019): 520–26.

Carter, Nathan T., Li Guan, Jessica L. Maples, Rachel L. Williamson, and Joshua D. Miller. "The Downsides of Extreme Conscientiousness for Psychological Well-Being: The Role of Obsessive Compulsive Tendencies." *Journal of Personality* 84 (2016): 510–22.

Catapano, Francesco, Francesco Perris, Mariangela Masella, Flavia Rossano, Marco Cigliano, Lorenza Magliano, and Mario Maj. "Obsessive-Compulsive Disorder: A 3-Year Prospective Follow-Up Study of Patients Treated with Serotonin Reuptake Inhibitors OCD Follow-Up Study." *Journal of Psychiatric Research* 40 (2006): 502–10.

Cefalu, Paul. "What's So Funny about Obsessive-Compulsive Disorder?" *PMLA* 124 (2009): 44–58.

Challacombe, Fiona L., and Abigail L. Wroe. "A Hidden Problem: Consequences of the Misdiagnosis of Perinatal Obsessive-Compulsive Disorder." *British Journal of General Practice* 63 (2013): 275–76.

Charmaz, Kathy. *Good Days, Bad Days: The Self in Chronic Illness in Time.* New Brunswick, NJ: Rutgers University Press, 1997. Kindle.

Chaudoir, Stephenie, Valerie A. Earnshaw, and Stephanie Andel. "'Discredited' versus 'Discreditable': Understanding How Shared and Unique Stigma Mechanisms Affect Psychological and Physical Health Disparities." *Basic and Applied Social Psychology* 35 (2013): 75–87.

Cicourel, Aaron V. *Cognitive Sociology* New York: Free Press, 1974.

Clark, David A. "Focus on 'Cognition' in Cognitive Behavior Therapy for OCD: Is It Really Necessary?" *Cognitive Behaviour Therapy* 34 (2005): 131–39.

Clark, David A., and Shelley Rhyno. "Unwanted Intrusive Thoughts in Nonclinical Individuals." In *Intrusive Thoughts in Clinical Disorders: Theory, Research, and Treatment*, edited by David A. Clark, 1–29. New York: Guilford Press, 2005.

Climacus, John. *The Ladder of Divine Ascent*. Translated by Colm Luibheid and Norman Russell. Mahwah, NJ: Paulist Press, 1982.

Cobb, Katherine Fohn. "Understanding Scrupulosity: Psychopathological and Catholic Perspectives." Master's thesis, University of Iowa, 2014.

Cockerham, William C. *Sociology of Mental Disorder*. 11th ed. New York: Routledge, 2021.

Cole, Jennifer L., and Debbie M. Warman. "An Examination of Continuum Beliefs versus Biogenetic Beliefs in Reducing Stigma toward Violent Intrusive Thoughts in OCD." *Journal of Obsessive-Compulsive and Related Disorders* 23 (2019): n.p.

Coles, Meredith E., Richard G. Heimberg, and Barry D. Weiss. "The Public's Knowledge and Beliefs about Obsessive Compulsive Disorder." *Depression and Anxiety* 30 (2013): 778–85.

Coles, Meredith E., and Ariel Ravid. "Clinical Presentation of Not-Just Right Experiences (NJREs) in Individuals with OCD: Characteristics and Response to Treatment." *Behaviour Research and Therapy* 87 (2016): 182–87.

Coles, Meredith E., Carle Jordan Wirshba, Jacob Nota, Jessica Schubert, and Breanna A. Grunthal. "Obsessive Compulsive Disorder Prevalence Increases with Latitude." *Journal of Obsessive-Compulsive and Related Disorders* 18 (2018): 25–30.

Conrad, Peter. "Medicalization and Social Control." *Annual Review of Sociology* 18 (1992): 209–32.

Conrad, Peter, Julia Bandini, and Alexandria Vasquez. "Illness and the Internet: From Private to Public Experience." *Health* 20 (2016): 22–32.

Conrad, Peter, and Deborah Potter. "From Hyperactive Children to ADHD Adults: Observations on the Expansion of Medical Categories." *Social Problems* 47 (2000): 559–82.

Conrad, Peter, and Joseph W. Schneider. *Deviance and Medicalization: From Badness to Sickness*. Philadelphia: Temple University Press, 1992. Kindle.

Corker, E., S. Hamilton, E. Robinson, J. Cotney, V. Pinfold, D. Rose, G. Thornicroft, and C. Henderson. "Viewpoint Survey of Mental Health Service Users' Experiences of Discrimination in England 2008–2014." *Acta Psychiatrica Scandinavica* 134 (2016): 6–13.

Corrigan, Patrick W., and Mandy W. M. Fong. "Competing Perspectives on Erasing the Stigma of Illness: What Says the Dodo Bird?" *Social Science and Medicine* 103 (2014): 110–17.

Corrigan, Patrick W., and Deepa Rao. "On the Self-Stigma of Mental Illness: Stages, Disclosure, and Strategies for Change." *Canadian Journal of Psychiatry* 57 (2012): 464–69.

Crino, Rocco, Tim Slade, and Gavin Andrews. "The Changing Prevalence and Severity of Obsessive-Compulsive Disorder Criteria from *DSM-III* to *DSM-IV*." *American Journal of Psychiatry* 162 (2005): 876–82.

Crossley, Nick. *In the Gym: Motives, Meanings and Moral Careers*. CRESC Working Paper No. 6. Milton Keynes, UK: University of Manchester, 2005.

Cullen, K. L., E. Irvin, A. Collie, F. Clay, U. Gensby, P. A. Jennings, S. Hogg-Johnson, et al. "Effectiveness of Workplace Interventions in Return-to-Work for Musculoskeletal, Pain-Related and Mental Health Conditions: An Update of the Evidence and Messages for Practitioners." *Journal of Occupational Rehabilitation* 28 (2018): 1–15.

Cummings, Janet R., Stephen M. Lucas, and Benjamin G. Druss. "Addressing Public Stigma and Disparities among Persons with Mental Illness: The Role of Federal Policy." *American Journal of Public Health* 103 (2013): 781–85.

D'Amico, Davide, Xavier Estivill, and Javier Terriente. "Switching to Zebrafish Neurobehavioral Models: The Obsessive Compulsive Disorder Paradigm." *European Journal of Pharmacology* 759 (2015): 142–50.

Davis, Lennard J. *Obsession: A History*. Chicago: University of Chicago Press, 2008.

Davis, Michelle L., Matthew McCann, Wayne K. Goodman, and Eric A. Storch. "Impact of the 2016 US Presidential Election on OCD Symptom Presentation: A Case Illustration." *Journal of Clinical Psychology* 74 (2018): 750–54.

de la Cruz, L. Fernández, M. Rydell, B. Runeson, B. M. D'Onofrio, G. Brander, C. Rück, P. Lichtenstein, H. Larsson, and D. Mataix-Cols. "Suicide in Obsessive-Compulsive Disorder: A Population-Based Study of 36,788 Swedish Patients." *Molecular Psychology* 22 (2017): 1626–32.

Diefenbach, Donald L., and Mark D. West. "Television and Attitudes toward Mental Health Issues: Cultivation Analysis and the Third-Person Effect." *Journal of Community Psychology* 35 (2007): 181–95.

DuBois, W. E. B. *The Souls of Black Folk*. New York: Oxford University Press, 2007.

Dumit, Joseph. *Drugs for Life: How Pharmaceutical Companies Define Our Health*. Durham, NC: Duke University Press, 2012. Kindle.

Durkheim, Émile. *Suicide: A Study in Sociology*. 1897; New York: Free Press, 1979.

Eisen, Jane L., Nicholas J. Sibrava, Christina L. Boisseau, Maria C. Mancebo, Robert L. Stout, Anthony Pinto, and Steven A. Rasmussen. "Five-Year Course of Obsessive-Compulsive Disorder: Predictors of Remission and Relapse." *Journal of Clinical Psychiatry* 74 (2013): 233–39.

Elraz, Hadar. "Identity, Mental Health and Work: How Employees with Mental Health Conditions Recount Stigma and the Pejorative Discourse of Mental Illness." *Human Relations* 71 (2018): 722–41.

Esman, Aaron H. "Obsessive-Compulsive Disorder: Current Views." *Psychoanalytic Inquiry* 21 (2001): 145–56.

Farrell, Lara J., and Paula M. Barrett. "The Function of the Family in Childhood Obsessive-Compulsive Disorder: Family Interactions and Accommodation." In *Handbook of Child and Adolescent Obsessive-Compulsive Disorder*, edited by Eric A. Storch, Gary R. Geffken, and Tanya K. Murphy, 313–32. Mahwah, NJ: Lawrence Erlbaum, 2007.

Fawcett, Emily J., Hilary Power, and Jonathan M. Fawcett. "Women Are at Greater Risk of OCD Than Men: A Meta-analytic Review of OCD Prevalence Worldwide." *Journal of Clinical Psychiatry* 81 (2020): 19r13085.

Fennell, Dana. "Explorations of Silence in the Religious Rituals of Buddhists and Quakers." *Religion* 42 (2012): 1–26.

———. "If You're 'So OCD,' What Does That Make Me?" In *Routledge Handbook on Deviance*, edited by Stephen E. Brown and Ophir Sefiha, 383–95. New York: Routledge, 2018.

Fennell, Dana, and Michael Boyd. "Obsessive-Compulsive Disorder in the Media." Deviant Behavior 35 (2014): 669–86.

Fennell, Dana, and Ana S. Q. Liberato. "Learning to Live with OCD: Labeling, the Self, and Stigma." *Deviant Behavior* 28 (2007): 305–31.

Ferlander, Sara. "The Importance of Different Forms of Social Capital for Health." *Acta Sociologica* 50 (2007): 115–28.

Fingelkurts, Andrew A., and Alexander A. Fingelkurts. "Brain Space and Time in Mental Disorders: Paradigm Shift in Biological Psychiatry." *International Journal of Psychiatry in Medicine* 54 (2019): 53–63.

Fisher, Peter L., and Adrian Wells. "Metacognitive Therapy for Obsessive-Compulsive Disorder: A Case Series." *Journal of Behavior Therapy* 39 (2008): 117–32.

Fleischer, Doris Zames, and Frieda Zames. *The Disability Rights Movement*. Philadelphia: Temple University Press, 2011.

Foa, Edna B., Jonathan D. Huppert, Susanne Leiberg, Robert Langner, Rafael Kichic, Greg Hajcak, and Paul M. Salkovskis. "The Obsessive-Compulsive Inventory: Development and Validation of a Short Version." *Psychological Assessment* 14 (2002): 485–96.

Foa, Edna B., and Reid Wilson. *Stop Obsessing! How to Overcome Your Obsessions and Compulsions*. Rev. ed. New York: Bantam Books, 2001.

Fontenelle, Leonardo F., Mauro V. Mendlowicz, and Marcio Versiani. "The Descriptive Epidemiology of Obsessive-Compulsive Disorder." *Progress in Neuro-Psychopharmacology and Biological Psychiatry* 30 (2006): 327–37.

Fontenelle, Leonardo F., and Murat Yücel. "A Clinical Staging Model for Obsessive-Compulsive Disorder: Is It Ready for Prime Time?" *EclinicalMedicine* 7 (2019): 65–72.

Foucault, Michel. "About the Beginning of the Hermeneutics of the Self: Two Lectures at Dartmouth." *Political Theory* 21 (1993): 198–227.

Fradkin, Isaac, Rick A. Adams, Thomas Parr, Jonathan P. Roiser, and Jonathan D. Huppert. "Searching for an Anchor in an Unpredictable World: A Computational Model of Obsessive Compulsive Disorder." *Psychological Review* 127 (2020): 672–99.

Francazio, Sarah K., Christopher A. Flessner, Christina L. Boisseau, Nicholas J. Sibrava, Maria C. Mancebo, Jane L. Eisen, and Steven A. Rasmussen. "Parental Accommodation Predicts Symptom Severity at Long-Term Follow-Up in Children with Obsessive-Compulsive Disorder: A Preliminary Investigation." *Journal of Child and Family Studies* 25 (2016): 2562–70.

Frances, Allen. "*DSM5* in Distress." *Psychology Today*. Accessed June 8, 2010. http://psychologytoday.com.

Frank, Arthur R. *The Wounded Storyteller: Body, Illness, and Ethics*. Chicago: University of Chicago Press, 1995.

Franks, David D. *Neurosociology: The Nexus between Neuroscience and Social Psychology*. New York: Springer, 2010.

Friedrich, Patricia. *The Literary and Linguistic Construction of Obsessive-Compulsive Disorder: No Ordinary Doubt*. New York: Palgrave Macmillan, 2015.

Fullana, Miguel A., David Mataix-Cols, Avshalom Caspi, Honalee Harrington, Jessica R. Grisham, Terrie E. Moffitt, and Richie Poulton. "Obsessions and Compulsions in the Community: Prevalence, Interference, Help-Seeking, Developmental Stability, and Co-occurring Psychiatric Conditions." *American Journal of Psychiatry* 166 (2009): 329–36.

Furedi, Frank. *Culture of Fear Revisited*. 4th ed. New York: Continuum Books, 2006.

Gagné, Jean-Philippe, and Adam S. Radomsky. "Manipulating Beliefs about Losing Control Causes Checking Behavior." *Journal of Obsessive-Compulsive and Related Disorders* 15 (2017): 34–42.

García-Soriano, Gemma, and María Roncero, "What Do Spanish Adolescents Think about Obsessive-Compulsive Disorder: Mental Health Literacy and Stigma Associated with Symmetry/Order and Aggression-Related Symptoms." *Psychiatry Research* 250 (2017): 193–99.

García-Soriano, Gemma, Michael Rufer, Aba Delsignore, and Steffi Weidt. "Factors Associated with Non-treatment or Delayed Treatment Seeking in OCD Sufferers: A Review of the Literature." *Psychiatry Research* 220 (2014): 1–10.

Garfinkel, Harold. 1964. "Studies of the Routine Grounds of Everyday Activities." *Social Problems* 11 (1964): 225–50.

Gentsch, Antje, Simone Schütz-Bosbach, Tanja Endrass, and Norbert Kathmann. "Dysfunctional Forward Model Mechanisms and Aberrant Sense of Agency in Obsessive-Compulsive Disorder." *Biological Psychiatry* 71 (2012): 652–59.

Gergel, Tania Louise. "Too Similar, Too Different: The Paradoxical Dualism of Psychiatric Stigma." *Psychiatric Bulletin* 38 (2014): 148–51.

Gershkovich, Marina, Rachel Middleton, Dianne M. Hezel, Stephanie Grimaldi, Megan Renna, Cale Basaraba, Sapana Patel, et al. "Integrating Exposure and Response Prevention with a Mobile App to Treat Obsessive-Compulsive Disorder: Feasibility, Acceptability, and Preliminary Effects." *Behavior Therapy* 52 (2021): 394–405.

Giddens, Anthony. *Modernity and Self-Identity: Self and Society in the Late Modern Age*. Cambridge, UK: Polity Press, 1991. Kindle.

Glazier, Kimberly, Rachelle M. Calixte, Rachel Rothschild, and Anthony Pinto. "High Rates of OCD Symptom Misidentification by Mental Health Professionals." *Annals of Clinical Psychology* 25 (2013): 201–09.

Goddard, Andrew W., Anantha Shekhar, Aaron F. Whiteman, and Christopher J. McDougle. "Serotoninergic Mechanisms in the Treatment of Obsessive-Compulsive Disorder." *Drug Discovery Today* 13 (2008): 325–32.

Goffman, Erving. "The Moral Career of the Mental Patient." *Psychiatry* 22 (1959): 123–42.

———. *The Presentation of Self in Everyday Life*. New York: Anchor Books, 1959.

———. *Stigma: Notes on the Management of Spoiled Identity*. New York: Touchstone, 1986.

Golden, Timothy D., and Kimberly A. Eddleston. "Is There a Price Telecommuters Pay? Examining the Relationship between Telecommuting and Objective Career Success." *Journal of Vocational Behavior* 116 (2020). https://www.sciencedirect.com/.

Gönner, Sascha, Willi Ecker, and Rainer Leonhart. "Diagnostic Discrimination of Patients with Different OCD Main Symptom Domains from Each Other and from Anxious and Depressive Controls." *Journal of Psychopathology and Behavioral Assessment* 31 (2009): 159–67.

Goodman, Wayne K., Lawrence H. Price, Steven A. Rasmussen, Carolyn Mazure, Roberta L. Fleischmann, Candy L. Hill, George R. Heninger, and Dennis S. Charney. "The Yale-Brown Obsessive Compulsive Scale. I. Development, Use, and Reliability." *Archives of General Psychiatry* 46 (1989): 1006–11.

Goodwin, Renee, Karestan C. Koenen, Fred Hellman, Mary Guardino, and Elmer Struening. "Helpseeking and Access to Mental Health Treatment for Obsessive-Compulsive Disorder." *Acta Psychiatrica Scandinavica* 106 (2002): 143–49.

Gordon, Beth Omansky, and Karen E. Rosenblum. "Bringing Disability into the Sociological Frame: A Comparison of Disability with Race, Sex, and Sexual Orientation Statuses." *Disability and Society* 16 (2001): 5–19.

Graby, Steve. "Neurodiversity: Bridging the Gap between the Disabled People's Movement and the Mental Health System Survivors' Movement?" In *Madness, Distress and the Politics of Disablement*, edited by Helen Spandler, Jill Anderson, and Bob Sapey, 231–43. Bristol: Policy Press, 2015.

Grant, Jon E., and Samuel R. Chamberlain. "Exploring the Neurobiology of OCD: Clinical Implications." *Psychiatric Times*, March 2, 2020. https://www.psychiatric-times.com/.

Grayson, Jonathan. *Freedom from Obsessive-Compulsive Disorder*. New York: Berkeley Books, 2014. Kindle.

———. "Series Response: Compliance and Understanding OCD." *Cognitive and Behavioral Practice* 6 (1999): 415–21.

Green, Gill. *The End of Stigma: Changes in the Social Experience of Long-Term Illness*. New York: Routledge, 2009.

Greist, J. H. "The Comparative Effectiveness of Treatments for Obsessive-Compulsive Disorder." *Bulletin of the Menninger Clinic* 62 (1998): A65–A81.

Grimes, Susan, Jill Scevak, Erica Southgate, and Rachel Buchanan. "Non-disclosing Students with Disabilities or Learning Challenges: Characteristics and Size of a Hidden Population." *Australian Education Researcher* 44 (2017): 425–41.

Grineski, Sara E. "Parental Accounts of Children's Asthma Care: The Role of Cultural and Social Capital in Health Disparities." *Sociological Focus* 42 (2009): 107–32.

Guthman, Julie. *Obesity, Food Justice, and the Limits of Capitalism*. Berkeley: University of California Press, 2011.

Guzick, Andrew G., Adam M. Reid, Amanda M. Balki, Cindi Flores, Anyaliese
D. Hancock-Smith, Brian Olsen, Greg Muller, Gary R. Geffken, and Joseph P. H.
McNamara. "Diagnostic Description and Prevalence." In *The Wiley Handbook of
Obsessive Compulsive Disorders*, edited by Jonathan S. Abramowitz, Dean McKay,
and Eric A. Storch, 24–43. Hoboken: John Wiley, 2017.

Haciomeroglu, Bikem. "The Role of Reassurance Seeking in Obsessive Compulsive
Disorder: The Associations between Reassurance Seeking, Dysfunctional Beliefs,
Negative Emotions, and Obsessive-Compulsive Symptoms." *BMC Psychiatry* 20
(2020): n.p.

Harrington, Anne. *Cure Within*. New York: W. W. Norton, 2008. Kindle.

Harrison, Natalie. "Regressing or Progressing: What Next for the Doctor-Patient."
Lancet Respiratory Medicine 6 (2018): 178–80.

Hauschildt, Marit, and Reuven Dar. "On the Relevance of Experimental Studies of
Cognitive Processes for Understanding and Treating Obsessive-Compulsive Disorder." *Journal of Obsessive-Compulsive and Related Disorders* 20 (2019): 1–3.

Hayes, Steven C., Kirk D. Strosahl, and Kelly G. Wilson. *Acceptance and Commitment
Therapy: The Process and Practice of Mindful Change*. 2nd ed. New York: Guilford
Press, 2012. Kindle.

Heritage, John. *Garfinkel and Ethnomethodology*. Cambridge: Polity Press, 1984.

Hershfield, Jon. "Mistaken Beliefs about Uncertainty Acceptance and OCD." Accessed
December 17, 2020. https://www.madeofmillions.com/.

Hershfield, Jon, and Tom Corboy. *The Mindfulness Workbook for OCD*. Oakland, CA:
New Harbinger Publications, 2013. Kindle.

Hilbert, Richard A. "The Acultural Dimensions of Chronic Pain: Flawed Reality Construction and the Problem of Meaning." *Social Problems* 31 (1984): 365–78.

Hinshaw, Stephen P., and Dante Cicchetti. "Stigma and Mental Disorder: Conceptions
of Illness, Public Attitudes, Personal Disclosure, and Social Policy." *Development
and Psychopathology* 12 (2000): 555–98.

Hipes, Crosby, Jeffrey Lucas, Jo C. Phelan, and Richard C. White. "The Stigma of Mental Illness in the Labor Market." *Social Science Research* 56 (2016): 16–25.

Hirschtritt, Matthew E., Michael H. Bloch, and Carol A. Mathews. "Obsessive-
Compulsive Disorder Advances in Diagnosis and Treatment." *JAMA* 317 (2017):
1358–67.

Hochschild, Arlie Russell. *The Managed Heart: Commercialization of Human Feeling*.
Berkeley: University of California Press, 1983. Kindle.

Hollander, Eric, Ashley Braun, and Daphne Simeon. "Should OCD Leave the Anxiety
Disorders in *DSM-V*? The Case for Obsessive Compulsive–Related Disorders."
Depression and Anxiety 25 (2008): 317–29.

Holstein, James A., and Jaber F. Gubrium. *The Self We Live By: Narrative Identity in a
Postmodern World*. New York: Oxford University Press, 2000.

Hult, Helena Vallo, Anders Hansson, Lars Svensson, and Martin Gellerstedt. "Flipped
Healthcare for Better or Worse." *Health Informatics Journal* 25 (2019): 587–97.

Huppert, Jonathan D., H. Blair Simpson, Kore J. Nissenson, Michael R. Liebowitz, and Edna B. Foa. "Quality of Life and Functional Impairment in Obsessive-Compulsive Disorder: A Comparison of Patients with and without Comorbidity, Patients in Remission, and Healthy Controls." *Depression and Anxiety* 26 (2009): 39–45.

Ilic, Marie, Jost Reinecke, Gerd Bohner, Röttgers Hans-Onno, Thomas Beblo, Martin Driessen, Ulrich Frommberger, and Patrick William Corrigan. "Protecting Self-Esteem from Stigma: A Test of Different Strategies for Coping with the Stigma of Mental Illness." *International Journal of Social Psychiatry* 58 (2012): 246–57.

Inference Based Approach. "What Is IBA?" Accessed November 15, 2020. http://ibaocs .com/.

International OCD Foundation. "Ineffective and Potentially Harmful Psychological Interventions for Obsessive-Compulsive Disorder." Accessed November 19, 2020. https://iocdf.org.

Isin, Engin F. "The Neurotic Citizen." *Citizenship Studies* 8 (2004): 217–35.

Jenike, Michael A. "Obsessive-Compulsive and Related Disorders: A Hidden Epidemic." *New England Journal of Medicine* 321 (1989): 539–41.

———. "Obsessive-Compulsive Disorder." *New England Journal of Medicine* 350 (2004): 259–65.

Johnson, Davi A. "Managing Mr. Monk: Control and the Politics of Madness." *Critical Studies in Media Communication* 25 (2008): 28–47.

Johnson and Johnson. "Employee Resource Groups." Accessed January 30, 2020. https://www.jnj.com/.

Johnson, Jessie M. Quintero, and Julius Riles. "'He Acted Like a Crazy Person': Exploring the Influence of College Students' Recall of Stereotypic Media Representations of Mental Illness." *Psychology of Popular Media Culture* 7 (2018): 146–63.

Jorm, Anthony F. "Mental Health Literacy: Public Knowledge and Beliefs about Mental Disorders." *British Journal of Psychiatry* 177 (2000): 396–401.

Jorm, Anthony F., Scott B. Patten, Traolach S. Brugha, and Ramin Mojtabai. "Has Increased Provision of Treatment Reduced the Prevalence of Common Mental Disorders? Review of Evidence from Four Countries." *World Psychiatry* 16 (2017): 90–99.

Julien, Dominic, Kieron O'Connor, and Frederick Aardema. "The Inference-Based Approach to Obsessive-Compulsive Disorder: A Comprehensive Review of Its Etiological Model, Treatment Efficacy, and Model of Change." *Journal of Affective Disorders* 202 (2016): 187–96.

———. "Intrusions Related to Obsessive-Compulsive Disorder: A Question of Content or Context?" *Journal of Clinical Psychology* 65 (2009): 709–22.

Jutel, Annemarie Goldstein. *Putting a Name to It: Diagnosis in Contemporary Society.* Baltimore, MD: Johns Hopkins University Press, 2011. Kindle.

Karcı, Canan Kuygun, and Gonca Gül Celik. "Nutritional and Herbal Supplements in the Treatment of Obsessive Compulsive Disorder." *General Psychiatry* 33 (2020): 1–6.

Karp, David A. *Is It Me or My Meds? Living with Antidepressants.* Cambridge, MA: Harvard University Press, 2006.

————. *Speaking of Sadness: Depression, Disconnection, and the Meanings of Illness*. New York: Oxford University Press, 1997.

Keleher, Julia, Amita Jassi, and Georgina Krebs. "Clinician-Reported Barriers to Using Exposure with Response Prevention in the Treatment of Paediatric Obsessive-Compulsive Disorder." *Journal of Obsessive-Compulsive and Related Disorders* 24 (2020): n.p.

Kelly, Brendan D. "Buddhist Psychology, Psychotherapy and the Brain: A Critical Introduction." *Transcultural Psychiatry* 45 (2008): 5–30.

Kelly, Michael P., and David Field. "Medical Sociology, Chronic Illness and the Body." *Sociology of Health and Illness* 18 (1996): 241–57.

Keyes, Carly, Lizette Nolte, and Timothy I. Williams. "The Battle of Living with Obsessive Compulsive Disorder: A Qualitative Study of Young People's Experiences." *Child and Adolescent Mental Health* 23 (2018): 177–84.

Khosravani, Vahid, Frederick Aardema, Seyed Mehdi Samimi Ardestani, and Farangis Sharifi Bastan. "The Impact of the Coronavirus Pandemic on Specific Symptom Dimensions and Severity in OCD: A Comparison before and during COVID-19 in the Context of Stress Responses." Journal of Obsessive-Compulsive and Related Disorders 29 (2021): n.p.

Kirsch, Irving, Bruce Wampold, and John M. Kelley. "Controlling for the Placebo Effect in Psychotherapy: Noble Quest or Tilting at Windmills?" *Psychology of Consciousness: Theory, Research, and Practice* 3 (2016): 121–31.

Koçak, Orhan Murat, Ayşegül Yılmaz Özpolat, Cem Atbaşoğlu, and Metehan Çiçek. "Cognitive Control of a Simple Mental Image in Patients with Obsessive-Compulsive Disorder." *Brain and Cognition* 76 (2011): 390–99.

Kotapati, Vijaya Padma, Ali M. Khan, Sara Dar, Gulshan Begum, Ramya Bachu, Mahwish Adnan, Aarij Zubair, and Rizwan A. Ahmed. "The Effectiveness of Selective Serotonin Reuptake Inhibitors for Treatment of Obsessive-Compulsive Disorder in Adolescents and Children: A Systematic Review and Meta-analysis." *Frontiers in Psychiatry* 10 (2019). https://www.frontiersin.org/.

Koutoufa, Iakovina, and Adrian Furnham. "Mental Health Literacy and Obsessive-Compulsive Personality Disorder." *Psychiatry Research* 215 (2014): 223–28.

Kramer, Peter D. *Listening to Prozac*. New York: Viking Press, 1993.

Kroll-Smith, Steve, and H. Hugh Floyd. *Bodies in Protest: Environmental Illness and the Struggle over Medical Knowledge*. New York: New York University Press, 1997. Kindle.

Kumar, Kevin K., Geoffrey Appelboom, Layton Lamsam, Arthur L. Caplan, Nolan R. Williams, Mahendra T. Bhati, Sherman C. Stein, and Casey H. Halpern. "Comparative Effectiveness of Neuroablation and Deep Brain Stimulation for Treatment-Resistant Obsessive-Compulsive Disorder: A Meta-analytic Study." *Journal of Neurology, Neurosurgery, and Psychiatry* 90 (2019): 469–73.

Kusalaruk, Pichaya, Ratana Saipanish, and Thanita Hiranyatheb. "Attitudes of Psychiatrists toward Obsessive-Compulsive Disorder Patients." *Neuropsychiatric Disease and Treatment* 11 (2015): 1703–11.

Kvaale, Erlend P., William H. Gottdiener, and Nick Haslam. "Biogenetic Explanations and Stigma: A Meta-analytic Review of Associations among Laypeople." *Social Science and Medicine* 96 (2013): 95–103.

Lakoff, Andrew. *Pharmaceutical Reason: Knowledge and Value in Global Psychiatry.* New York: Cambridge University Press, 2005. Kindle.

Lamont, Michele, and Annette Lareau. "Cultural Capital: Allusions, Gaps and Glissandos in Recent Theoretical Developments." *Sociological Theory* 6 (1998): 153–68.

Lazarus, R., and S. Folkman. *Stress, Appraisal, and Coping.* New York: Springer, 1984.

Lebowitz, Eli R., Kaitlyn E. Panza, and Michael H. Bloch. "Family Accommodation in Obsessive-Compulsive and Anxiety Disorders: A Five-Year Update." *Expert Review of Neurotherapeutics* 16 (2016): 45–53.

Levy, Hannah C., Carmen P. McLean, Elna Yadin, and Edna B. Foa. "Characteristics of Individuals Seeking Treatment for Obsessive-Compulsive Disorder." *Behavior Therapy* 44 (2013): 408–16.

Levy, Jordan. "Am I a Monster? An Overview of Common Features, Typical Course, Shame and Treatment of Pedophilia OCD (pOCD)." International OCD Foundation. Accessed October 28, 2020. https://iocdf.org.

Lewis, Tania. "DIY Selves?" *European Journal of Cultural Studies* 9 (2006): 461–79.

Li, Ying, Luana Marques, Devon E. Hinton, Yuan Wang, and Ze-Ping Xiao. "Symptom Dimensions in Chinese Patients with Obsessive-Compulsive Disorder." *CNS Neuroscience and Therapeutics* 15 (2009): 276–82.

Liegghio, Maria. "Too Young to Be Mad: Disabling Encounters with 'Normal' from the Perspectives of Psychiatrized Youth." *Intersectionalities: A Global Journal of Social Work Analysis, Research, Polity, and Practice* 5 (2016): 110–29.

Linardon, Jake, Pim Cuijpers, Per Carlbring, Mariel Messer, and Matthew Fuller-Tyskiewicz. "The Efficacy of App-Supported Smartphone Interventions for Mental Health Problems: A Meta-analysis of Randomized Controlled Trials." *World Psychiatry* 18 (2019): 325–36.

Linden, David. "Biological Psychiatry: Time for New Paradigms." *British Journal of Psychiatry* 202 (2013): 166–67.

Link, Bruce G., and Jo C. Phelan. "Labeling and Stigma." In *Handbook of the Sociology of Mental Health*, 2nd ed., edited by Carol S. Aneshensel, Jo C. Phelan, and Alex Bierman, 525–41. Dordrecht: Springer, 2013.

Link, Bruce G., Jo C. Phelan, and Greer Sullivan. "Mental and Physical Health Consequences of the Stigma Associated with Mental Illnesses." In *The Oxford Handbook of Stigma, Discrimination, and Health*, edited by Brenda Major, John F. Dovidio, and Bruce G. Link, 521–40. New York: Oxford University Press, 2018.

Llorens-Aguilar, Sara, Gemma García-Soriano, Sandra Arnáez, Frederick Aardema, and Kieron O'Connor. "Is Context a Crucial Factor in Distinguishing between Intrusions and Obsessions in Patients with Obsessive-Compulsive Disorder?" *Journal of Clinical Psychology* 77 (2021): 804–17.

Loughman, Amy, and Nick Haslam. "Neuroscientific Explanations and the Stigma of Mental Disorder: A Meta-analytic Study." *Cognitive Research: Principles and Implications* 3 (2018). https://link.springer.com.

Lupton, Deborah. "Digitized Health Promotion." In *To Fix or To Heal: Patient Care, Public Health, and the Limits of Biomedicine*, edited by Joseph E. Davis and Ana Marta González, 152–76. New York: New York University Press, 2016.

———. "Sociology and Risk." In *Beyond the Risk Society: Critical Reflections on Risk and Human Security*, edited by Sandra Walklate and Gabe Mythen, 11–24. Berkshire, UK: Open University Press, 2006.

Luu, John, Michael Millard, Jill Newby, Hila Haskelberg, Megan J. Hobbs, and Alison E. J. Mahoney. "Internet-Based Cognitive Behavioural Therapy for Treating Symptoms of Obsessive Compulsive Disorder in Routine Care." Journal of Obsessive-Compulsive and Related Disorders 26 (2020): n.p.

MacDonald, Joanna, Sangsu Sohn, and Pete Ellis. "Privacy, Professionalism and Facebook: A Dilemma for Young Doctors." *Medical Education* 44 (2010): 805–13.

Maggini, Carlo, P. Ampollini, S. Gariboldi, P. L. Cella, L. Pelizza, and C. Marchesi. "The Parma High School Epidemiological Survey: Obsessive-Compulsive Symptoms." *Acta Psychiatrica Scandinavica* 103 (2001): 441–46.

Maier, Julia A., Douglas A. Gentile, David L. Vogel, and Scott A. Kaplan. "Media Influences on Self-Stigma of Seeking Psychological Services: The Importance of Media Portrayals and Person Perception." *Psychology of Popular Media Culture* 3 (2014): 239–56.

Maiorano, Alessandra, Antonio Lasalvia, Gaia Sampogna, Benedetta Pocai, Mirella Ruggeri, and Claire Henderson. "Reducing Stigma in Media Professionals: Is There Room for Improvement? Results from a Systematic Review." *Canadian Journal of Psychiatry* 62 (2017): 702–15.

Makowski, Anna C., Eva E. Mnich, Matthias C. Angermeyer, and Olaf von dem Knesebeck. "Continuum Beliefs in the Stigma Process Regarding Persons with Schizophrenia and Depression: Results of Path Analyses." *PeerJ* 4 (2016): e2360. https://peerj.com/.

Manjula, M., and Paulomi M. Sudhir. "New-Wave Behavioral Therapies in Obsessive-Compulsive Disorder: Moving toward Integrated Behavioral Therapies." *Indian Journal of Psychiatry* 61 (2019): S104–S113.

March, John S., and Christine M. Benton. *Talking Back to OCD: The Program That Helps Kids and Teens Say "No Way"—and Parents Say "Way to Go."* New York: Guilford Press, 2007. Kindle.

Marcussen, Kristen, Mary Gallagher, and Christian Ritter. "Mental Illness as a Stigmatized Identity." *Society and Mental Health* 9 (2019): 211–27.

Marques, Luana, Nicole J. LeBlanc, Hilary M. Weingarden, Kiara R. Timpano, Michael Jenike, and Sabine Wilhelm. "Barriers to Treatment and Service Utilization in an Internet Sample of Individuals with Obsessive-Compulsive Symptoms." *Depression and Anxiety* 27 (2010): 470–75.

Martin, Jack, and Ann-Marie McLellan. The *Education of Selves: How Psychology Transformed Students*. New York: Oxford University Press, 2013.

Mataix-Cols, David, Randy O. Frost, Alberto Pertusa, Lee Anna Clark, Sanjaya Saxena, James F. Leckman, Dan J. Stein, Hisato Matsunaga, and Sabine Wilhelm. "Hoarding Disorder: A New Diagnosis for *DSM-V*?" *Depression and Anxiety* 27 (2010): 556–72.

Mataix-Cols, David, and Isaac M. Marks. "Self-Help for Obsessive-Compulsive Disorder: How Much Therapist Contact Is Necessary?" *Clinical Neuropsychiatry* 3 (2006): 404–9.

Mayerovitch, Jamie I., Guillaume Galbaud du Fort, Ritsuko Kakuma, Roger C. Bland, Stephen C. Newman, and Gilbert Pinard. "Treatment Seeking for Obsessive-Compulsive Disorder: Role of Obsessive-Compulsive Disorder Symptoms and Comorbid Psychiatric Diagnoses." *Comprehensive Psychiatry* 44 (2003): 162–68.

McGuire, Joan M., and Sally S. Scott. "Universal Design for Instruction: Extending the Universal Design Paradigm to College Instruction." *Journal of Postsecondary Education and Disability* 19 (2006): 124–34.

McGuire, Joseph F., Eric A. Storch, Adam B. Lewin, Lawrence H. Price, Steven A. Rasmussen, and Wayne K. Goodman. "The Role of Avoidance in the Phenomenology of Obsessive-Compulsive Disorder." *Comprehensive Psychiatry* 53 (2012): 187–94.

McKay, Dean, Jonathan Abramowitz, and Eric Storch. "Ineffective and Potentially Harmful Psychological Interventions for Obsessive-Compulsive Disorder." Accessed November 18, 2020. https://iocdf.org.

McLean Hospital. "Living with OCD during the Coronavirus Crisis." Accessed October 24, 2020. https://www.mcleanhospital.org.

Mead, George Herbert. *Mind, Self and Society from the Standpoint of a Social Behaviorist*. Edited by Charles W. Morris. Chicago: University of Chicago Press, 1934.

Meier, Adrian, and Svenja Schäfer. "Positive Side of Social Comparison on Social Network Sites: How Envy Can Drive Inspiration on Instagram." *Cyberpsychology, Behavior, and Social Networking* 21 (2018): 411–17.

Meyer, A., D. H. Rose, and D. Gordon. *Universal Design for Learning*. Wakefield, MA: CAST Publishing, 2014.

Mian, Matthew K., Michael Campos, Sameer A. Sheth, and Emad N. Eskandar. "Deep Brain Stimulation for Obsessive-Compulsive Disorder: Past, Present, and Future." *Neurosurgical Focus* 29 (2010). https://thejns.org/.

Miles, Matthew B., and A. Michael Huberman. *Qualitative Data Analysis*. 2nd ed. Thousand Oaks, CA: Sage, 1994.

Moerman, Daniel E., and Wayne B. Jonas. "Deconstructing the Placebo Effect and Finding the Meaning Response." *Annals of Internal Medicine* 136 (2002): 471–76.

Mulvany, Julie. "Disability, Impairment or Illness? The Relevance of the Social Model of Disability to the Study of Mental Disorder." *Sociology of Health and Illness* 22 (2000): 582–601.

Myrick, Jessica Gall, Lesa Hatley Major, and Stacie Meihaus Jankowski. "The Sources and Frames Used to Tell Stories about Depression and Anxiety: A Content Analysis of 18 Years of National Television News Coverage." *Electronic News* 8 (2014): 49–63.

Myrick, Jessica Gall, and Rachelle L. Pavelko. "Examining Differences in Audience Recall and Reaction between Mediated Portrayals of Mental Illness as Trivializing versus Stigmatizing." *Journal of Health Communication* 22 (2017): 876–84.

Mythen, Gabe, and Sandra Walklate. "Introduction: Thinking beyond the Risk Society." In *Beyond the Risk Society: Critical Reflections on Risk and Human Security*, edited by Sandra Walklate and Gabe Mythen, 1–7. Berkshire, UK: Open University Press, 2006.

Ñāṇamoli, Bhikkhu, and Bhikkhu Bodhi, trans. *The Middle Length Discourses of the Buddha: A Translation of the Majjhima Nikāya*. 3rd ed. Boston: Wisdom Publications, 2005. Kindle.

National Institute of Mental Health. "Statistics." Last modified January 2021. https://www.nimh.nih.gov.

Nicolini, Humberto, Rafael Salin-Pascual, Brenda Cabrera, and Nuria Lanzagorta. "Influence of Culture in Obsessive-Compulsive Disorder and Its Treatment." *Current Psychiatric Reviews* 13 (2017): 285–92.

Nikodijevic, Alexandra, Richard Moulding, Jeromy Anglim, Frederick Aardema, and Maja Nedeljkovic. "Fear of Self, Doubt and Obsessive Compulsive Symptoms." *Journal of Behavior Therapy and Experimental Psychiatry* 49 (2015): 164–72.

Nissen, J. B., D. R. M. A. Højgaard, and P. H. Thomsen. "The Immediate Effect of COVID-19 Pandemic on Children and Adolescents with Obsessive Compulsive Disorder." *BMC Psychiatry* 20 (2020): n.p.

Nuñez, Mia, Richard E. Zinbarg, and Vijay A. Mittal. "Efficacy and Mechanisms of Non-invasive Brain Stimulation to Enhance Exposure Therapy: A Review." *Clinical Psychology Review* 70 (2019): 64–78.

OCD Center of Los Angeles. "Doubt, Denial and OCD." Accessed January 20, 2020. https://ocdla.com.

———. "Harm OCD: Symptoms and Treatment." Accessed January 15, 2016. https://ocdla.com.

———. "HOCD/Gay OCD: Common Subtypes." Accessed December 7, 2020. https://ocdla.com.

———. "Imaginal Exposure for OCD and Anxiety." Accessed January 15, 2016. https://ocdla.com.

———. "ROCD: Relationship OCD and the Myth of 'The One.'" Accessed January 20, 2016. https://ocdla.com.

O'Connor, Kieron, and Jean-Sébastien Audet. "OCD Is Not a Phobia: An Alternative Conceptualization of OCD." *Clinical Neuropsychiatry* 16 (2019): 39–46.

Olatunji, Bunmi O., Caroline Christian, Leigh Brosof, David F. Tolin, and Cheri A. Levinson. "What Is at the Core of OCD? A Network Analysis of Selected Obsessive-Compulsive Symptoms and Beliefs." *Journal of Affective Disorders* 2019 (257): 45–54.

Olbrich, Hanife, Katarina Stengler, and Sebastian Olbrich. "Smartphone Based Geo-Feedback in Obsessive Compulsive Disorder as Facilitatory Intervention: A Case Report." *Journal of Obsessive-Compulsive and Related Disorders* 8 (2016): 75–78.

Olson, Tom. "Buddhism, Behavior Change, and OCD." *Journal of Holistic Nursing* 21 (2003): 149–62.

Olson, Tom, Oriana Perez, Sergio Tapia, and Beatriz Vera. "Culturally Sensitive OCD Research: Lessons from the U.S.-Mexico Border." *Issues in Mental Health Nursing* 40 (2019): 760–67.

Ong, Clarissa W., Joseph W. Clyde, Ellen J. Bluett, Michael E. Levin, and Michael P. Twohig. "Dropout Rates in Exposure and Response Prevention for Obsessive-Compulsive Disorder: What Do the Data Really Say?" Journal of Anxiety Disorders 40 (2016): 8–17.

Ong, L. M. L., J. C. J. M. De Haes, A. M. Hoos, and F. B. Lammes. "Doctor-Patient Communication: A Review of the Literature." *Social Science and Medicine* 40 (1995): 903–18.

Osborn, Ian. *Can Christianity Cure Obsessive-Compulsive Disorder? A Psychiatrist Explores the Role of Faith in Treatment.* Grand Rapids, MI: Brazos Press, 2008.

Ostrow, Laysha, and Neal Adams. "Recovery in the USA: From Politics to Peer Support." *International Review of Psychiatry* 24 (2012): 70–78.

Ouellet-Courtois, Catherine, Samantha Wilson, and Kieron O'Connor. "Cognitive Confidence in Obsessive-Compulsive Disorder: A Systematic Review and Meta-analysis." *Journal of Obsessive-Compulsive and Related Disorders* 19 (2018): 77–86.

Ouimet, Allison, Andrea R. Ashbaugh, and Adam S. Radomsky. "Hoping for More: How Cognitive Science Has and Hasn't Been Helpful to the OCD Clinician." *Clinical Psychology Review* 69 (2019): 14–29.

Ozcanli, Fulya, Eva Ceulemans, Dirk Hermans, Laurence Claes, and Batja Mesquita. "Obsessions across Two Cultures: A Comparison of Belgian and Turkish Nonclinical Samples." *Frontiers in Psychology* 10 (2019): 1–13.

Pachankis, John E., Mark L. Hatzenbuehler, Katie Wang, Charles L. Burton, Forrest W. Crawford, Jo C. Phelan, and Bruce G. Link. "The Burden of Stigma on Health and Well-Being: A Taxonomy of Concealment, Course, Disruptiveness, Aesthetics, Origin, and Peril across 93 Stigmas." *Psychology Bulletin* 44 (2018): 451–74.

Parsons, Talcott. *The Social System.* London: Free Press of Glencoe, 1951.

Pattyn, E., M. Verhaeghe, C. Sercu, and P. Bracke. "Medicalizing versus Psychologizing Mental Illness: What Are the Implications for Help Seeking and Stigma? A General Population Study." *Social Psychiatry and Psychiatric Epidemiology* 48 (2013): 1637–45.

Pavelko, Rachelle L., and Jessica Gall Myrick. "Measuring Trivialization of Mental Illness: Developing a Scale of Perceptions That Mental Illness Symptoms Are Beneficial." *Health Communication* 35 (2020): 576–84.

———. "Tweeting and Trivializing: How the Trivialization of Obsessive-Compulsive Disorder via Social Media Impacts User Perceptions, Emotions, and Behaviors." *Imagination, Cognition and Personality: Consciousness in Theory, Research and Clinical Practice* 36 (2016): 41–63.

Penzel, Fred. "'But I Love My Kids . . .'—Parents Who Think about Harming Their Children." International OCD Foundation. Accessed January 8, 2020. https://iocdf .org/.

———. "To Be or Not to Be, That Is the Obsession: Existential and Philosophical OCD." International OCD Foundation. Accessed January 6, 2021. https://iocdf.org/.

Peris, Tara S., Mina Yadegar, Joan R. Asarnow, and John Piacentini. "Pediatric Obsessive Compulsive Disorder: Family Climate as a Predictor of Treatment Outcome." *Journal of Obsessive-Compulsive and Related Disorders* 1 (2012): 267–73.

Pescosolido, Bernice A. "The Public Stigma of Mental Illness: What Do We Think; What Do We Know; What Can We Prove?" *Journal of Health and Social Behavior* 54 (2013): 1–21.

Pescosolido, Bernice A., and Carol A. Boyer. "The American Health Care System: Entering the Twenty-First Century with High Risk, Major Challenges, and Great Opportunities." In *The Blackwell Companion to Medical Sociology*, edited by William C. Cockerham, 180–98. Malden, MA: Blackwell, 2001.

Pescosolido, Bernice A., Tait R. Medina, Jack K. Martin, and J. Scott Long. "The 'Backbone' of Stigma: Identifying the Global Core of Public Prejudice Associated with Mental Illness." *American Journal of Public Health* 103 (2013): 853–60.

Peter, Lina-Jolien, Stephanie Schindler, Christian Sander, Silke Schmidt, Holger Muehlan, Thomas McLaren, Samuel Tomczyk, Sven Speerforck, and Georg Schomerus. "Continuum Beliefs and Mental Illness Stigma: A Systematic Review and Meta-analysis of Correlation and Intervention Studies." Psychological Medicine 51 (2021): 716–26.

Petersen, Alan R. "Risk and the Regulated Self: The Discourse of Health Promotion as Politics of Uncertainty." *Australian and New Zealand Journal of Sociology* 32 (1996): 44–57.

Philo, Greg, and Glasgow University Media Group. *Media and Mental Distress*. New York: Longman, 1996.

Picco, L., E. Abdin, S. Pang, J. A. Vaingankar, A. Jeyagurunathan, S. A. Chong, and M. Subramaniam. "Association between Recognition and Help-Seeking Preferences and Stigma towards People with Mental Illness." *Epidemiology and Psychiatric Services* 27 (2018): 84–93.

Pirkis, Jane, R. Warwick Blood, Catherine Francis, and Kerry McCallum. "On-Screen Portrayals of Mental Illness: Extent, Nature, and Impacts." *Journal of Health Communication* 11 (2006): 523–41.

Pittenger, Christopher, and Michael H. Bloch. "Pharmacological Treatment of Obsessive-Compulsive Disorder." *Psychiatric Clinics of North America* 37 (2014): 375–91.

Polimeni, Joseph, Jeffrey P. Reiss, and Jitender Sareen. "Could Obsessive-Compulsive Disorder Have Originated as a Group-Selected Adaptive Trait in Traditional Societies?" *Medical Hypotheses* 65 (2005): 655–64.

Pollan, Michael. *The Omnivore's Dilemma: A Natural History of Four Meals*. New York: Penguin, 2007.

Porter, Roy. *Madness: A Brief History*. New York: Oxford University Press, 2002. Kindle.

Priebe, Stefan, Tom Burns, and Tom K. J. Craig. "The Future of Academic Psychiatry May Be Social." *British Journal of Psychiatry* 202 (2013): 319–20.

Purdon, Christine. "Empirical Investigations of Thought Suppression in OCD." *Journal of Behavior Therapy and Experimental Psychiatry* 35 (2004): 121–36.

Purdon, Christine, and David A. Clark. *Overcoming Obsessive Thoughts*. Oakland, CA: New Harbinger Publications, 2005.

Purdon, Christine, Emily Cripps, Matthew Faull, Stephen Joseph, and Karen Rowa. "Development of a Measure of Egodystonicity." *Journal of Cognitive Psychotherapy* 21 (2007): 198–216.

Rachman, S. "A Cognitive Theory of Compulsive Checking." *Behaviour Research and Therapy* 40 (2002): 625–39.

———. "A Cognitive Theory of Obsessions." *Behaviour Research and Therapy* 35 (1997): 793–802.

———. "The Evolution of Cognitive Behaviour Therapy." In *Science and Practice of Cognitive Behaviour Therapy*, edited by David M. Clark and Christopher G. Fairburn, 3–26. Oxford: Oxford University Press, 1997.

Rachman, Stanley J., and Padmal De Silva. *Obsessive-Compulsive Disorder*. New York: Oxford University Press, 2009.

Rachman, S., and Ray J. Hodgson. *Obsessions and Compulsions*. Englewood Cliffs, NJ: Prentice-Hall, 1980.

Rachman, S., Adam S. Radomsky, and Roz Shafran. "Safety Behaviour: A Reconsideration." *Behaviour Research and Therapy* 46 (2008): 163–73.

Rachman, S., R. Shafran, D. Mitchell, J. Trant, and B. Teachman. "How to Remain Neutral: An Experimental Analysis of Neutralization." *Behaviour Research and Therapy* 34 (1996): 889–98.

Radomsky, Adam S., and Gillian M. Alcolado. "Don't Even *Think* about Checking: Mental Checking Causes Memory Distrust." *Journal of Behavior Therapy and Experimental Psychiatry* 41 (2010): 345–51.

Radomsky, Adam S., Gillian M. Alcolado, Jonathan S. Abramowitz, Pino Alonso, Amparo Belloch, Martine Bouvard, David A. Clark, et al. "Part 1—You Can Run But You Can't Hide: Intrusive Thoughts on Six Continents." *Journal of Obsessive-Compulsive and Related Disorders* 3 (2014): 269–79.

Raiola, Alyssa. "Why You Need to Stop Saying You're 'So OCD.'" *Greatist*. Accessed December 15, 2019. https://greatist.com.

Ramos-Cerqueira, Ana Teresa de Abreu, Albina Rodrigues Torres, Ricardo Cezar Torresan, Ana Paula Maranhão Negreiros, and Caroline Nakano Vitorino. "Emotional Burden in Caregivers of Patients with Obsessive-Compulsive Disorder." *Depression and Anxiety* 25 (2008): 1020–27.

Rapoport, Judith L. *The Boy Who Couldn't Stop Washing: The Experience and Treatment of Obsessive-Compulsive Disorder*. New York: Plume, 1990.

Rasmussen, Steven A., and Jane L. Eisen. "The Epidemiology and Clinical Features of Obsessive Compulsive Disorder." *Psychiatric Clinics of North America* 15 (1992): 743–58.

Rathbun-Grubb, Susan. "The Lived Experience of Work and Career among Individuals with Bipolar Disorder: A Phenomenological Study of Discussion Forum Narratives." *International Journal of Information, Diversity, and Inclusion* 3 (2019): 20–44.

Remmerswaal, Karin C. P., Neeltje M. Batelaan, and Anton J. L. M. van Balkom. "Relieving the Burden of Family Members of Patients with Obsessive-Compulsive Disorder." *Clinical Neuropsychiatry* 16 (2019): 47–52.

Richter, D., A. Wall, A. Bruen, and R. Whittington. "Is the Global Prevalence Rate of Adult Mental Illness Increasing? Systematic Review and Meta-analysis." *Acta Psychiatrica Scandinavia* 140 (2019): 393–407.

Rigney, Daniel. *The Metaphorical Society: An Invitation to Social Theory.* Lanham, MD: Rowman and Littlefield, 2001.

Roberts, Clark, Barbara J. Sahakian, and Trevor W. Robbins. "Psychological Mechanisms and Functions of 5-HT and SSRIs in Potential Therapeutic Change: Lessons from the Serotonergic Modulation of Action Selection, Learning, Affect, and Social Cognition." *Neuroscience and Biobehavioral Reviews* 119 (2020): 138–67.

Robinson, Patrick, Daniel Turk, Sagar Jilka, and Matteo Cella. "Measuring Attitudes towards Mental Health Using Social Media: Investigating Stigma and Trivialisation." *Social Psychiatry and Psychiatric Epidemiology* 54 (2019): 51–58.

Rose, Diana. "The Mainstreaming of Recovery." *Journal of Mental Health* 23 (2014): 217–18.

Rose, Nikolas. *Our Psychiatric Future: The Politics of Mental Health.* Cambridge, UK: Polity Press, 2019. Kindle.

———. *The Politics of Life Itself: Biomedicine, Power, and Subjectivity in the Twenty-First Century.* Princeton, NJ: Princeton University Press, 2007. Kindle.

Rosmarin, David H., Steven Pirutinsky, and Jedidiah Siev. "Recognition of Scrupulosity and Non-religious OCD by Orthodox and Non-Orthodox Jews." *Journal of Social and Clinical Psychology* 29 (2010): 930–44.

Ross, Anna M., Amy J. Morgan, Anthony F. Jorm, and Nicola J. Reavley. "A Systematic Review of the Impact of Media Reports of Severe Mental Illness on Stigma and Discrimination, and Interventions That Aim to Mitigate Any Adverse Impact." Social Psychiatry and Psychiatric Epidemiology 54 (2019): 11–31.

Rosso, Gianluca, Umberto Albert, Giovanni Francesco Asinari, Filippo Bogetto, and Giuseppe Maina. "Stressful Life Events and Obsessive-Compulsive Disorder: Clinical Features and Symptom Dimensions." *Psychiatry Research* 197 (2012): 259–64.

Rüsch, Nicolas, Matthias C. Angermeyer, and Patrick W. Corrigan. "Mental Illness Stigma: Concepts, Consequences, and Initiatives to Reduce Stigma." *European Psychiatry* 20 (2005): 529–39.

Ruscio, A. M., D. J. Stein, W. T. Chiu, and R. C. Kessler. "The Epidemiology of Obsessive-Compulsive Disorder in the National Comorbidity Survey Replication." *Molecular Psychiatry* 15 (2010): 53–63.

Salkovskis, Paul M., and Joan Kirk. "Obsessive-Compulsive Disorder." In *Science and Practice of Cognitive Behaviour Therapy*, edited by David M. Clark and Christopher G. Fairburn, 179–208. Oxford: Oxford University Press, 1996.

Salkovskis, Paul M., and Osamu Kobori. "Reassuringly Calm? Self-Reported Patterns of Responses to Reassurance Seeking in Obsessive Compulsive Disorder." *Journal of Behavior Therapy and Experimental Psychiatry* 49 (2015): 203–8.

Samerski, Silja. "Health Literacy as a Social Practice: Social and Empirical Dimensions of Knowledge on Health and Healthcare." *Social Science and Medicine* 226 (2019): 1–8.

Sarris, Jerome, David Camfield, and Michael Berk. "Complementary Medicine, Self-Help, and Lifestyle Interventions for Obsessive Compulsive Disorder (OCD) and the OCD Spectrum: A Systematic Review." *Journal of Affective Disorders* 138 (2012): 213–21.

Schmelkin, Liora Pedhazur. "Hierarchy of Preferences toward Disabled Groups: A Reanalysis." *Perceptual and Motor Skills* 59 (1984): 151–57.

Schneider, Joseph W., and Peter Conrad. *Having Epilepsy: The Experience and Control of Illness*. Philadelphia: Temple University Press, 1983.

Schneider, Sophie C., Lindsey Knott, Sandra L. Cepeda, Lynn M. Hana, Elizabeth Mc-Ingvale, Wayne K. Goodman, and Eric A. Storch. "Serious Negative Consequences Associated with Exposure and Response Prevention for Obsessive-Compulsive Disorder: A Survey of Therapist Attitudes and Experiences." *Depression and Anxiety* 37 (2020): 418–28.

Schomerus, Georg, Herbert Matschinger, and Matthias C. Angermeyer. "Continuum Beliefs and Stigmatizing Attitudes towards Persons with Schizophrenia, Depression and Alcohol Dependence." *Psychiatry Research* 209 (2013): 665–69.

Schur, Edwin M. *Labeling Deviant Behavior: Its Sociological Implications*. New York: Harper and Row, 1971.

Schürmann, Jan, and Jürgen Margraf. "Age of Anxiety and Depression Revisited: A Meta-analysis of Two European Community Samples (1964–2015)." *International Journal of Clinical and Health Psychology* 18 (2018): 102–12.

Schuster, Sarah. "16 Hilarious OCD Memes (That Don't Make Fun of People with OCD)." *The Mighty*. Accessed April 28, 2018. https://themighty.com/.

Schwartz, Caroline, Sandra Schlegl, Anne Katrin Kuelz, and Ulrich Voderholzer. "Treatment-Seeking in OCD Community Cases and Psychological Treatment Actually Provided to Treatment-Seeking Patients: A Systematic Review." *Journal of Obsessive-Compulsive and Related Disorders* 2 (2013): 448–56.

Schwartz, Jeffrey, and Beverly Beyette. *Brain Lock: Free Yourself from Obsessive-Compulsive Behavior*. New York: Regan Books, 1997.

Schwartz, Jeffrey, and Rebecca Gladding. *You Are Not Your Brain: The 4-Step Solution for Changing Bad Habits, Ending Unhealthy Thinking, and Taking Control of Your Life*. New York: Penguin, 2012.

Seay, Steven J. "Suicide Obsessions: Fear of Killing/Harming Yourself." Last modified July 20, 2012. http://www.steveseay.com/suicide-obsessions-fear-killing-yourself/.

Shapiro, Leslie J. *Understanding OCD: Skills to Control the Conscience and Outsmart Obsessive Compulsive Disorder*. Santa Barbara, CA: Praeger, 2015. Kindle.

Shim, Janet K. "Cultural Health Capital: A Theoretical Approach to Understanding Health Care Interactions and the Dynamics of Unequal Treatment." *Journal of Health and Social Behavior* 51 (2010): 1–15.

Siegel, Dustin E. "The Portrayal of Characters with Obsessive-Compulsive Disorder in American films." PsyD diss., University of Hartford, 2014.

Siev, Jedidiah, Jonathan D. Huppert, and Shelby E. Zuckerman. "Understanding and Treating Scrupulosity." In *The Wiley Handbook of Obsessive Compulsive Disorders*, edited by Jonathan S. Abramowitz, Dean McKay, and Eric A. Storch, 527–46. Hoboken, NJ: Wiley Blackwell, 2017.

Simonds, Laura M., and Sandra A. Elliott. "OCD Patients and Non-patient Groups Reporting Obsessions and Compulsions: Phenomenology, Help-Seeking, and Access to Treatment." *British Journal of Medical Psychology* 74 (2001): 431–49.

Singh, Ilina. "A Disorder of Anger and Aggression: Children's Perspectives on Attention Deficit/Hyperactivity Disorder in the UK." *Social Science and Medicine* 73 (2011): 889–96.

Siu, Judy Yuen-man. " 'Seeing a Doctor Is Just Like Having a Date': A Qualitative Study on Doctor Shopping among Overactive Bladder Patients in Hong Kong." *BMC Family Practice* 15 (2014). https://bmcfampract.biomedcentral.com/.

Skapinakis Petros, Deborah Caldwell, William Hollingworth, Peter Bryden, Naomi Fineberg, Paul Salkovskis, et al. "A Systematic Review of the Clinical Effectiveness and Cost-Effectiveness of Pharmacological and Psychological Interventions for the Management of Obsessive-Compulsive Disorder in Children/Adolescents and Adults." *Health Technology Assessment* 20 (2016): vii–360.

Skoog, Gunnar, and Ingmar Skoog. "A 40-Year Follow-Up of Patients with Obsessive-Compulsive Disorder." *Archives of General Psychiatry* 56 (1999): 121–27.

Sontag, Susan. *Illness as Metaphor and AIDS and Its Metaphors*. New York: Picador USA, 1989.

Springer, Kristen S., Hannah C. Levy, and David F. Tolin. "Remission in CBT for Adult Anxiety Disorders: A Meta Analysis." *Clinical Psychology Review* 61 (2018): 1–8.

Stein, Dan J., Damiaan Denys, Andrew T. Gloster, Eric Hollander, James F. Leckman, Scott L. Rauch, and Katharine A. Phillips. "Obsessive-Compulsive Disorder: Diagnostic and Treatment Issues." *Psychiatric Clinics of North America* 32 (2009): 665–85.

Steinberg, Daniel S., and Chad T. Wetterneck. "OCD Taboo Thoughts and Stigmatizing Attitudes in Clinicians." *Community Mental Health Journal* 53 (2017): 275–80.

Steketee, Gail, Teresa A. Pigott, and Todd Schemmel. *Obsessive Compulsive Disorder: The Latest Assessment and Treatment Strategies*. Kansas City, MO: Compact Clinicals, 2006.

Steketee, Gail, and Barbara van Noppen. "Family Approaches to Treatment for Obsessive Compulsive Disorder." *Revista Brasileira de Psiquiatria* 25 (2003): 43–50.

Stengler, Katarina, Sebastian Olbrich, Dirk Heider, Sandra Dietrich, Steffi Riedel-Heller, and Ina Jahn. "Mental Health Treatment Seeking among Patients with OCD:

Impact of Age of Onset." *Social Psychiatry and Psychiatric Epidemiology* 48 (2013): 813–19.

Stengler-Wenzke, Katarina, Michael Kroll, Herbert Matschinger, and Matthias C. Angermeyer. "Subjective Quality of Life of Patients with Obsessive-Compulsive Disorder." *Social Psychiatry and Psychiatric Epidemiology* 41 (2006): 662–68.

Stengler-Wenzke, Katarina, Johanna Trosbach, Sandra Dietrich, and Matthias C. Angermeyer. "Coping Strategies Used by the Relatives of People with Obsessive-Compulsive Disorder." *Journal of Advanced Nursing* 48 (2004): s35–s42.

Stokes, Peter E., and Aliza Holtz. "Fluoxetine Tenth Anniversary Update: The Progress Continues." *Clinical Therapeutics* 19 (1997): 1135–250.

Stoppard, Janet, and Linda McMullen, eds. *Situating Sadness: Women and Depression in Social Context.* New York: New York University Press, 2003.

Storch, Eric A., Gary R. Geffken, and Tanya K. Murphy, eds. *Handbook of Child and Adolescent Obsessive-Compulsive Disorder.* Mahwah, NJ: Lawrence Erlbaum, 2007.

Stout, Patricia A., Jorge Villegas, and Nancy A. Jennings. "Images of Mental Illness in the Media: Identifying Gaps in the Research." *Schizophrenia Bulletin* 30 (2004): 543–61.

Strauss, Anselm L. *Chronic Illness and the Quality of Life.* St. Louis, MO: C. V. Mosby, 1975.

Subramaniam, Mythily, Edimansyah Abdin, Louisa Picco, Shazana Shahwan, Anitha Jeyagurunathan, Janhavi Ajit Vaingankar, and Siow Ann Chong. "Continuum Beliefs and Stigmatising Beliefs about Mental Illness: Results from an Asian Community Survey." *BMJ Open* 7 (2017). https://mc.manuscriptcentral.com.

Subramaniam, Mythily, Edimansyah Abdin, Janhavi Ajit Vaingankar, and Siow Ann Chong. "Obsessive-Compulsive Disorder: Prevalence, Correlates, Help-Seeking and Quality of Life in a Multiracial Asian Population." *Social Psychiatry and Psychiatric Epidemiology* 47 (2012): 2035–43.

Subramaniam, Mythily, Pauline Soh, Janhavi Ajit Vaingankar, Louisa Picco, and Siow Ann Chong. "Quality of Life in Obsessive-Compulsive Disorder: Impact of the Disorder and of Treatment." *CNS Drugs* 27 (2013): 367–83.

Suchman, Edward A. "Stages of Illness and Medical Care." *Journal of Health and Human Behavior* 6 (1965): 114–28.

Taylor, Danielle M. *Americans with Disabilities: 2014.* Published 2018, United States Census Bureau. https://www.census.gov/.

Taylor, Steven. "Etiology of Obsessions and Compulsions: A Meta-analysis and Narrative Review of Twin Studies." *Clinical Psychology Review* 31 (2011): 1361–72.

Thibodeau, Ryan, Lindsay N. Shanks, and Brian P. Smith. "Do Continuum Beliefs Reduce Schizophrenia Stigma? Effects of a Laboratory Intervention on Behavioral and Self-Reported Stigma." *Journal of Behavior Therapy and Experimental Psychiatry* 58 (2017): 29–35.

Thoits, Peggy A. "Disentangling Mental Illness Labeling Effects from Treatment Effects on Well-Being." *Society and Mental Health* OnlineFirst (2020): 1–18.

Thomas, Carol. "Medical Sociology and Disability Theory." In *New Directions in the Sociology of Chronic and Disabling Conditions*, edited by Graham Scambler and Sasha Scambler, 37–56. New York: Palgrave Macmillan, 2010.

Thompson, Anna, Cathy Issakidis, and Caroline Hunt. "Delay to Seek Treatment for Anxiety and Mood Disorders in an Australian Clinical Sample." *Behaviour Change* 25 (2008): 71–84.

Thornicroft, Graham. *Shunned: Discrimination against People with Mental Illness*. New York: Oxford University Press, 2006.

Time to Change. Accessed January 8, 2020. https://www.time-to-change.org.uk.

Timpano, Kiara R., and Norman B. Schmidt. "The Relationship between Self-Control Deficits and Hoarding: A Multimethod Investigation across Three Samples." *Journal of Abnormal Psychology* 122 (2013): 13–25.

Torres, Albina R., Martin J. Prince, Paul E. Bebbington, Dinesh K. Bhugra, Traolach S. Brugha, Michael Farrell, Rachel Jenkins, Glyn Lewis, Howard Meltzer, and Nicola Singleton. "Treatment Seeking by Individuals with Obsessive-Compulsive Disorder from the British Psychiatric Morbidity Survey of 2000." *Psychiatric Services* 58 (2007): 977–82.

Traynor, Michael, Maggie Boland, Niels Buus. "Professional Autonomy in 21st Century Healthcare: Nurses' Accounts of Clinical Decision-Making." *Social Science and Medicine* 71 (2010): 1506–12.

Tringo, J. L. "The Hierarchy of Preference toward Disability Groups." *Journal of Special Education* 4 (1970): 295–306.

Twenge, Jean M. "Age of Anxiety? Birth Cohort Change in Anxiety and Neuroticism, 1952–1993." *Journal of Personality and Social Psychology* 79 (2000): 1007–21.

Uhre, Camilla Funch, Valdemar Funch Uhre, Nicole Nadine Lønfeldt, Linea Pretzmann, Signe Vangkilde, Kerstin Jessica Plessen, Christian Gludd, Janus Christian Jakobsen, and Anne Katrine Pagsberg. "Systematic Review and Meta-analysis: Cognitive-Behavioral Therapy for Obsessive-Compulsive Disorder in Children and Adolescents." *Journal of the American Academy of Child and Adolescent Psychiatry* 59 (2020): 64–77.

Union of the Physically Impaired Against Segregation and Disability Alliance. *Fundamental Principles of Disability*. https://disability-studies.leeds.ac.uk/.

UNM Center for Social Policy. "The Medicalization of Society." Accessed January 8, 2020. https://www.youtube.com/watch?v=9l8LJjy5B2g&list=WL&index=7&t=3925s.

van Dis, Eva Anna Maria, and Marcel A. van den Hout. "Not Just Right Experiences as Ironic Result of Perseverative Checking." *Clinical Neuropsychiatry* 13 (2016): 100–107.

Veale, David. "Psychopathology of Obsessive-Compulsive Disorder." *Psychiatry* 3 (2004): 65–68.

Verlinde, Evelyn, Nele De Laender, Stéphanie De Maesschalck, Myriam Deveugele, and Sara Willems. "The Social Gradient in Doctor-Patient Communication." *International Journal for Equity in Health* 11 (2012). https://equityhealthj.biomedcentral.com/.

Wahl, Otto F. *Media Madness: Public Images of Mental Illness*. New Brunswick, NJ: Rutgers University Press, 1995.

———. "Obsessive-Compulsive Disorder in Popular Magazines." *Community Mental Health Journal* 36 (2000): 307–12.

Walseth, Liv Tveit, Vegard Øksendal Haaland, Gunvor Launes, Joseph Himle, and Åshild Tellefsen Håland. "Obsessive-Compulsive Disorder's Impact on Partner Relationships: A Qualitative Study." *Journal of Family Psychotherapy* 28 (2017): 205–21.

Wang, Philip S., Sergio Aguilar-Gaxiola, Jordi Alonso, Matthias C. Angermeyer, Guilherme Borges, Evelyn J. Bromet, Ronny Bruffaerts, Giovanni de Girolamo, Ron de Graaf, and Oye Gureje. "Use of Mental Health Services for Anxiety, Mood, and Substance Disorders in 17 Countries in the WHO World Mental Health Surveys." *Lancet* 370 (2007): 841–50.

Warman, Debbie M., Peter L. Phalen, and Joel M. Martin. "Impact of a Brief Education about Mental Illness on Stigma of OCD and Violent Thoughts." *Journal of Obsessive-Compulsive and Related Disorders* 5 (2015): 16–23.

Watson, James L., ed. *Golden Arches East: McDonald's in East Asia*. Stanford, CA: Stanford University Press, 1997.

Wegner, Daniel M., David J. Schneider, Samuel R. Carter III, and Teri L. White. "Paradoxical Effects of Thought Suppression." *Journal of Personality and Social Psychology* 53 (1987): 5–13.

Weiss, Marjorie, and Ray Fitzpatrick. "Challenges to Medicine: The Case of Prescribing." *Sociology of Health and Illness* 19 (1997): 297–327.

Weitz, Rose. *Life with AIDS*. New Brunswick, NJ: Rutgers University Press, 1991.

Welkowitz, Lawrence A., Elmer L. Struening, John Pittman, Mary Guardino, and Joan Welkowitz. "Obsessive-Compulsive Disorder and Comorbid Anxiety Problems in a National Anxiety Screening Sample." *Journal of Anxiety Disorders* 14 (2000): 471–82.

Wheaton, Michael G., Brittain Mahaffey, Kiara R. Timpano, Noah C. Berman, and Jonathan S. Abramowitz. "The Relationship between Anxiety Sensitivity and Obsessive-Compulsive Symptom Dimensions." *Journal of Behavior Therapy and Experimental Psychiatry* 43 (2012): 891–96.

Whittal, Maureen L., and Peter D. McLean. "CBT for OCD: The Rationale, Protocol, and Challenges." *Cognitive and Behavioral Practice* 6 (1999): 383–96.

Wilhelm, Sabine, Noah C. Berman, Aparna Keshaviah, Rachel A. Schwartz, and Gail Steketee. "Mechanisms of Change in Cognitive Therapy for Obsessive Compulsive Disorder: Role of Maladaptive Beliefs and Schemas." *Behaviour Research and Therapy* 65 (2015): 5–10.

Wilkinson, Iain. *Anxiety in a Risk Society*. London: Routledge, 2001.

Williams, M. T., L. K. Chapman, J. V. Simms, and G. Tellawi. "Cross-Cultural Phenomenology of Obsessive-Compulsive Disorder." In *The Wiley Handbook of Obsessive Compulsive Disorders*, edited by Jonathan S. Abramowitz, Dean McKay, and Eric A. Storch, 56–74. Hoboken, NJ: Wiley Blackwell, 2017.

Williams, Monnica T., and Matthew E. Jahn. "Obsessive-Compulsive Disorder in African American Children and Adolescents: Risks, Resiliency, and Barriers to Treatment." *American Journal of Orthopsychiatry* 87 (2017): 291–303.

Williams, Simon J. "Chronic Illness as Biographical Disruption or Biographical Disruption as Chronic Illness? Reflections on a Core Concept." *Sociology of Health and Illness* 22 (2000): 40–67.

Willis, Evan. "Introduction: Taking Stock of Medical Dominance." *Health Sociology Review* 15 (2006): 421–31.

Wilson, Adriana, and Kayla Thayer. "Cross-Cultural Differences in the Presentation and Expression of OCD in Black Individuals: A Systematic Review." *Journal of Obsessive-Compulsive and Related Disorders* 27 (2020): n.p.

Winnick, Terri A. "From Quackery to 'Complementary' Medicine: The American Medical Profession Confronts Alternative Therapies." *Social Problems* 52 (2005): 38–61.

Wolfensberger, Wolf. *The Principle of Normalization in Human Services.* Toronto: National Institute on Mental Retardation, 1972.

Wong, Bernie. "What Companies Like Google, Johnson & Johnson, RetailMeNot and SAP Are Doing to Change the Culture of Workplace Mental Health." *Forbes.* Accessed January 30, 2020. https://www.forbes.com.

Wong, Eunice C., Rebecca L. Collins, Jennifer L. Cerully, Jennifer W. Yu, and Rachana Seelam. "Effects of Contact-Based Mental Illness Stigma Reduction Programs: Age, Gender, and Asian, Latino, and White American Differences." *Social Psychiatry and Psychiatric Epidemiology* 53 (2018): 299–308.

World Health Organization. "International Classification of Diseases (ICD-11)." Accessed June 17, 2018. http://www.who.int/classifications/icd/en/.

Wu, Monica S., Rebecca Hamblin, Joshua Nadeau, Jessica Simmons, Ashley Smith, Meredith Wilson, Stephanie Eken, Brent Small, Vicky Phares, and Eric A. Storch. "Quality of Life and Burden in Caregivers of Youth with Obsessive-Compulsive Disorder Presenting for Intensive Treatment." *Comprehensive Psychiatry* 80 (2018): 46–56.

Yorulmaz, Orçun, Tülin Gençöz, and Shelia Woody. "Vulnerability Factors in OCD Symptoms: Cross-Cultural Comparisons between Turkish and Canadian Samples." *Clinical Psychology and Psychotherapy* 17 (2010): 110–21.

Zedner, Lucia. "Too Much Security?" *International Journal of the Sociology of Law* 31 (2003): 155–84.

Ziebland, Sue. "The Importance of Being Expert: The Quest for Cancer Information on the Internet." *Social Science and Medicine* 59 (2004): 1783–93.

Zion, Sean R., and Alia J. Crum. "Mindsets Matter: A New Framework for Harnessing the Placebo Effect in Modern Medicine." *International Review of Neurobiology* 138 (2018): 137–60.

INDEX

Page numbers in *italics* indicate Figures.

hair cutting and shaving, symptoms, 51

harm: fear of, symptoms, 1, 3, 17, 28, 30, 35, 41–43, 45–46, 48, 73, 82, 84–85, 95, 109, 111–15, 117–18, 131–32, 134, 136, 202–3, 224n50, 225n50, 226n55, 226nn54–55; self-, 28, 46

healthcare system. *See* access to help; doctor-patient relationships; psychiatric hospital; treatment

help-seeking: access to help, 20, 120, 147, 151, 155, 182–83, 188, 204; age of onset and, 79, 81–82; career contingencies, 72–73; delays in, and onset of symptoms, 79; doctor-shopping, 150; influenced by media, 27; the internet and, 144–48, 151, 154, 157–59; mental health literacy and, 93–96; non-, 9; perceiving oneself as not having a problem and, 73–74, 77–81; social networks and, 79–80, 88, 144–48, 159–62; stage in illness career, 19–20. *See also* barriers to help-seeking

Hershfield, Jon, 64

heterogeneity, of OCD, 41–43, 51–53

hidden disorder, 14, 38–39

hiding: concealing and, 40–41, 83, 172–78, 231n16; in plain sight, 173–74. *See also* inner world

Hillam, Hannah, 54, 168

historical context: OCD in, 35–38, 198–203; treatment in, 58–66

hit-and-run OCD, 48

hoarding disorder: classification of, 9–10; media representations of, 26

hoarding symptoms, 9–10, 35, 77–78, 81, 122, 158, 173, 212n27, 218n8

Hodgson, Ray J., 37

Holstein, James A., 77, 86, 89

homosexual OCD. *See* symptoms: involving sexual thoughts

Honneth, Axel, 178

hospitalization. *See* psychiatric hospital

humor, 3, 26–27, 107, 153, 169; coping and, 206; social support and, 179; stereotypes and, 194; trivialization and, 27. *See also* joke

Huppert, Jonathan D., 59

Hyman, Bruce, 136

IBA. *See* inference-based approach
IBT. *See* inference-based therapy
ICD. *See* International Statistical Classification of Diseases and Related Health Problems

identity: -based movement, 185–86; chronicity and, 166–70; labeling and, 166, 185–89. *See also* the self

illness career: confidants and, 136–43; defined, 12–14, 72–74; depression and, 12–13, 78, 102; description of stages in OCD, 69–71; diagnosis of OCD as part of, 90–96; family and, 79–80, 137–43, 179–80, 185; help-seeking stage in, 19–20; problem recognition stage in, 69–89

illness metaphor, 1–2, 19–20, 53–56, 119–20, 122, 126, 164–65, 167

imaginal exposure script, 134–35

imperfection, feelings of, 50–51

impression management, 172–73, 177

individualism, 205–6

inference-based approach (IBA), 33, 62–63

inference-based therapy (IBT), 62–63

inner world *vs.* outer, 39–41, 78, 141, 170–71, 173–74, 183–84. *See also* hiding

insight, and OCD, 4, 55–56, 84–85

interactional strategies, 172–78

International OCD Foundation, 58, 106, 188

International Statistical Classification of Diseases and Related Health Problems (ICD), 29

the internet: exacerbating OCD, 149; flexibility of, 157–59; help-seeking and, 144–48, 151, 154, 157–59; stigma minimized by, use of, 158–62

spiritual symptoms (including religious/ scrupulosity and morality OCD), 3, 30, 35–37, 40, 44, 47, 57, 82, 109, 111–16, 134, 136, 140, 156–57, 181, 225n50
SPSS, 226n54
SRI. *See* serotonin reuptake inhibitor
SSRIs. *See* selective serotonin reuptake inhibitors
Steketee, Gail, 59
stereotypes, 2, 15–16, 27–28, 86, 93–95, 103, 106–8, 105–106, 111, 159, 196; continuum beliefs and, 197; humor and, 27, 102, 194; stigma grounded in, 102–4, 194; trivialization grounded in, 195; used to avoid stigma, 93, 176–77
stereotypical revealing, 175–76
stigma, 102–5, 173, 194–95; biologisation of mental illness and, 196; challenging, 183, 187, 195–206; confidants and, 180–82; consciousness, 104; contact and reducing, 196; continuum beliefs and, 17–18, 21, 195–98, 204; courtesy, 140–41; diagnosis and, 102–3, 192; discredited vs. discreditable, 173; experienced, 20, 81, 99, 164, 180–82; fear of, 8, 73–74, 83, 90, 101, 126–27, 141, 178; Goffman on, 103–4, 173, 222n12, 231n9; grounded in stereotypes, 102–4, 194; hierarchy, 15, 19, 105–6, 113–16, 141; interactional strategies and, 173–78; media representations and, 27–29; medicalization and, 13, 19, 95–96, 102, 153; of mental disorder, 102–5; mental health literacy and, 93, 106–16; minimized by use of the internet, 158–62; self-, 15–16, 69–71, 74, *100*, 104–5, 164–65, 179, 194, 222n12; tangled web of trivialization and, 14–17, 93, 106–9, 144, 193–98; and technology, 146, 154, 158–60, 183
stress: coping and, 123; OCD exacerbated by, 18, 32, 166, 198, 202, 205–6; mindfulness for, 198
student survey, 109–16

subthreshold symptoms, 4, 30, 80, 198
suicide, 4, 46, 71, 124. *See also* symptoms: thoughts involving self-harm or suicide
supernormals, 30
support group, 8, 74–75, 158–62, 179, 183
symbolic interaction, 11, 76–77, 206
symmetry (including ordering and arranging), symptoms 28, 30, 41, 43, 47, 77, 81, 109, 111–17, 131, 138, 176, 188, 225n50
symptoms: anxiety, 1, 3–4, 18, 33, 43, 45, 49, 62, 76, 99, 112, 117, 119, 123, 128, 131–34, 202, 205, 218n8, 227n10; avoidance, 1–2, 4, 18–19, 25, 41, 49–50, 52, 62, 91–92, 109, 131–32, 134–35, 173–74; checking, 1–2, 4, 28, 30, 41–42, 44–45, 47–49, 62, 78, 81–82, 117–18, 131–32, 135, 138–39, 145–46, 177; confessing, 225n50; contamination (including symptoms involving germs/illness/health), 3, 15, 18, 28, 30, 33–34, 36–37, 40–42, 46–47, 49–50, 52, 81, 84–85, 90–91, 95–96, 109, 111–15, 119, 131, 141, 149, 173, 179, 202, 225n50; counting or numerical, 4, 26, 48, 53, 69–70, 77, 145, 154, 174; delays in help-seeking and onset of, 79; with existential content, 41, 44, 57; fear of harm, 1, 3, 17, 28, 30, 35, 41–43, 45–46, 48, 73, 82, 84–85, 95, 109, 111–15, 117–18, 131–32, 134, 136, 202–3, 225n50, 226nn54–55; hair cutting and shaving, 51; hoarding, 9–10, 35, 77–78, 81, 122, 158, 173, 212n27, 218n8; magical thinking, 4, 48, 56, 70, 84–85, 225n50; musical, 41; neutralizing, 29, 131–32; about not being anxious enough (backdoor spike), 136, 229n46; not just right, 3, 50–51; past event (false memory OCD), 135; of perfectionism, 119, 170, 177, 181–82, 185; involving relationship, 3, 41, 44–45, 109, 111–15, 134, 161, 174, 225n50;

DANA FENNELL is professor of sociology at the University of Southern Mississippi. She studies health and well-being and has published articles on food marketing, complementary medicine, religion, fitness, and mental health.

Made in United States
Orlando, FL
08 January 2022

12733427R00171